This book is dedicated to the memory of Dave Cook

OROGENIC ZONES

THE FIRST FIVE YEARS OF THE
INTERNATIONAL FESTIVAL OF
MOUNTAINEERING LITERATURE

Compiled by
Terry Gifford and Rosie Smith

Bretton Hall

UK Copyright Information

British Library and Cataloguing Data available

ISBN 0 9524693 0 8

Published in Great Britain in 1994 by Bretton Hall College of the University of Leeds, West Bretton, Wakefield, West Yorkshire, WF4 4LG, England, U.K.

All trade enquiries in U.K., Europe and the Commonwealth to Cordee, 3a De Montfort Street, Leicester, LE1 7HD, England, U.K.

Printed and bound in Great Britain by The Guernsey Press Company Limited

illustrations on pages 6, 24, 43, 54, 73, 81, 120, 135, 194 and 196 by Kevin Borman
illustrations on pages 14 and 161 by Dubbo

cover photograph: *Héros de Lumière (detail) 1986, Carrara Marble; Igor Mitoraj. © Yorkshire Sculpture Park. Photographer: Norman Elliott. The photograph was taken on the day of the first Festival and was used as an inspirational subject for writing in the first Festival/* High *writing competition, 1989. The hand is Al Churcher's.*

orogenesis, *n.* mountain-
building. [Gr. *oros,* mountain,
genesis, production.]

Yorkshire & Humberside
ARTS

Acknowledgements

In addition to the organisations and individuals acknowledged in
the Introduction, we would like to thank the following people for
their help in production of this book:

Chris Bonington for support; Kevin Borman for ten orogenic
vignettes; Dubbo for Festival posters; Norman Elliott for the cover
photograph; Dave Gregory for proof-reading; Danuta Holata for
research; Bernard Newman for technical advice; *On the Edge* for
assistance with the cover; Audrey Salkeld for research; Richard
Sammels for suggesting the title; Anne Sauvy for research; Ian Smith
for research; Ken Vickers and Ken Wilson for their publishing
expertise, and Derek Walker of the BMC for support.

FOREWORD

by Chris Bonington

The annual International Festival of Mountaineering Literature at Bretton Hall is no longer unique. It has spawned a fellow festival in Banff, Canada and there is now another in Passy, France. But it remains unique in its celebratory yet rigorous spirit, and it has firmly established itself on the British climbing calendar, providing not just a live performance from new books, but an open forum for the exchange of views about developments in the literature of our sport and the sport's development of our literature. Its support for young and new writers is as committed as its determination to raise the profile of the most creative and experimental climbing writing. The Festival has blown the cobwebs out of the mountaineering library and made the books spring into often unpredictable life. I have been struck by the enthusiasm and originality in evidence at the Festival, that nevertheless allows plenty of space for healthy dissent and debunking humour.

As Chairman of the Boardman Tasker Award Committee, I am delighted that the Festival provides an opportunity to hear both the Chair of Judges and an excerpt from the winning book each year. The ensuing debate often throws up practical suggestions that are brought back by Dorothy Boardman to the committee. That this present book is able to put into print some of those judges' adjudication speeches is only part of the book's important contribution to the climbing record. I am sure that *Orogenic Zones* will become a collector's item for its authoritative accounts of French mountaineering literature, Polish climbing writing under the constraints of communism, women's mountaineering writing, its commitment to climbing fiction, to the historical attitudes of climbers to writing, and to much new work which would not have been written but for the Festival's invitation. Long may it continue to commission, to listen, to debate and to celebrate the long and flourishing tradition of mountaineering literature.

Contents

INTRODUCTION

by Terry Gifford

We were driving across Anglesey heading for Castell Helen and an evidently rain-threatened adventure on Lighthouse Arete. It was June 1987. David Craig and I were talking about the poet Ed Drummond, recently returned to England with his new performance, delivered, it was said, whilst climbing a twenty-foot tripod. Drummond had a book coming out and by coincidence so did both David and I. So it began, I confess, as a celebration of our new books, *Native Stones* and *The Stone Spiral*. But who can blame us? We were climbing poets out beyond the fringe of the scene, mere 'camp-followers', as Jim Perrin reminded us in *Mountain* 122 after our first event.

Whilst I drove, David Craig wrote down the details of our plans for the first Festival. We needed a provocative speaker to stir up the smugness around at the time. Dave Cook, popular heretic and idealist, was the obvious choice. Dave's 'Mountaineering Literature: Running On Empty' became a manifesto for the Festivals that followed each year and we are proud to open this book with Dave's seminal essay. Dave Cook's tragic death after a cycling accident in Turkey before his own first book, *Breaking Loose*, was published, hit us whilst we were preparing this collection of material from the first five Festivals. This book is dedicated to Dave's spirit of critical, imaginative, good-natured support.

So there has developed with each Festival a heady mix of celebration and debate, readings and argument from authors, publishers and readers - a kind of creative turbulence that might be compared with the making of mountains themselves. This book therefore records a series of literary orogenic zones. And it is no accident that these Festivals are generated each year from the School of English at Bretton Hall where this very combination of creativity and criticism characterises its unique approach to teaching and research in both creating and studying literature. Out of the mountains of mountaineering literature is created each year a forum for creativity and criticism in this vigorous area of literary endeavour.

Following Dave Cook's critique of the state of the art in 1987, the aim of each successive Festival has been to widen the content and forms of current climbing writing, from keeping alive neglected traditions to encouraging the renewed interest in climbing fiction and poetry. Whilst inviting fresh reflections from senior figures like Janet Adam Smith, Harold Drasdo and Paul Nunn, we have commissioned new writing from younger activists like Kevin Howett. In fact, of the youngest writers published here, poet Chris Briggs was sixteen and Ian Vickers was fourteen when they wrote their respective contributions for the Festival. International perspectives have been opened up in the first five years by major overviews of mountaineering literature from France and Poland. The wit and authority of these intelligent surveyors of their very different national mountaineering literatures will become important documents of their time and cultures.

A lot of creativity has been generated throughout Britain each year by the Festival writing competition, run in conjunction with *High* magazine. The winning entries are included here and they are well worth re-reading for their lively surprises and knowing insights. We have also been delighted to give a public airing to the Boardman Tasker Award a month after its announcement at the Alpine Club in London. So we are able to publish here for the first time two of the Chair of Judges' adjudication addresses which have been followed at every Festival since 1990 by a reading from the winning author and a rigorous open debate on the judgement. The quality and intensity of discussion, often between legendary international writers, which is one of the attractions of the Festival, can only be guessed at by readers who did not attend. So we are re-publishing the lively, and sometimes critical, reports of events which have appeared in the climbing magazines.

It ought to be remembered that some important contributions to the first five Festivals were not written papers and therefore do not appear here: Chris Bonington's candid extemporizing on the writing of his books, Ian Smith's stepping into the gap at a night's notice to give advice on writing for the magazines, and Mike Harding's hilarious stories about making his Himalayan books. Also missing, of course, are the readings from some of the new books which are celebrated and debated each year. But the bulk of the remarkable diversity that enlivens each Festival is represented between these pages.

For those who were present, many of these essays, stories and poems will evoke the fun and unexpectedness of their presentation: Steve Ashton climbing a step ladder to suggest his ascent of the Chamonix Aiguilles, Rosie Smith's Band of Hope giving us Patey's 'Onward Christian Bonington', or the discovery of Dermot Somers as a brilliant storyteller who quickly had the audience crying with laughter. Hopefully those who have not been to a Festival before will want to come and join the fun, the open debates, the unpredictable glimpses of live genius that climbing writers, unlike any others, can produce in the presence of their peers. As this goes to press we are planning the ninth Festival and no end to the series is in sight.

What this book demonstrates is that Dave Cook's initial hopes for the future of mountaineering literature were not in vain. The doors have been flung wider and 'the rest of life' has 'flooded into the world of climbing literature'. The British climbing community thinks of itself as a kind of invisible mobile village, surrounded, when at home or at work, by a green belt of crags and mountains where it actually meets. Its writers have to pass muster firstly for readers in the climbing village, then for outsiders. Mountaineering literature has to work first for climbing readers in order to have integrity within the village, however big a best-seller it might become outside. One of the doors that the village ought to open wider is to its potential place in the larger exciting literary and cultural developments of our time. In many ways climbing writing is a primary form of travel writing, as Harold Drasdo and Moira Viggers, for example, show us in very different ways in this book. Mountaineering is one of the areas of activity producing lively new writing in literature today. As this book shows, the exploration of self and partnerships through an active relationship with mountain landscapes is asking important new questions of content and form - of politics, history, gender, environmentalism, and of fiction, documentary, poetry. These are also questions about the nature of the sport itself.

This is a time when the sport is asking what its essential relationship really is with the natural environment. The debates about the long-term effects of indoor climbing walls, climbing competitions, bolts in our rock heritage and fees for access are all about attitudes towards the climbing environment which can be informed by mountaineering literature. The School of English at Bretton Hall has strong research interests in literature that engages with the environment and in creative writing in all its forms. Through the publication of this book the School is hoping to put some of these new developments on record for both the climbing village and a wider audience.

This book is arranged in chronological order of Festivals. By the time of planning the fifth event I realised that we always had enough climbing poets in the audience to have a lively and varied reading if each person read one of their poems. The unique collection of fourteen poems that resulted is distributed throughout the book.

Part of the cost of every Festival is borne by our sponsors, who deserve our grateful acknowledgement for putting something back into an annual attempt to make mountaineering literature live. Sponsoring the Festival at least once have been: *High, Mountain, Climber and Hillwalker, On The Edge, Mountain Review,* Patrick Stephens, Jonathan Cape, Hodder and Stoughton, Diadem, Secker and Warburg, Victor Gollancz, Michael Joseph, Methuen, The Ernest Press and Mountain Klub Wysokogorski, Gliwice, Poland. But without generous grant aid from The Foundation for Sport and The Arts, and from Yorkshire and Humberside Arts, the publication of this book would not have been possible. We gratefully acknowledge their crucial support for this book.

A festival only exists for its audience, and those who have supported the event are the people who have made it a friendly and lively meeting place for readers and writers, editors and publishers, collectors and detractors. This is the place to say thanks for your letters suggesting improvements (keep them coming) and thanks for the good word you have put out on the grapevine.

Finally we must thank Bretton Hall for appointing Rosie Smith as a Research Assistant to see this book through to publication and distribution. More particularly we all owe a debt of thanks to Andrew Tatham, Head of the Faculty of Art, Design and Humanities for helping to get the first event off the ground, and to Mary Mobley, Margaret Noble and Clare Faulkner for continued and cheerful administrative support.

Terry Gifford
Bretton Hall
September 1994

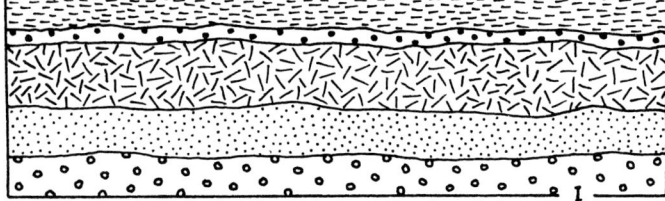

Running on Empty:
Climbing Literature in the '80s

by Dave Cook

"**A** fierce and savage wind tore at us - we were there." Even though it is 30 years ago I can remember both the exact words Maurice Herzog used to describe his arrival on the summit of Annapurna and the excitement they evoked in me with astonishing clarity. Many climbers have told me how influenced they were by inspirational passages from the literature of our sport; indeed some were recruited to it by the enthusiasm and passion of such writing. Books like *Nanga Parbat Pilgrimage* by Herman Buhl, Bill Murray's great accounts of Scottish mountain days, *The White Spider* by Heinrich Harrer, *Savage Arena* by Joe Tasker, *Annapurna, a Woman's Place* by Arlene Blum - these books spoke to the outside world. In a sense they were no more *for* mountaineers than *Moby Dick* was a book for whalers.

However, although climbing has become one of the largest participation sports in Britain, and now supports an unprecedented number of books and magazines, I believe that this sort of writing has become depressingly rare. The focus of climbing literature concerns has become narrower at a time when its volume has expanded. In a big bookshop today the 'mountaineering' section takes up quite a few shelves, but it will be tucked away with motor racing and home brewing, on the escapist margins of life.

That is not to say that it's not alive and kicking, but it is to say that its narrowed focus has had a heavy cost. David Craig in his book *Native Stones* used Yeats' four-word description of Ireland to characterise the situation on our crags today. "Great hatred, little room." It is no accident that the criticisms most commonly expressed about the climbing magazines today also suggest this sense of making a lot out of a little - 'elitist' - 'incestuous' - 'the beautiful people pissing in each other's pockets' - 'almost exclusively written by men'.

I would like to suggest some reasons why our climbing literature has become so lightweight and what the cost of its marginalisation has been. Then I want to express some grounds for optimism about the future.

An important question is why climbing literature is so large compared with that of other adventure sports like skiing, sailing, yachting, motor racing, canoeing, caving and gliding. Climbing is in a different league when it comes to writing. Whether we are speaking about books, journals, magazines, even instructional books and guides, these other sports produce far less. Why?

Those who began the sport were an exceptionally literary breed: upper class, from the 'Liberal Professions', and university backgrounds. A standard and a style was set. Then, even though social composition changed, there was the influence of the clubs. Clubs have a collective life, and how is this embodied? Often in a venture like a hut, or a journal, through which this tradition has been encouraged. A rather flattering idea for climbers is that there are characteristics of our sport which encourage writing - namely that we are not just creatures of brawn and instinct, but that the requirements for efficiency are also intellectual. This is certainly the conventional wisdom. Mental control is as important as physical prowess on harder routes. At least this is what older climbers tell themselves!

For most of human history mountains were viewed with fear and abhorrence. In the Bible Isaiah prophesied: "Every mountain and hill shall be made low... the crooked shall be made straight, and the rough places made plain." (Isaiah 40.4.) Not until the industrial revolution, when men had already begun to operate Isaiah's prophecy, were mountains and nature as a whole regarded differently. The Romantics began to project hills as beautiful and ethereal images far out of reach of mere mortals. Rousseau portrayed them as sources of romantic awe and joy, expressions of the mobility of savage experience. This tradition runs through the lyrical ballads of Coleridge and Wordsworth and finds expression in some of the first mountaineering literature, the books of Leslie Stephen, Edward Whymper, Mummery, Winthrop Young and Paccard.

Of course this writing had the stamp of upper class Oxbridge all over it. It was about a restricted experience - restricted in terms of class, sex and race, but nonetheless because it was at the tail end of wider romantic tradition, it was not a totally tunnelled vision. Wider concerns sometimes featured even if they only had a walk-on part.

Beginning between the wars, and at a rush after 1945, the social composition of climbers changed dramatically. This shift was reflected in mountaineering writing, just as it was in all else to do with the sport, most notably in the explosion of standards. There was a rejection of the romanticism of the previous era. The focus of writing narrowed into the technical concern with the movement. Literary references went out of the window. Climbing began to be treated as separate from life. There were stylistic aspects to this. Terse understatement and irony became the rule. Writing that represented an outpouring of emotion, never a strong point of the 'muscular Christianity' that dominated the sport at the start of the century, came to be regarded as embarrassing - uncontrolled self-indulgence.

We have seen expressed in climbing writing a fatal flaw of British sporting literature in general that inevitably makes it seem impoverished and lightweight. I refer to the dichotomy summed up in the slogan "Keeping politics out of sport", that pet slogan of the small-witted. Imagine saying keep politics out of sex, work, class, war or any of the other human activities that are also major literary subjects. This approach has relegated sport to the escapist margins of life, and it has become a self-fulfilling prediction that, with rare exceptions, literature about it has been similarly relegated.

Most British climbing writing contains this weakness and

what a cost it has been. Although our sport abounds with great dramas, passions, jealousies, issues and conflicts, rarely do these intrude into the bland and sanitised pages of our journals and magazines. Just think how rare it is for the explosive conflicts that often break out on climbing expeditions to blaze onto the pages of books about them. It is precisely because *Red Peak* by Malcolm Slesser allowed this to happen that it stands out among a notoriously formula-ridden branch of the genre - books about expeditions. This is not to say that there are not great strengths contained within this dominant and often hermetically sealed tradition of writing. For a start it represents all the advantages of direct involvement. As Jim Perrin put it, "The more closely a writer is involved personally, in his or her moments of action, the more cleverly are their truths perceived, both in essence and context."

Then there are the mags and journals. Well, I've been an avid reader of both the qualities and the tabloids since the days of *Mountain Craft* in the 1950s and their discoloured remains litter the shelves of my home. A random spot-check revealed the following:

Articles by women are few and far between. On ethical dilemmas within the sport (e.g. competition, education, aid, bolts, style of ascent) - growing number but almost no connection between these and wider issues in society. Similarly with environmental and access concerns, which again are mostly treated in isolation. Race - never a mention, a non-issue, although in a multiracial Britain, climbing has fewer black participants than almost any other sport.

Obviously books - whether anthologies, histories, biographies and autobiographies, expedition accounts or mountain travel books, range more widely, but again there is a feeling of little writing of substance, of overworked and predictable themes, as often as not images of heroic male conquest.

One interesting question is why fictional writing about climbing is so weak? There is a long tradition - James Ramsey

Ullman, Elizabeth Coxhead, Gwen Moffat, Dougal Haston, Lucy Rees - but it has always been peripheral. Is this not very strange? After all, a climbing trip, especially an expedition, as a subject for a book has a very clear structure: a beginning, an objective and an end, with the main characters having to deal with all manner of excitements and passions. Yet no novels of any stature. Why not? Perhaps part of the reason is that the truth has already been told. "Truth is stranger than fiction" is the old adage.

Contrast the concentration camps in World War Two with the Gulags of Stalinism. From the former a million true stories and no fiction; from the latter a hidden story from which the Gorbachev revolution is only now lifting the veil - yet remarkable fiction. Maybe the reality of climbing has been so well described as to narrow the scope for the likes of a Solzhenitsyn.

I want now to consider a particular problem of a great deal of climbing writing. Its domination by what I'm going to call the 'being totally alive' syndrome. The definition of the greatest moment is total absorption. Climbing is a simplified reality, but it is real! So goes the argument. The greatest gift that climbing can give is when everything else is blotted out and focus on a few square feet of rock or ice is complete.

Is not this definition, so common in writing about our sport, somewhat limiting? In what other form of human activity would being 'totally alive' mean being cut off from family, friends, work? These things are usually considered to be enhancers of sensibility, not a hindrance.

I think we can now begin to pinpoint some of the *costs* to climbing literature of its location on the escapist margins - the sources of nourishment are pretty thin. This is what the separation of our sport from politics, that is to say from wider society and its almost total domination by men, has meant. Climbing literature is close to 'running on empty'. It urgently needs to take on some fuel. Climbing writing is crying out for the interconnections between work, relationships, art and scaling mountains. It's crying out for outpourings of emotion, not buttoned-down stiff upper lippery. It's crying out for the reassertion of some of the values of humanity and fellowship against the imperial colonisation of the hills by hi-tech climbers. It's crying out for the insights of feminism to challenge its restrictive and dehumanising male imagery. It's crying out for a bit of poetry, even. *Total Control* is the name of one of the latest climbing videos. Above all, climbing writing needs to risk pressing the hyperspace button. After all, probing to the edge of control is what climbing is all about. Maybe these are vain hopes.

Perhaps the concept of a common tradition both in climbing and mountaineering literature is already a thing of the past. Is not the athleticism of the super-fit rock specialists so far apart from traditional mountaineering or even lower standard rock climbing that it is nonsense to categorise them as the same sport? David Craig has described a clear divergence from the mid '60s or thereabouts. One branch leads to the world of the moderns - who siege, bolt and clean the cliffs to order, and make their climbs "like electricians trying to follow a new piece of circuitry." The other is a continuation of the original romantic route. He contrasts the names of some recent climbs - *Colostomy, Hysterectomy, Sexcrime, Mass Murderer, Cystitis by Proxy* - with those of earlier generations that did not display the same contempts for women and nature.

I'm not convinced that the cleavage of sensibility is quite as dramatic as Craig claims. Many of the writers of *Extreme Rock*, who presumably can be taken as representative of the new wave, seem to go out of their way to reaffirm their attachment to the older, more romantic traditions.

Listen to this writer, beginning his chapter on *Strawberries* - for a while considered to be the country's hardest route:

Flitting through the hand-written pages of my climbing diary brings innumerable memories of past adventures flooding back. With these come moments of sentimentality... [Speaking of

Tremadog!] *Set back a mile or so from the sea by a wide, pancake-flat, flood plain, the cliffs rise majestically from dense vegetation, clean and almost plant-like in their quest for the sun.*

Not some old romantic like Paul Nunn or Ed Drummond - but young Andy Pollitt, who has put up more modern desperates than most on roadside crags.

There are other grounds for optimism. Tunnelled vision is under challenge. Writers like Jim Perrin insist on the interconnections that exist between climbing and everything that we do. *Menlove* stands out in this respect. Anthologies of climbing poetry are being published, privatisation of Britain's wilderness areas may be sending a politicising shiver down even the most cocooned spine. Women writers like Elaine Brook and Julie Tullis have placed a wider range of concerns and emotions on the agenda.

If these partially-opened doors can be flung wider, the rest of life will flood into the world of climbing literature. Then our sport will be restored to its rightful place - right at the centre of things. I'll leave the last word to Norman Nicholson, introducing *Speak to the Hills* - an anthology of mountain poetry.

Mountains should not serve as an escape from reality. They are surely an escape back to reality.

That is the route I hope climbing literature is going to follow.

A Quotes Quiz

by Mike and Marjorie Mortimer

When Terry Gifford rang to ask if Marjorie and I could make a contribution to his Mountaineering Literature Extravaganza, I must confess to having been more than a little surprised. "You see," he explained, "I have these intellectual heavy-weights lined up - Dave Cook, David Craig and Ed Drummond. I need somebody to dilute the serious stuff and inject a bit of humour into the proceedings." "Why us?" was my immediate response. "Well, for a start, neither of you are famous so I don't have to pay you so much, and you're a guide-book writer - you're used to using plain numbers that climbers understand."

Anyway, here we are with a very avant-garde look at climbing literature and anybody who knows anything about The Arts in the Modern World knows that it is all about Audience Participation. This means that you all have to get involved in this effort. Knowing what competitive bastards climbers are, we decided that the best way to wake you up was to organise a competition in which you are required to identify the authors of the unattributed quotations with which we are going to illustrate our offering. There will be prizes awarded, these being:

First Prize	A copy of Terry Gifford's *The Stone Spiral*
Second Prize	A copy of Ed Drummond's *A Dream of White Horses*
Third Prize	Signed copies of each of these books

Climbers and mountaineers have many different outlets for their urge to express themselves in the printed word, from the commercial magazines through the club journals, right up to the pinnacle of achievement epitomised by the latest Ken Wilson coffee-table special. However, if you have spent much time reading this wealth of literature, you may have come to the conclusion that climbers take themselves very seriously, in fact so seriously that in many a case we have a source of unintentional humour, especially when there is a tendency to exaggerate just a little. For instance, a famous foreign mountaineer describes an ascent of the Pilastro di Rozes in his autobiography:

A *I saw a ledge above me and promised myself a stance on it. I would get there somehow; but the last few feet were utterly smooth wall, which I managed to surmount without holds.*

Anybody who has done the route will recognise more than a little poetic licence there.

Of course it always has been a risky venture to put one's thoughts and opinions down on paper - it's a permanent record which can be made foolish by the passage of time and subsequent developments. A past president of the Climbers' Club once wrote to *Mountain* magazine complaining of the use of chalk on his local crags at Frodsham. Nowadays, this same climber is never to be seen on the crags without a large chalk-bag and has been known to apply (to his fingers) a sticky substance known as 'Sure-grip'.

A good source of laughs are the writings of British Alpinists attacking the teutonic extremists of the pre-Second World War era. They were regarded as having an unduly mechanistic approach to mountaineering (they were scathingly referred to as 'steeplejack climbers') and yet were prepared to risk all in pursuit of glory for the Fatherland. Here is an extract from a chapter entitled 'Mechanisation and the Cult of Danger':

B *The great invention with which this mechanical age has* *endowed the climber is the piton, which varies from a rough, stout peg of iron to an elegant, fragile leaf of steel. It can be adorned with a ring, so that the proudest rock-faces and the most domineering of profiles suffer degradation foretold by the prophet: "Behold I will put a ring in thy nose." This ring opens like the clip at the end of a watch-chain, hence the name* **Mousqueton** *in French,* **Moschettone** *in Italian; in German it is a* **Karabiner***. There is no English word for it. It is, in fact, decidedly un-English in name and in nature.*

British climbers of this period were not immune to the temptation to cheat. A famous incident on Cloggy is recorded thus:

C *Our leader having arrived exhausted at this point stood up on the ledge and called for a man with guts. Having none to spare below we sent up two chockstones slung in a handkerchief, one of which he inserted in the crack above, and secured himself by passing his rope through another six feet of Beale.*

Few climbing guide-books can be recommended as a good read (Paul Williams' new Llanberis guide is a brilliant exception) but if you leaf through those old cloth-bound versions of yesteryear, there are a few gems to be found. The whimsical style illustrated here (all from the same guide) has long since passed away:

D *a)   The climb has a certain good variety about it, is playful in type but not too simple.*
b)   An excellent climb for a good beginner, having the quality of romance; toiling painfully for a long time, then, for one short instant the struggle out into the sun.
c)   The long crack gives a fine exercise in nail technique. The rest gives good clean climbing, rather discrete and ephemeral.
d)   A good climb of its kind, rather artificial and discrete

like some of the Tryfan ridges, but with five good pitches and five good halts between.

e) *This is an indefinite article. The rocks on the left of Bracket Gully rise in discontinuous and brief series with innumerable incidental factors and no common factors.*

Alas, modern climbing does not allow this approach to its guide-books. Here is a more recent, but still dated, guide-book style:

E a) *The steepness of the climbing demands fast movement, using jams in the ascent to the half way break...
It is tiring to rest here, almost easier to press on. Pulling round the vile bulge is hard and the ascent mildly desperate on sparse holds until the angle eases and the summit soon reached.*

b) *The route is superb with an unforgettable character; it faces east and so catches morning sunlight - to the dawn it is dedicated.*

Whilst we are on the subject of guide-books, can anybody recognise the author of the letter to *Crags* concerning my guide to Tremadog? He complained: "Altogether I thought it to be a very poor guide, the worst I've ever seen."

The category which I would vote the biggest yawn of all is the great expedition book with its predictable formula so much criticised over the years. One of the best and most classic of the genre includes a macabre episode which only those with a sick sense of humour will find amusing:

F *Great beads of sweat were pouring off Oudot. He trimmed and trimmed again without paying attention to poor Biscante's cries: there was only half an hour and he still had another toe to cut. Altogether it made a considerable number since he started. This time the scissors were too big. "Quick, Matha, the little scissors"....*
This was not at all to Lachenal's liking; but that big toe had to be

done. *"But I don't want you to do it! Gently, gently..."* he said between sobs...

"No, Oudot, please!"

This time Oudot was at the end of his patience. He stopped and looked at Lachenal:

"Really, it's a bit much! You might be a little more obliging!"

This left Lachenal speechless. *If it is a matter of being obliging, he said to himself, he can cut off both arms and both legs!*

The train was due to leave in a few seconds. Crowds were moving about all the time on the platforms, and getting in our way. The moment the bandages were on, Terray seized Lachenal and carried him off. We just had time to call: *"Good-bye, Biscante! Cheer up! See you in Delhi!"*

Things had to be cleaned up now; the nauseating smell drove even the natives away. Sarki and Phutharkay set to: they opened the door wide and with a sort of old broom made of twigs they pushed everything on to the floor. In the midst of a whole heap of rubbish rolled an amazing number of toes of all sizes which were then swept on to the platform before the startled eyes of the natives. Whistles blew, the carriages jolted, and amid cries and shouts the train started. We drew out alongside a mass of humanity. I just had time to spot Terray, who waved us good-bye with a pair of boots.

One of the best expedition books of recent years includes the following exchange which kept me chuckling for days:

G *"Joe, have you still got The Seven Pillars of Wisdom?"*

"No, Ang Phurba's reading it."

Ang Phurba often spent a long time inside his tent, reading, and I went over and disturbed him. *"Ang Phurba, have you finished The Seven Pillars of Wisdom?"*

"Yes."

"Did you enjoy it?"

"Yes."

"What was it about?"

"Arabs."

As I have already mentioned, climbers take their sport very seriously, agonising over why they climb, their attitudes to ethics and so on, but there is only one who writes in great detail about trying to give it up:

H *Yet, believe me, I've tried very hard to give it up. Oh yes, so very, very hard. And this stern moral overseer, whom I call my malefactor, implanted in me during a Catholic childhood, whispers to me continually, "you must choose not to climb, it is mere hedonism, wilful, the self-destructive portion of man, the sin of Lucifer, Godless, and too much on a Sunday." And if it's not him it's soft spoken Belial whispering, counselling, tempting with visions of Sunday mornings spent in slothful ease, toast and marmalade, the Sunday papers, a warm bed and a voluptuous woman, and believe me, that is a style of life which I would not affect to despise.*

I would like to finish on a serious note. I have always thought that climbing on crags and mountains is the greatest recreation of all but also it is important to remember that it is no more than that. There is a fine balance to be found between the level of commitment that is necessary to get the most out of the sport and the prudence that enables one to stay alive, for, make no mistake, the biggest failure of all is to get killed. This thought leads me to conclude with one of my favourite passages in climbing literature:

I *Still, the last, sad memory hovers around, and sometimes drifts across like floating mist, cutting off sunshine, and chilling the remembrance of happier times. There have been joys too great to be described in words and there have been griefs upon which I have not dared to dwell; and with these in mind I say, Climb if you will, but remember that courage and strength are nought without prudence, and that a momentary negligence may destroy the happiness of a lifetime. Do nothing in haste; look well to each step; and from the beginning think what may be the end.*

Report of the First Festival of Mountaineering Literature

by Terry Gifford

'Running on Empty: British Climbing Writing in the '80s' was the title Dave Cook chose for his keynote address at the first British Festival of Mountaineering Literature held at Bretton Hall, West Yorkshire, on Saturday 10 October 1987. An audience of 70 heard Dave Cook argue that climbing writing has become narrower and more lightweight at a time when its volume has expanded. An intense focus on technical concerns has resulted in a marginalisation from the climber's real context in relationships, work, politics and the climbing environment itself. In much of the writing, climbing has become separated from life. The interaction of people and place had been the source of richness in a literature which had, in the past, drawn many people into the sport in the first place.

Climbing writing, Cook suggested, is crying out for an injection of emotion, the values of fellowship, the insights of feminism, even a bit of poetry. Some women writers such as Arlene Blum and Elaine Brook have placed a wider range of concerns and emotions on the agenda and here is an indication of the way forward, Cook concluded.

The presence of many well-known writers in the audience ensured a lively and well-informed debate which considered amongst other things Gary Gibson's suggestion that he and Dave Cook were not participating in the same sport.

It was perhaps significant that those present representing climbing magazines agreed with Cook's analysis and made a plea for writing that made connections between climbing and the rest of life.

"Why isn't there a single British guide-book written by a

woman?" Dave Cook had asked. The next speaker, Marjorie Mortimer, suggested that they were too busy laughing at competitive male egos trying to out-manoeuvre each other in print. Her tongue-in-cheek analysis of mountaineering writing included the Mine is Bigger Than Yours display and the NIGYYSOB exchange (Now I've Got You You Son of a Bitch). Mike Mortimer then proved how badly-read the audience actually was when he tested their identification of humorous quotations, including "This is the worst guide-book I have ever read", which turned out to be referring to one of his own.

Terry Gifford had compiled a brief anthology of mountaineering writing which wove in and out of his own book, *The Stone Spiral* (Giant Steps). This presentation included Al Churcher reading his poem *The Face* from *Mountain* 117. David Craig followed, reading from *Native Stones* (which is already being reprinted in paperback for next Spring). The Festival also launched David Craig's new collection of climbing/environmental poems, *Against Looting* (Giant Steps). The opening of an exhibition of water-colours by David F. Wilson provided an excuse for a bar. David Wilson was artist-in-residence on the 1986 Sickle Moon Expedition. The Festival closed with Ed Drummond's poetry performance on his twenty-foot tripod.

The warm reception given to the readings was an indication not only of the appreciation of the 'live performance' of literature, but of the way in which Dave Cook had struck a chord for the audience. The next Festival of Mountaineering Literature at Bretton Hall on Saturday 12th November 1988 will take Dave Cook's challenge further. Jill Lawrence will open the Festival with a personal view of *Women and Mountaineering Writing*, there will be a reading from the 1988 Boardman Tasker Award winning book, together with an audio-visual presentation of poetry about the Lake District. The 1987 Festival seemed informal yet rigorous, both thought-provoking and amusing. Has it set a pattern for the future?

Doomsville

by Chris Briggs

And there were big fish out at sea,
As he quivered in the groove,
And world just fell away
On the wall below his perch:
A hellish nightmare in that groove.

I didn't want to follow at all.
I hated Gogarth;
Its rotten and crusty core, its walls bowing threats,
And each green ledge not meant for people at all.

I shook awfully,
Muscles filled with a canker, thrilled
By the painful cyst of sea and
Hidden zawns.

Yet choiceless I stirred and climbed,
Forcing rigid fingers into vague holes,
Applying body to cliff crudely
On a rising tide of fear.
And despite betrayal by bogus gifts of rock,
That forced a film of tears,
I arrived.

A blanket of white light
Fell on the heather slope
Above the cliff.

The cliff sank, gurgling, away,
Into the foamy sea
And into bliss of limbs.

Yet even now it hangs, poised, malignant,
And through the dirty half-light
I can tell -
Above that sordid, brutal smell,
That dizzies brain and lowers me on knee -
There are still big fish out at sea.

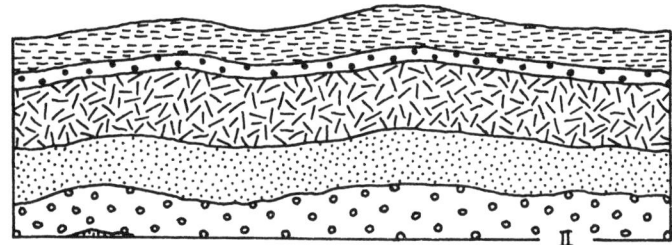

Report of the Second Festival of Mountaineering Literature

by Tim Noble

How does raw writing about climbing mature into vintage 'Mountaineering Literature'? And if it does, who controls the process? The speakers at the Second Festival of Mountaineering Literature held at Bretton Hall on the 12th November 1988 offered a small but discerning audience a taste of these issues.

For Jill Lawrence, who had the keynote address entitled *Women and Climbing Writing*, the answer to the latter question was obvious: male editors, publishers and advertisers. Her closely-argued thesis was that men's perceptions of women's psychology and physiology provide the bulk of writing about women climbing. Many writers, she claimed, adducing some (im)potent examples from the patronising pens of men, deal in stereotypes - and the magazines support them. Why, Jill wanted to know, did men not write about women's physical strength and power rather than their 'elegance and grace'. Women like Catherine Destivelle and Arlene Blum did not get where they have got by being elegant or 'glowing slightly'.

Ian Smith, stepping in to fill the Magazine Editor's slot at short notice from another magazine, defended *High's* policy on publishing women's writing and pleaded with women to send in more unsolicited manuscripts. He outlined the role of the editor and discussed the real constraints operating on a commercial venture. Writing is for readers, he concluded, so tell us stories that take us places we can 'see'. As a guide to beginning (women) writers this was all worthwhile inside information, but the heated conversation in the bar and cafeteria afterwards was as much about the Curran boobagram as about advertisers' pressure on magazine editors.

Janet Adam Smith uncorked some vintage writing by nineteenth century women mountaineers. She claimed that in a life-time's alpinism she'd never been discriminated against; but her heroines obviously had been - or had repressed the fact. Many of them, like the 'Lady Pioneer', had written anonymously or else recorded other sorts of humiliation from the male mountaineering establishment.

The audience warmed to Janet's subtle ironies remembering, perhaps, how some 'great mountaineering writers' like Tilman have vilified independent women. "The trouble with women," the 'great writer' had once said to his interviewer, one Jim Perrin, "is they get in the damned way." Had Jim listened to Janet Adam Smith, he would never have been able to say that "There's nothing in the least sexist about this."

But the elixir of the day was certainly Nick Shearman's powerful reading of two extracts from Joe Simpson's Boardman Tasker prize-winning account of disaster in the Andes, *Touching the Void*. Janet Adam Smith gave her chair of the judges' introduction to the book and gave more advice to would-be writers as she did: no gratuitous swear words, get petty squabbles into proportion, be careful about reconstructed conversations.

Jim Curran's well-oiled humorous look at parody followed a bar, a display of John Cambell's powerful paintings and a moving compilation of words and images about the Lake District by Bretton Hall students. Curran -'writer, literary judge, wit and psychopath' - first offered to kill himself for offending women with the infamous boobagram and then, reprieved by Jill, proceeded to drop his notes. His scrounged jokes, scurrilous anecdotes and self-parody were a perfect end to the evening. If the third Festival is as good as the first two, then *anyone* who enjoys reading and writing about climbing will need to come to Bretton next year for another taste of writing old and nouveau.

Women and Climbing Writing

by Jill Lawrence

Last year, Dave Cook had this particular talk slot that I am now occupying, and in fact that is probably one of the main reasons for my presence this year. Dave was critical of the fact that he thought climbing writing was stagnating: 'Running on Empty' was his actual catchphrase. The crux of his criticism was that much climbing literature is presented in a style and format that takes little or no account of social changes or influences: in that sense climbing literature becomes an escapist diversion that appears to reflect very little of what goes on in wider society. Whilst I think that diversions are necessary strategies for gaining both relief and relaxation from the many stresses that face us in the 1980s, I agree with Dave that an over-emphasis on escapist 'fantasy' means that much climbing literature is presented as though the sport operates in a vacuum, which of course it definitely does not. Social and economic factors impinge on us all, and rather than ignoring them, we could be exploring the interrelationship between social conditions and changes and their very real impact on the sport of climbing. Socially, the position of women appears to have changed quite dramatically during the last twenty years and certainly many more women are participating in an ever-widening range of sporting activities, including the sport of climbing. Concurrent with this is a tremendous rise in their performance standards.

Whilst on the surface it does appear that women are gaining ground, in both access and acceptance into areas previously considered to be the prerogative and domain of men, I think the premise that equality of opportunity abounds needs to be considered carefully. I propose to attempt to use that premise as the starting point for exploring women and climbing writing as a topic.

It has felt quite difficult considering how best to approach this topic to an unknown audience who may very well be at best disinterested, at the worst hostile to the topic. I decided to be optimistic and assume that those of you who are still listening at this point are the totally supportive 'right on' types who represent the best of the breed of climbers and writers.

Climbing writing exhibits itself through different outlets; there are many of us who keep personal records and reflections of climbs and trips, but it is the public outlets that I am most interested in, the magazines and books. These provide information and images for public scrutiny, in both a positive and a negative form. They have a very real impact in the formation of an individual's view of participating groups and individuals, in this case women participants. I want to take a three-pronged approach:

- Look at men's presentation of women and climbing.
- Look at women's presentation of themselves in climbing.
- Finally to look at access to publication: who controls it?

Before going any further, I should point out that I do recognise that women in climbing are in the minority in relation to the bulk of the participants, who are men. This is also reflected in the written material about climbing; it is in fact dominated by men. However, recognising this factor, whilst perhaps necessary, is not in itself useful. What would be more useful would be to explore *why*?

The presentation of women by both themselves and by men within the climbing literature does not occur in isolation; it stems from views held generally about women in our society. These actually impinge on women participants in all sports and I feel it would be useful to summarise these before looking specifically at climbing.

Firstly, let's look at the influence of the so-called ideal

shape: slender but not too bony; toned but not too muscular; slim-hipped, long-legged and glowing ever so slightly from exertion, and, of course, smiling sweetly. In reality few women can achieve this particular ideal; women, like men, come in a whole range of shapes and sizes. However, because of the current vogue of the wholesome athletic female presented by the media in all its forms, many women who feel pounds and inches away from the ideal lack the confidence to start to participate in sport. It must be remembered that most sports require a very public display of the body. Climbing falls into this category. Women's bodies are constantly being compared, commented on, and often found lacking when compared to the 'ideal'. The same kind of pressure is not exerted around men's bodies and the whole range of shapes and sizes tends to be on public display in a variety of venues. Climbing is no different; a visit to any popular Derbyshire edge shows a tremendous variety of lycra-clad male bodies in a somewhat bizarre and occasionally gruesome range of shapes and sizes.

Equally daunting for women is the pressure to look good at all times. The 'Feminine' image is an idealised glamorous one that most women know full well to be unobtainable. But whilst they are aware of the ethereal elusive nature of this image they have also been told that they have a duty as women to make every attempt possible to get as near as they can to achieving this. It would be easy for a predominantly male audience to dismiss this preoccupation with one's looks as something women bring on themselves; however unless one has actually been on the receiving end of such comments as "ugly bitch", "fat cow", "are you a man or a woman?", it is hard to fully understand the oppressive yet effective message of the media to look good. In choosing examples, it must be noted that I have selected some of the more overt terms of abuse reserved for women; there are many more subtle yet relentless images that constantly bombard women which are equally as effective and oppressive.

As a case in point, a week spent camping in Llanberis pass in order to experience the delights of Welsh rock hinders rather than enhances the attainment of the ideal feminine image, as does a couple of weeks' grotting on Snell's field in Chamonix, with bivouacs at the foot of routes. Also not to be missed are the delights of slogging up mountains at altitude with the concurrent drain on both physical and mental resources that leave one looking a complete wreck. However for men all of these examples can be enhancers of their image. The tough, hardy, self-reliant, adventuresome, unwashed and unkempt look is an enhancer of masculinity adding to the macho image; there is certainly not the same kind of conflict as there is for women.

Lastly, but linked to my previous barriers for women, is the effect of sport on the body: it actually changes both its shape and size. Repetitive physical movement and exercise of body parts does lead to muscular development. I said earlier that 'toned' muscles were okay, but producing actual real muscle is trickier and far from acceptable for many women.

Within any sport there may well be a subculture that supports this kind of development and encourages women to discover their muscular potential, and this is true of climbing. However, I would suggest that those who show support in this way are not representative of men in general. Also, women who are able to break out of the feminine stereotype know they are taking a very real risk, and are generally those women who have very stable support systems from their women or men friends.

Coupled with these conflicts that affect women's participation in sports are pervasive attitudes and assumptions by men about women's physical, psychological and emotional capacity to engage in a risk sport like climbing. Women are often assumed to be passive, timid and technically incompetent to the extent that they begin to believe this about themselves.

Their motivation for engaging in such activities is even

scrutinised by some writers:

It is of primary importance to ensure that the motives of female expeditioners are based on a genuine wish to participate in the expedition and not on making a point for the female cause. Nigel Gifford, *Expeditions and Explorations*.

Later in his book he goes on to explain how "personal ambition and commitment were open to question." However this time he is talking about a group of men and when deliberating about the reasons for this he blames lack of time to get to know each other. I wondered on reading this how come he wasn't prepared to look more closely at their reasons for participating: were they in it for just the 'masculine cause' or doesn't that actually need to be stated as it's accepted as given that masculinity and climbing go together?

Certainly according to Jim Masters femininity and expeditions don't go together:

I well remember an all-women's expedition that went off to Central America, and it turned out to be an absolute and total disaster. It is as if there is something odd about a group of women trying to achieve something in the expeditionary sense, which is not true about men for some reason. The only opinion or theory that I can offer for this all-women expedition being such a failure is as follows. If you have men on an expedition, they do tend to accept orders in an emergency and get on with whatever they are told to do to solve the particular problem at the time. Girls tend to need reasons for doing things - they seem to have this need to discuss what it is they have to do before they actually do it, and in emergency situations this often doesn't work, although in a mixed group, this is no quite so.

Women are in a double bind because when they do succeed some writers suggest it is not to do just with their climbing abilities; women have been known to use their 'feminine charms' to actually aid them up the route.

Coco soothed it, seduced it, and it fell easy prey to her charms.

John Barry's article *A Couple of Climbs with Coco* is so riddled with sexual innuendo as to be more at home in *Playboy* than in a climbing magazine.

Where now Coco demanded, the upper of a pair of lips a half size too big - dew-drop moistened by heat and svelte exertion.
...with subtle sleights of hand and foot and subtle shifts of bum and boob.

There's more too:

What she did now was rude, positively rude; damn well just went and seduced it.

Actually, on close scrutiny of the article, all John is really trying to say is that she got up the route in far better style than he did and with less effort. However it seems that some men when describing women's climbing have a hard time separating their own sexual response from the situation.

In an interview of Alison Hargreaves by Bill Birkett in *Climber and Rambler*, one of the questions he asks is: "You're very pretty and very feminine; climbing routes which are mentally and physically extremely demanding. Do you find it a special problem to be a woman and a climber?"

Imagine if he were interviewing John Barry, and started off with: "You're very handsome and very masculine", apart from its being a complete lie.

Even when men are well intentioned, and let it be said that some writers are, they fall easily into the trap of generalities rather than actualities about women's climbing ability and style. How many accounts of women's rock climbing wax lyrical about their gracefulness, nimbleness and rhythm on the rock? Okay, these may well be factors, but women are also powerful, strong, determined and competitive in their approach to climbing, so why not round out the descriptions? There's no way Lynn Hill, Catherine Destivelle or Louise Sheppard get up the hard routes they do by just being graceful. Think about it this way: how often are Ron Fawcett or John Dunne described as being graceful?

It may seem niggling to be so pedantic about words and how they are applied, but that's what writing is about: *words*, the meanings they both convey and imply. Talking to people on the crags and eavesdropping on some younger climbers, I do think there has been an expansion in men's attitudes and thinking toward women who climb. Generally I feel this reflects changes in the wider society about women's roles and abilities, not least because women are finding their own voices and demanding changes in attitudes and more equality. However at the moment this does not seem to be reflected in the writing or, for that matter, the photographs. In a recent edition, *High* magazine thought it quite appropriate to publish Jim Curran receiving a naked woman delivering a boobagram message on its index page. This is perhaps a reflection of the entrenched position of the editors rather than the readers; someone should tell them it's 1988 and that things are changing.

When *women* write and talk about their climbing experiences, the quality and style is completely different; it's fuller, more balanced, and more risk-taking because they dare to explore emotions and show vulnerability and apprehension as well as strength, commitment and the ability to co-operate.

But first, to counter the suggestion that women don't get on or work well together on expeditions, I'd like you to consider these extracts from Elaine Brook's book *Land of the Snow Lion*:

Although I found the aggressive atmosphere depressing when I was in the midst of it, from a safe distance I found it quite interesting. Perhaps it was the inevitable result of having more than one prima donna in a single camp. Individually they were used to dominating those around by force of personality, and this was inevitably causing friction as each jockeyed for position in the pecking order. Experienced mountaineers like Doug were inevitably a little sensitive to younger, dynamic climbers challenging their authority and wanting to do things their own way. Usually Doug automatically took control, because of his experience and forceful personality. On occasion, however, other forceful personalities would emerge, and things would not be so simple. It was clear that Alex was measuring himself against Doug, testing his strength and experience against those of a man fourteen years older. The arguments began to sound not unlike the clash of antlers in the contest for the leadership of the herd.

There was so much backbiting and petty bickering on this expedition to Shishapangma amongst the men who were posturing for positions of power with each other that I marvelled at Elaine's ability to stay with the bad-tempered, mean-minded group for as long as she did.

Maybe it is in some ways inevitable that ambitious disparate groups of people, who have as a common factor only a desire to climb a mountain, should produce conflict. Certainly there are a great many stress factors involved in expedition climbing, both physical and mental, as well as emotional; however in men's writing it is the emotional conflict that is so barren and unprobed.

Arlene Blum in her book *Annapurna. A Woman's Place* gives a lot of detail about the emotional complexities and inter-relationships within her team: exposing her own weaknesses and daring to be vulnerable in order to show 'how it was'. Example:

I had climbed several times with Joan in the rugged N. Cascades and had great respect for her toughness, self-sufficiency and route-finding ability. If I hadn't been the leader, I was sure we would have become better friends.

I suppose Joan got to me because in some ways she was what I wanted to be - a natural leader, charismatic, decisive. We disagreed, it seemed, over virtually every issue that arose, and we both feared that factions might form around each of us and destroy the unity of the team. Before leaving for Nepal, we had discussed our conflict at length. She finally promised to support my decisions, yet the feelings between us had remained tense.

One cannot help but admire the openness and honesty in this book. There are problems, but they are discussed and written about. We also learn a great deal about the participants - not just their climbing abilities and accomplishments; rather, Blum gives us a fuller version of her companions. This wider perspective makes it easier to recognise the extraordinariness of the ordinariness of these women's lives, personalities and histories, thus drawing one into the characters and enabling the reader to understand and identify with their strengths and weaknesses as one would a character in a novel. Examples:

When she got older, Alison's (Chadwick) parents even sent her away to boarding school because they felt she was not strong enough to make the daily bus and train trip to the local grammar school.
"At school I was totally unathletic, and I hated all games," Alison recalled with amusement. "When we had gymnastics, I would hide behind the piano so I wouldn't have to take my turn at vaulting over the horse. I did like climbing the ropes and wall bars, but that wasn't considered serious stuff at our school - just playing."

Another snippet about Alison preparing to get off to set up Camp 1 gives us insights into the contrasts between herself and Arlene:

Alison got a bowl of water from the kitchen, then carefully washed her face and brushed her teeth. Next she cleaned all of her camera lenses and slowly and neatly packed her gear. I watched impatiently, thinking what different types we were. I would have thrown my things together haphazardly and hurried off. Despite Alison's meticulousness, both she and Liz were ready to set off by 9.30, wearing large packs and big smiles.

We also gain insights into the worries and stresses that Arlene feels are there precisely because they are an all-women team. For example, one of the team, Joan, was ill and there was a debate about whether to call a helicopter in:

"If it's necessary, of course, we'll call a helicopter," I agreed. My worry about Joan's health was complicated by my awareness of the spotlight of publicity focused on us. I knew from experience that the media tend to emphasize women's weaknesses rather than our strengths. Coverage of a helicopter evacuation might receive more notoriety than an announcement of our reaching the summit.

"Two years ago when I had dysentery on Mount Everest," I told everyone, "it was reported on national television on the six o'clock news. All the men on the team had dysentery at one time or another, but that wasn't mentioned. Strangers still come up to me and sympathize about my famous dysentery." The older members of the team had been denied many climbing opportunities because of their sex and they were quite sensitive about how the world would judge us. The younger climbers had experienced little or no discrimination and were less concerned about public opinion.

This highlights the need to perform well: they felt the media would be looking for the smallest incident to blow up into the "I told you so! Women shouldn't go on such dangerous trips especially without men" rhetoric.

On top of this worry they were having some trouble with the men who were there, the Sherpas, who were starting to make sexual innuendoes:

"Besides, they're getting awfully obnoxious," Liz added. "They keep pointing at us and giggling all the time. I know they're making obscene comments."

"How do you know?" I asked.

"Well, for one thing, they keep drawing phallic symbols in the snow," Liz said, "And when Vera W. asked them to stop, they just

said, 'Yeti make pictures in snow - not Sherpas.'"
We all laughed, easing the tension a little.

The Sherpa men felt they had the right to pass comments on the team members' abilities based on assumptions of what was or was not considered appropriate for them because they were women rather than on any assessment of their climbing abilities; naturally enough, the women got pretty sick of this.

However, there were also conflicts within the group: these too are fully and openly documented in the book:

"We'll never reach a consensus," Annie interrupted. "You're supposed to be the leader and decide what's going to happen."
Their anger and the loss of support hurt me a lot. But the strain and unhappiness I saw now among the group was even worse.
"I'm sick to death of this wrangling about who's going to lead."

However, they do decide to sit down and try to sort out the growing tensions amongst the climbing members:

Fortunately we had not simply buried our hurt feelings and gone marching stoically up the mountain. It had been worth it to take the time to face each other and expose our vulnerability, hurt, and anger, and then our fears. We realized again how much we cared about each other, and our shared laughter had been the final healing touch.

Compare this airing of conflict with Elaine Brook's description of making attempts to discuss problems with Doug Scott:

Now Doug was an unknown quantity. His sudden outbursts of temper could occur again at any time, and on the mountain that would be not only unpleasant but also dangerous....
I found myself speaking generally as a metaphor for what concerned him personally, and trying to work the conversation round

to the reasons for his fury of the previous day. Whenever we got too close to the subject his anger would rise again, confirming my fears that I would be climbing with a human time-bomb. I realised I was only making things worse by trying to discuss the problem. So I backed off, saying I was just depressed by the aggressive atmosphere.

When women write about climbing with men, there are certainly conflicts that come up above and beyond those created by the climbing itself.

Land of the Snow Lion, Elaine Brook:

"You're looking cold, Mr. Wu, you need warming up! Come on Elaine, get into his sleeping bag and rub his chest for him."

I gave Paul a furious glare, but it was lost in the gloom. It made me angry to be referred to as if I were the expedition groupie. He did not mean it spitefully, but when it came down to it, none of them could conceive of a woman on this sort of trip in any other context. Doug had confided quite cheerfully to me that both he and Alex had discussed my presence with their respective ladies. They had given their assurances that they would not sleep with me during the trip - as if it was their decision, not mine! Few men seem able to accept women climbing on equal terms. Women are there 'to soften the atmosphere for men...' Long ago I had learned from pub talk after a day's rock-climbing that women are of three types: wives are 'hags', single girls are 'tarts' and good climbers are 'dykes'. God, I thought, they're probably expecting me to be their cook and potwasher for three months.

Climbing with other women would seem to be the solution, but even then men have a lot of comments to make. This extract is from Miriam Underhill's *Give Me the Hills:*

Henry de Ségogne went to some pains to explain to me why a woman could never lead a climb. There is a lot more to leading, said Henry, than first meets the eye, a lot that must be learned, and that is best learned by watching competent leaders attentively and coming to understand their decisions. Women, however, never bother to do this. Since they know that they will never be allowed to lead anyway, they just come walking along behind, looking at the scenery. Therefore, even if they were given an opportunity to lead, they would be completely unprepared. I didn't find this argument too convincing, but I did realize that if women were really to lead, that is, to take the entire responsibility for the climb, there couldn't be any man at all in the party. For back in the 1920's women were perhaps a bit more sheltered than they are today. And in any emergency, particularly in an outdoor sport like mountaineering, what man wouldn't spring to the front and take over? I decided to try some climbs not only guideless but manless.

Miriam's chapter on *Manless Climbing* is full of little snippets that give insights into men's attitudes of the day to women climbing together.

Whilst gaining the Mummery crack on the Grépon, which had a reputation for difficulty, they had knocked a few stones onto a party below them in the couloir. Miriam says:

... the boys poked their heads out from behind their rock and I was immensely amused to watch the expressions on their faces when they saw where Alice was, and that there was no-one above her. (She was high up in the Mummery crack.)

Earlier they had arrived on the col on the north bank of the couloir where the rocks were steep, icy and loose. When the porter Alfred Burnet, who was on the col, saw them, he excitedly shouted he would throw down a rope, assuming they were stuck. Miriam's one-liner summary of their response tells us a great deal.

We declined with thanks this superfluous rescue.

At a time when most parties in the Alps were still accompanied by a guide and porters, this was not to be the only incident of men wanting to rescue or assist Miriam's women-only parties. However the women were determined to climb manless and even when unsure of the route on one climb due to poor visibility they couldn't allow themselves to ask for directions from male climbers:

We wouldn't have asked directions of any of those men for the world! We were playing a game and we must abide by the rules: no help from men!

Miriam's sense of humour, her independence and determination, come over very strongly throughout this wonderful book. Miriam's book is about climbing in the late 1920s and '30s, when women-only ropes were exceptional. Today there are far more women who climb together gaining support from each other.

Rosie Andrews in her article *No Spare Rib* published in *Mountain 97*, talks about the difficulties and conflicts that the male/female dynamic of protector and protected often creates within a mixed partnership. She goes on to say: "Because such dynamics are so deeply ingrained in us many women find that climbing with other women can be an important part of learning to climb well." ... it leads to... "companionship, a greater sense of equality and a higher degree of self-reliance, valuable experience is gained in making decisions and taking charge in situations where women have to rely on themselves."

This climbing 'sisterhood' is becoming more available on the crags as more women enter the sport. But it also needs to be available in the literature in order to reach a wider audience.

Access to publication/Utopian visions:
I have spent quite a lot of time earlier looking at the social relations between women and men and I feel this is necessary if we are to understand the power relationships and imbalances that occur. It is only by understanding that power differential and how it operates, sometimes consciously, sometimes unconsciously, to maintain the status quo, that we are able to suggest strategies for change. Dorothy Smith

in an article entitled *A Peculiar Eclipsing: Women's Exclusion from Man's Culture*, 1978, points out that there are gatekeepers in the academic community. She argues that these are the ones who set the standards, produce the social knowledge and monitor what is admitted to the system for distribution, thereby decreeing the innovations in thought and knowledge and not least values. I feel the same could be said of climbing: climbing writing not only reflects that which is written about, it also reflects that which gets published.

So who are the gatekeepers of climbing writing?

Many of them are to be found as editors of the magazines and club journals, and as advisors to publishers and as publishers themselves. They are the ones in a position to determine what gets published and what does not, and in relation to climbing these are almost exclusively men. A visit to the Alpine Club Library in London reveals thousands of books on hundreds of shelves and within these there are probably few books by women. Why? This needs further exploration.

First, in a very fundamental sense articles and books about climbing that are not in print do not exist. Secondly, what gets published can and does influence not only those who read but those who write. This is because the published literature sets the parameters and is instrumental in establishing the guidelines and values of what and how climbing should be written about. In other words, it sets a style for aspirants. The style, as Dave Cook said last year, "has little of substance, it's impoverished, running on empty, and existing on the escapist margins."

It could be argued that the gatekeepers have a vested interest in keeping it that way; if it truly does reflect their values then they will wish to legitimate and preserve their authority as the upholders of established values. One way of doing this is to trivialise and marginalise any criticisms. Recently *High* did this when criticised for being sexist: they made fun of antisexism by means of cartoons and with a photo of Jerry Moffat's bum, which was to redress the balance for the boobagram photo in the previous issue. This is not equality, this is not giving a platform to alternative or different views, rather it is a blatant display of abuse of power.

The gatekeepers reinforce their own position by exercising sponsorship and patronage towards those who agree with their own views of the climbing world. Women are an 'outside' group, they are not the only one but they are a significant one. Whilst it may not be deliberate policy to exclude women, they do have a scattering of articles in all the magazines; nonetheless they are not well represented, therefore their views are seldom heard in debates around climbing. This conference does go some way towards a redress of the balance; however it will be a small ripple unless the gatekeepers allow it to build into a tide for positive change. (Change means more writing by women being published.)

There is a silence around the process of selection for publication; it's often not what one has to say but who you know. It's not what I have to say that has got me up in front of you but who I am that allows me access to this platform today. There must be many women out there, some in this particular audience, that would have done a better job given this title than myself. How are they to be allowed a voice?

One thing Dave Cook said last year about climbing writing was, "It's crying out for the insights of feminism to challenge its restrictive and dehumanising male imagery." Well I'm not so sure about that myself; the IT is not some faceless flesh and bloodless mishmash of words, the IT is a small cross-section of white males who are not actually crying out for change or to be challenged. In fact I don't think they like it at all.

The climbing media often reject material that smacks even faintly of feminism. Even women who write for climbing magazines tend to be greatly concerned by feminism and certainly make attempts to disassociate themselves from it. Stella Adams in her review of the Women's issue of *Climbing*, an American magazine, starts off by saying she was anticipating banality and crassness mixed with a lot of hard-line feminism.

Gill Fawcett, now Kent, writes in the same vein, although she does also get some very amusing swingeing comments in about male posturing.

Generally it can be said that very little gets published, certainly in magazines, that challenges sexism, therefore the message to young women and men wishing to get published is not to write in that vein; hence little material of this nature gets presented for publication. This allows the gatekeepers to sit back complacently with the reassurance that their values are firmly established and representative of their readership, hence there is no need to change them. Back to 'Running on Empty'.

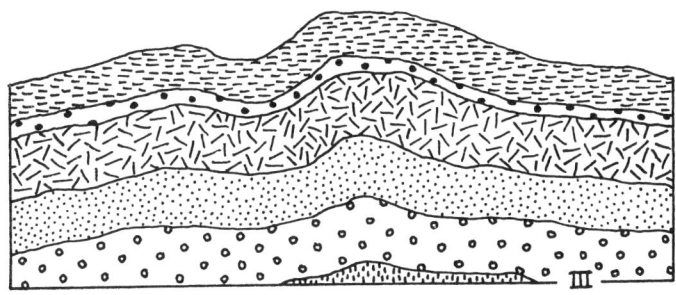

Caterina of the Rocks

by Kym Martindale

It is no myth: listen child, to me,
I saw the white woman climb.
Slow dancer on the rocks,
On this monster cliff ending in the sky.
Colours have faded around me with the years
But I see the madness and the brilliance of that day,
Feel the hearts of us all not daring to beat,
Our necks and shoulders breaking with the tilt of our
heads.
One breath would blow her away.

It began like a feast -
music, swaying; we chanted her name to her rhythm,
"Oye Caterina, oye Caterina".

As she set her face to the rock,
My belly was water inside; she was too small.
Our cliff would spit her out like I spit seeds,
But I saw her back ripple,
Her grip, child, left prints in the soft rock,
And she inched like a snake on its prey,
Into the folds and seams and up.

Then our voices fell away, the music tailed,
The wind shifted, a lizard darted,
And Caterina hung, by her heels,
By one hand,
Moving between each in slow curves.

The day slowed, stretched out
Into a time of no end,
When she lived only by her fingers on the rock.

Relief sighed like a breeze through us all
When she pulled high and stood in the sky.

Then we feasted and sang.
The men put on their costumes and danced,
But their hearts were small and their feet were dead.
She shrank their hearts.
But we swayed and called
Tall into the nights and days.
Yes, child, she came, the white woman who climbed to
climb,
Who needed no-one but herself.

Down the years of toiling,
Of bearing boys who want to be men,
When my back and heart ache,
I dream that day again,
Eyes closed,
My hand still on the warm rough stone.

Ladies' Mountaineering Books

by Janet Adam Smith

I emphasise *Ladies'* books, because the word Lady is - or anyway used to be - all-important in the mountain connection. When in 1838 Mlle Henriette d'Angeville reached the top of Mont Blanc, it was emphasised that she was the second *woman*, but first *lady* to have done so - she had been preceded by some peasant lass from Chamonix. Then in 1859 was published a book with the prettiest title-page, *A Lady's Tour round Monte Rosa*. She was a sensible lady, who found that "lady's dress is inconvenient for mountain-travelling and therefore any device which may render it less so should be adopted". One of these devices, which has rather puzzled me, is "a riding-skirt, without a body, which can be slipped on and off in a moment". But she is down to earth about the need for "a pair of easily-fitting strong treble-soled broad-footed boots, in which some hob-nails should be put - smaller, but of the same kind as those used for gentlemen's shooting boots". One complaint, echoed by many of the lady travellers of the time, was that side-saddles were unknown in Alpine valleys, so when the lady wanted to ride up the mule-track, there were difficulties; however, one lady discovered that "Whippy's portable side-saddles, which folded into a compact waterproof case, could be adapted with equal facility to horse, mule or donkey" - great relief.

Another matter that bothered these early lady travellers was delicately expressed by the Hon. Frederica Plunket, when she wrote in *Here and There Among the Alps*, 1875, about "the necessity of sleeping in a cave or small hut, containing but one room. Of course in this matter every lady must be the best judge for herself - of these places *I* only speak by hearsay."

A few years after the Monte Rosa Tour came *Alpine Byways*, by 'A Lady', 1861, with another pretty title-page. We know now that the Monte Rosa lady was a Mrs Cole, and the *Byways* one was Mrs. Freshfield, mother of Douglas Freshfield - as a lad, the future President of the Alpine Club went with his mother on many of her Alpine excursions.

In 1876 another lady produced a magnificent book, *The Indian Alps and How we Crossed Them*, by 'a Lady Pioneer'. A splendid Lady Pioneer - who travelled in Sikkim and Bhutan, and towards Kangchenjunga, sketched and painted - her book is full of her illustrations - and provided intriguing running headlines to her pages. I was caught by one: *I am seized with Alarm*. In fact, it was the old familiar story of two parties being temporarily separated; but she is resolute. "Now this would have been a fitting occasion for hysterics - high strikes as F_____ calls them - but I am not given to such demonstrations, so sitting down I quaked and trembled silently beneath my waterproof."

These ladies were coy about revealing their authorship; not so one remarkable lady climber who was also a prolific author - far from concealing her name, she had three. She was successively Mrs. Fred Burnaby (who wrote *The High Alps in Winter*), Mrs. Main (who wrote *My Home in the Alps*) and Mrs. Aubrey le Blond who wrote *True Tales of Mountain Adventure*, and founded the Ladies' Alpine Club in 1907.

I take special pleasure in owning many books by these ladies' successors, because many of them, Dorothy Pilley, Miriam Underhill, Micheline Morin, Nea Morin, have been my friends. Alas, their books are not so charming to look at as the *Lady's Tour round Monte Rosa*, though their photographs may be more accurate than the earlier prints. But note - Nea Morin's title is *A Woman's Reach* - and when she led me over the traverse of the Meije more than 30 years ago, we made a little record by being the first guideless British *women's* party to do it. We were no ladies that day.

Terracotta

by Dave Thomas

Someone inside me giggles with manic
anticipation of the game to be played out.
My body apes frantically around the inside
of my mind's cavity that has become
the Old Redoubt at Berry Head.
Crashing waters feed off signals from the rock,
secrets countless millennia old.
But I am out of reach, above all
that is confusion below me.
My body flows like the water,
feeding off energies of wind and rain.
Reading their message,
dancing to their signal.
Born into the halfway niche,
I am presented with life's gambol.
A pinch-grip shifts like a deck of cards
and only my inner web of self knows
how close my faith is to extinction
beneath the swamping swell below.
A boulder surfaces and I understand its smile,
as for six or seven metres my life
follows the course of a single rail.
The simplicity we all strive for.
I swing along, ecstatic with this freedom,
in control, knowing my life is in my own hands,
inverting to hang batlike
from a footjam above my head.
The stage is open, and the pretender
inside cannot refuse its lure.

My consciousness bows,
collects the flowers and retires,
seduced by dark whispers in the wings.
With no room for fear, only the blackest
of comedies can subdue daylight's reality,
waiting at the tunnel mouth.
The terracotta stains my flesh,
an acrid balm of baked earth
become my ritual device.
I craze at the rhythms of this ancient stone;
intoxicated, laughing in the face of fate.
The boulders below seem to rise and fall
in the swirling vortex of sea.
Echoing my ferment, as vulnerability surfaces and
control threatens to slip away with the tide.
No longer feeling around the vault inside my mind,
but groping for holds on the 'lip-trip',
I'm tripping on the brink of night,
hanging in, bridged across, pumping out...

Report of the Third Festival of Mountaineering Literature

by Roy Bennet

Unlike the British Grand Prix Climbing Competition held earlier in the year, on a sunny day when every self-respecting climber and walker wanted to be outside, the organisers of the Third Festival of Mountaineering Literature had the profound good sense to hold the event on a day when the same constituency were thankful of a legitimate excuse to stay indoors.

The weather was truly miserable and the only question was, "Would the journey be worth the effort and would the programme live up to expectations and my happy recollections of previous years?"

The Festival was held at Bretton Hall in West Yorkshire, England, a beautiful location, set lakeside in rolling parkland and littered with interesting and impressive sculptures. The fog and mist was so thick throughout the day that visitors would have to know this to be the case because none of its attractions could be seen.

The mixed and varied styles of contributors, a considerable amount of new writing, a bar and an exhibition of prints and paintings by the Cumbrian artist, Donald Wilkinson, succeeded in creating the relaxed and friendly atmosphere that the Festival is justifiably noted for.

The scope of the event ranged from a serious and studied analysis of mountain literature in fiction through the deliberately humorous to the eccentric, and was at all times entertaining and informative.

After introductions by Terry Gifford, organiser of the Festival and master of ceremonies for the day, Rosie Smith and Audrey Salkeld got the proceedings off to a stimulating and interesting start with a summary of their investigations and research into the whole genre of climbing fiction. Audrey is generally believed to have the most extensive collection of climbing literature and it was no doubt this remarkable personal library that had provided the raw material for their research.

I suspect that it came as a considerable surprise to many that climbing fiction encompasses everything from the adventure novel *The Jackson Route* through the Miss Pink detective novels of Gwen Moffat and on into the realms of science fiction with *Green Mars* by Kim Stanley Robinson. The surprising scope of the genre and the extensive selected readings were not only informative and illuminating in their own right, they also provided a rather handy catalogue into which it was possible to situate contributions later in the day. Reading extracts from the literature available, Rosie and Audrey were able to provide a focus by suggesting that, as in other fields of literature, the true distinction is that between good writing and bad. A good piece of work by an accomplished author will handle the medium and the detail with sensitivity, to tell a tale, to entertain, to inform, to educate, to challenge and perhaps even comment on the human condition.

Although climbing novels are plentiful, by comparison with other forms of literature they are rare, and there is plenty of opportunity for fledgling authors to submit short stories to the climbing press for consideration. All those present representing magazines were adamant that only a small number of unsolicited manuscripts were fiction and more would be welcome.

As a trailer to events to come later in the day, M. John Harrison's book *Climbers* was singled out by Rosie and Audrey as an excellent and brilliant novel dealing autobiographically with the life of Mike, a climber, and very much, it seemed, in the tradition of Al Harris and Lucy Rees' novel from the 1960s, *Take it to the Limit*.

After considerable discussion, much of it concentrating on whether Harrison's book really was brilliant, having received mixed reviews, Geoff Dutton, author of *The Ridiculous Mountains* treated us to a specially commissioned new story featuring The Doctor and The Apprentice, called *Midges*. With Geoff's light touch and remarkable sense of the absurd, the story tells of the Doctor's and the Apprentice's attempt at a Scottish new route. Beaten back on the first attempt by the indestructible Scottish midge, they later have to contend with the added complication of a rival expedition. After a number of twists, the story concludes with a sting in the tail as the midge repellent is exhausted. Geoff has a strong Scottish accent and the loss of a tooth or two in a recent accident carrying a ladder made it difficult to pick up all the subtleties of language, and so it is hoped that sooner rather than later the story is published so that we may again appreciate Geoff's outstanding story-telling ability.

A break for an early dinner was followed by Tim Noble reading from his first book *Great VS Climbs in the Lake District*. This was far more than a simple reading for the benefit of those who hadn't bought the book but might be persuaded, it was more of an introduction for aspiring writers. Tim emphasised the importance of being clear about your prospective audience, being able to tell the reader a story, and having a good editor.

Making his second appearance of the day, Geoff Dutton introduced a reading from M. John Harrison's' book *Climbers* as Judge of the Boardman Tasker Memorial Award for Mountain Literature, explaining why it had won and how it had been a close-run decision between *Climbers* and *Everest - Kangshung Face* by Stephen Venables.

With ghastly memories of some climbing novels in everyone's minds, Harrison's book stood out because it was a story which rose above tabloid imaginings and used fiction to extend realism, not to escape from it. With writing that was lean, crisp and compelling and language exercised with economy, *Climbers* was biting, sensitive and exploratory with a tightly-zipped compassion held ever in the background. Despite the absence of plot and largely undifferentiated characters, the book was felt by the judges to be difficult to put down, as the author explored a quite new route on unseen holds.

The reading was well received and convinced many of those listening that, in spite of the mixed reviews, the book was certainly worthy of closer inspection. A description of a route and a fall well-known to this writer certainly convinced me that here was an author who was well able to trigger memory and emotion to considerable effect.

Andy Fanshawe read a piece from the pen of the absent 'Slippery' Victor Saunders who was delayed ice climbing in Scotland. This was an extract from a book which may or may not end up being called *Five Go Mad in the Karakoram*.

Yet more new writing concluded the day as *Sean's Story* by Terry Storry was announced as the winner of the *High* Magazine writing competition. The story is an intricate tale of two separate but connected mountain deaths and how they affect those left behind. A special award was presented to 15 year-old Ian Vickers for his story *Mind Games*, telling of his real climb on Vector (E2 5c) as a 14 year-old with an imaginary Joe Brown as his guide. A part of Ian's prize is a chance to re-climb Vector with a real Joe Brown.

The day had been a virtual feast of new writing and as people made their way home one was struck by how much the event had captured the spirit of a good day cragging - a day full of fun, good humour, serious discussion and comradeship. It is to be hoped that the Festival, still in its infancy, can develop and grow into a major component on the climbing social scene, encouraging new writing and bringing mountain literature to a wider audience.

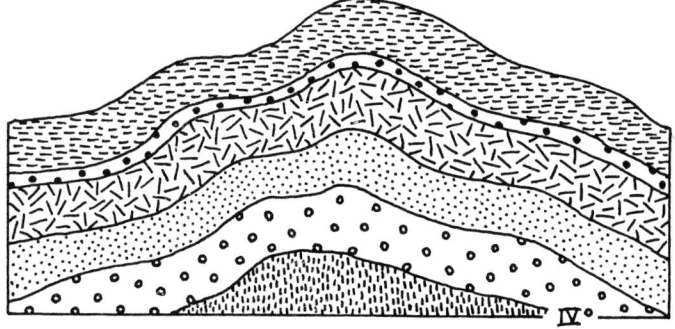

Climbing Fiction - The State of the Art

by Audrey Salkeld and Rosie Smith

There is wide subscription to the idea that 'most climbing fiction has failed'. However, considering that so much of this afternoon's programme is devoted to fiction, I am taking it that none of us here seriously hold to that belief. Let me say only that if Rosie and I felt - even for one moment, that 'most' climbing fiction had failed (or, more to the point, was failing), not only would we not be here now, but we certainly would never have embarked upon filling more than a thousand pages with the stuff. Our anthology includes four novels, two novellas, a play and thirty assorted short stories! And each and every item we have chosen because we felt it was a jolly good read.

I think the attitude we find hardest to swallow - and it is depressingly widespread - is that climbing is somehow too *sacred* to fictionalise... that its vivid real-life dramas, intense loyalties, its tales of heroism and all too frequent encounters with violent death are too precious, too much part of some private lore and myth - for any 'invented' plot to hope to match - and that moreover no-one should presume to try. I am sure this is why climbing fiction is so frequently given short shrift by climbing reviewers:

You'd have thought that by now writers would have given up trying to turn the climbing experience into a novel. The remainder bins are littered with failed attempts, at best serving only to provide a little literary light relief for climbers before they turn back to their usual reading matter - battered guidebooks and well-thumbed magazines.

From last month's *Climber* magazine!

Perhaps, though, our job here is not to make a case for the validity of climbing fiction - as I say, I am assuming us to be the enlightened few - but rather to give an idea of the vast choice and range that currently exists - state of the Art, the man said... It doesn't seem to me that there has ever been a *better* time for mountain fiction. Climbing stories go back at least a hundred years, but far more are being published now than ever before; they are getting better and better all the time, beginning at last to receive the critical attention they deserve - and (big AND, this) the majority are being written by authors who themselves have a first-hand commitment to climbing.

The amazing plot opportunities that mountaineering offers have never been lost on non-climbing authors. There has been an endless stream of tense, high action adventures - thrillers, mostly, and spy stories - enacted against spectacular mountain backdrops. A dozen or more novels must have been set on the North Wall of the Eiger alone, and hundreds of secret missions despatched to Himalayan frontiers. Other more 'general' fictional works have included climbing intrusions - Salman Rushdie's *Satanic Verses*, even, has among its characters a young woman who climbs Everest without oxygen, and thereafter keeps bumping into the shade of Maurice Wilson. In an ironic final twist, she falls to her death from the Everest Villas in Bombay.

We did wonder whether to consider novels and short stories separately - recognising them as very different - but equally valid - literary forms. Short stories tend so easily to be overlooked, and we wanted to make the point that it is particularly in the realm of the short story that so much of the vigorous new creativity is taking place. However... since many authors span both fields and indeed often venture into screen drama as well, it would probably be best to consider more generally who is behind this current surge of mountain writing.

It is no quirk of fate that the majority of authors pushing out climbing stories are based on the opposite side of the Atlantic: Greg Child, Geof Childs, Jeff Long, John Long, Dave Roberts, John Daniel, Guy Waterman, Charles Hood... just some of the many names that leap to mind. Having an outlet is the prime stimulus to new writing, and American climbing magazines (it has to be said) have a far better record than our own for publishing and reviewing works of fiction. *Climbing* magazine, *Rock and Ice*, and the late-lamented *Mountain Gazette* have all regularly printed short stories, nor should we forget the role played by *Ascent*, the Californian literary journal, which perhaps more than any other has introduced fiction writers to a receptive audience. Six stories are included in the latest edition - just out.

But in the States, the climbing short story has transcended even the climbing press. Peter Lars Sandberg published many of his pieces first in *Playboy* magazine, Kim Stanley Robinson appears regularly in sci-fi collections, and the *New Yorker*, too, from time to time has printed work by Al Alvarez, Stanislaw Lem and others.

The award this year of the Boardman Tasker to a work of fiction and the promise of more novels and collections of short stories from other writers next year should all make for a healthier climate over here too. (As with most things, the rest of the world eventually falls into step behind the Americans!)

What are all these authors finding to write about?

There are few formulae. You could not call mountain writing a *genre* in any real sense. All the sorts and styles of stories that exist can perfectly well have mountains or mountaineering as a major theme.

Although we want to concentrate particularly this afternoon on those authors who are pushing out work now, it would be no bad thing to take a quick look back first to a novel from 1951, which at the time was recognised as starting a new direction in mountain writing...

It certainly wasn't by the then Bishop of Chester, though. He condemned Elizabeth Coxhead's book, *One Green Bottle*, for its explicitness. After all, its heroine, Cathy Canning, didn't just indulge in *free sex*, she also took her own precautions against becoming pregnant, and this is, after all, truly shocking.

But the Bishop of Chester missed the point, anyway. Cathy's sexual awakening is only one theme of the book, which above all explores the breaking and retention of class barriers and, to some extent, female liberation, although here Coxhead ultimately fails her female characters, as we shall partly see.

Cathy comes from Tooley Street: a harsh, impoverished part of Birkenhead. Life is bleak: dull, grey and monotonous. So when she is invited by chance to North Wales for a weekend, and discovers rock climbing and a healthy, fresh-air environment, it brings about many changes in her life. Other climbers she meets are from differing backgrounds and this broadens her experience tremendously. Her climbing is increasingly good and hard and she has guts and determination. However...

After a relationship with a lad called Chris, which reaches a tortuous and hopelessly Hardyesque ending, Cathy decides to return to Tooley Street for good, to nurture her intellectually and emotionally weak ex-boyfriend on his return from borstal. And this, really, is where the novel falls down, because Cathy is *such* a strong character, and so many of her discoveries are so joyous, that you know such an ending *could not be*. If Cathy were male, Coxhead would have been accused of metaphorically castrating her. So incensing is the finish, it had to be put right in some way, and Jim Perrin in his *On the Rocks* series in *Climber and Hillwalker* gave Cathy something of a let-out with an optional ending. Thus has fiction spawned fiction.

Coxhead's middle class view of life somewhat oversimplifies the class distinctions, making them a little cardboard-cut-out to view, but for all this there is an eminent readability about this novel. You can't put it down, even if you're using it as a focus for socially moral outrage. And it is exceptional in that its themes predate all the social realism novels of the 'Angry Young Men' of the sixties.

Many people today still regard *One Green Bottle* as the finest climbing novel ever written. Good as it is, such a judgement does seem to wilfully ignore much that has been written since.

It might have been expected that, given the open-armed welcome from establishment climbers to *One Green Bottle*, Lucy Rees' *Take It to the Limit* would have been similarly embraced. If - in 1951 - Cathy Canning could sleep with a bounder in exchange for a pair of climbing boots, and with the man she loves, out of wedlock, and cause little affront (apart from to the Bishop), you would have thought that thirty permissive years later no eyebrows would be raised at further tales of North Wales goings-on. Wrong. *The Alpine Journal*:

Oh dear! Another exposé of what things are like at the high sharp end of the climbing scene where the main stimulus comes apparently from non-conformity, alcohol and sex. This may well be so, as the authors seem determined to point out. But the main body of mountaineers is much different from this, easier to accept and more pleasant by far to know. Do they care very much what motivates the lunatic fringe?

Lucy Rees - boosted by the recollections and fantasies of the legendary and now sadly-late Al Harris - had recreated the extrovert anarchism of Deiniolen in the late sixties. But it would be a shame if, believing it merely to be the cavortings of a lunatic fringe, readers were put off from discovering here a well-written, moving and essentially moral story. It looks back less with nostalgia or any glorification of hedonism than with bitterness for lost innocence and thwarted promise. The young, restless central figure, Luke, is the apex of a tragic love-triangle: he and his older, more stable climbing partner are both loved by the same woman. The action moves swiftly between Wales, Scotland and the Lakes to reach its climax on a big wall climb in Yosemite. Scenes are set with vivid economy. Conversations live. There are wistful echoes of Salinger, and the outcome is achingly sad. It is a book of a period, but equally, it is timeless. And long overdue for reappraisal.

Solo Faces by James Salter (1980) explores the problems and the ultimate loneliness of the hard climber. This book has been criticised for its minimalist style, unasham.d machismo and intensity-for-its-own-sake. Climbers have been dismissive, too, because they do not see the author as a 'true believer': he climbed for a while with Royal Robbins, largely, it seems, as research for this novel, and then went his way.

Polished to a fine shine, *Solo Faces* is plainly the work of a talented writer and, 'minimalist' or not, packs in a deceptive amount of detail. It has a compelling story-line, even if it can promise no happy ending. Salter was fascinated by the briefly incandescent career of the American climber Gary Hemming, who took the Alpine world by storm in the middle sixties with his bold climbs and even bolder rescues. Darling of the French press, *Le Beatnik* grabbed the headlines for one last time in 1969 when he plugged a bullet into his skull (do it the Hemingway). Salter's driven central character is clearly a Hemming figure, and the story examines his seesaw swoops between elation and despair, between fulfilling climbs and the brutal knocks climbing can deliver. Finally, he has to face the slow losing of grip as age and alienation take their toll:

His hand searched up and down. Everything was happening too fast, nothing was happening. The ice had weaknesses but he could not find them. His legs began to tremble. The secret one must keep despite everything had begun to spill, he could not prevent it. He was not going to be able to do this. He knew it. The will was draining from him.

He had the resignation of one condemned. He knew the outcome, he no longer cared, he merely wanted it to end. The wind had killed his fingers.

"You can do it," he said, "you can do it."

He was clinging to the face. Slowly his head bent forward to rest against it like a child resting against its mother. His eyes closed. "You can do it," he said.

***

They came up the meadow to find him. He was sitting in the sunlight in a long-sleeved undershirt and faded pants like a convalescent.

"What turned you back? Was it the weather?"

As a novel, the book did respectably well - satisfying such demanding critics as Alvarez, Norman Mailer and Graham Greene - but many climbers lost sight of the whole by getting hooked up on whether Salter had or had not explained climbing jargon fully (a perennial problem when making climbing stories accessible to a wide public). And that terse style, they found that uncomfortable, too - such a long way from dear Winthrop Young!

Having to come to terms with 'Age and a resultant loss of climbing powers' is a recurring preoccupation for both novelists and short story writers. An older man and a younger man climbing together - we see it in Alvarez's *Night Out*, which concerns an epic in the Dolomites and was inspired by a climb on Cima Grande which Alvarez made with Mo Anthoine. The theme reappears in Pat Ament's *Moments of Personal Peril*, Les Ellison's *Doubt*, and *Backing Off* by Dave Roberts, where the older man feels obliged to rein in his young companion's impetuosity, realising in so doing that their partnership can never again be one of equals.

John Long's *For Everything Its Season* is a bit more complicated. Here we have again the experienced guy and the younger climber, but a mystery as well - because the younger man's brother has earlier been chopped whilst climbing with the older man, and in circumstances which have never been fully explained.

John Long is one of the most invigorating of today's storytellers. He's a larger than life 'adventurer' and has been described as the man in the Camel ad just stepped off the page. His tales are gutsy and the prose often as crazed and breakneck as some of his own escapades. His job nowadays is writing film scripts; climbing stories are a diversion.

All these last-mentioned are short stories, by the way, as is *The White Graph* by Irish writer Dermot Somers. This centres on a climber recovering from the combined effects of his marriage failure, financial difficulties *and* emotional breakdown - a full-blown mid-life crisis in fact. However, he is now climbing again, in the Alps, and draws wisdom and the strength for survival from the experience. But he can only do this at the expense of other people's egos and in consequence his young, male partners have to be sort of one-climb stands, casual pick-ups in climbing areas.

Somers has been producing powerful stories like this for many years. Suppressed violence and betrayal are his especial strengths, as well as the evocation of historical outrage. He definitely deserves much wider recognition, and this will hopefully come next year when a full collection - *Mountains and Other Ghosts* - is expected to make an appearance.

Anne Sauvy is someone who already has two collections of short stories published and a novel on the way - but unfortunately they're in French. Not enough of her work has yet been translated. An exception, though, is *La Fourche*, which appeared in the 1985 *Alpine Journal*. It's a chilling Faustian fantasy (one of several we came across) in which her ageing hero buys back youth from the Devil, along with climbing skill the like of which has never been seen before. New routes, popularity, fasts cars, good looks, gorgeous women... he commands them all... *and* the first winter solo ascent of Everest - without oxygen - to boot. He leads a charmed life, but one day the only girl he has ever loved dies during a climb with him on the Grandes Jorasses. For the first time *Faustin* realises the worth of a soul... and time is running out...

It's heartening, anyway, to see that Steck and Roper have included another of Sauvy's stories, *The Collector*, in the latest *Ascent*. This excellently-written tale might make many a first ascensionist feel uncomfortable... I'll say no more...

Gwen Moffat - whose output has mostly been meaty detective stories - was another to choose the ageing theme when she ventured into 'straight' fiction. Owen Parry, the central figure of her novel *Hard Option*, is the leader of a mountain rescue team. He finds it increasingly hard to keep up with younger colleagues, but there is no way that he is prepared to relinquish to them any of the responsibility or glory that goes with his position. In the end, it is an adulterous liaison with a cool-headed, young woman climber that brings about his downfall. And what a downfall! With a relish bordering on vindictiveness (one is reminded of Charlotte Bronte's emasculation of Mr. Rochester), Gwen Moffat sees to it that poor Parry is brought very low indeed: he is made to confront all his inadequacies, as a climber and as a lover, and then, when his mental disintegration is almost complete - when he's lost his wife, his best friend, this girl that he loves and every last vestige of human pride - Moffat really puts the boot in. She strikes him down with a paralysing stroke - yet still manages to make the last line of the book sound hopeful!

Well, after all that, you'll be relieved to know that humour and farce live on! More, though, in short stories than long. We're all looking forward to Geoff Dutton's new story this afternoon and hope *More Ridiculous Mountains* are on the way...

His fellow countryman Robin Campbell has shown ingenuity in bringing a resuscitated Sherlock Holmes and Doctor Watson to the Highlands - and they're investigating mysteries that involve real-life mountaineers. Collie and Raeburn are integral to the action in *The Adventure of the Misplaced Eyeglasses*. There's a certain ironic neatness in this, since Collie may well have been Conan Doyle's model for Holmes himself and was certainly often addressed as 'Holmes' by his friends. A sequel, *The Case of the Great Grey Man* (set on Ben Macdhui, of course) is, we think, even better and features Munro of the Tables fame. We're hoping for more of these too.

A wonderful little one-off is Greg Child's story, *No Gentlemen in the Himalaya*. This has the unlikely scenario of a Catholic priest secretly organising an expedition to the Himalaya - as a cover for something sinister. He is investigating a new religion which has sprung up in one area, whose main symbolism centres on paper aeroplanes and whose main catchword is the mysterious 'Bool'. The answer lies in the past on Nanga Parbat...

Guy Waterman's amusing *The Gearfreak Caper* is written in the style of the American down-at-heel detective story. Nick Barrett's (very short) short story *Rescue at Stoney* is in the mould of Damon Runyon's *Guys and Dolls*, but Dave Gregory's style in his *Old Man* stories is uniquely his own, as in *Her Two Doors Up:*

He's on a good thing, is Batesie: Sonja following him about with sheepdoggy eyes and Her Two Doors Up *offering him all these spare-time jobs in the way of wiring. And her house is one of only four on our street in stone. All the others are brick but two pairs of semis are in gritstone. Mrs. Armthwaite lives in half of one but* Two Doors Up *lets Batesie use the side wall of hers by the gennel to practise on, providing he doesn't use chalk. It's the only training he does. All this pumping iron and doing pull-ups with weights on is all wrong. The only training for climbing is climbing, he says, and he can go three times one way and two back along* Her Two Doors Up's *side wall. When he's pumped he gets invited in for a cup of tea and a discussion on wiring and who knows what else besides. A very good thing he thought he was onto until Mrs. Armthwaite got suspicious.*

She doesn't need to see anything dubious to start a rumour, but

*pretty soon Batesie is going about with a face as long as a fiddle
because Mrs. Armthwaite is spreading rumours that he and* Her
Two Doors Up *are making Gomorrah look like a Sunday School
trip and Sonja is beginning to believe the rumours and starting to
give him a heavy measure of how-could-you glances and a fair bit of
earache. Besides, Sonja's Mam is dead and her Dad's really
protective about her, and he's the foreman electrician where Batesie
works.*

"I'll fix her," says Batesie, "I'll fix her a notice."

*Two nights later I'm round and he's climbing up the front of her
house with a couple of notices to hang on her guttering.*

'Nosey Nora', one said, and 'Scandalmonger', said the other.

*Clever little notices, they were, with hooks to catch on the
guttering. Up to the gutter in a twinkling he is and traversing left
to just beside the window. Something took his concentration for a
moment because the next thing his foot has slipped and he's done a
microsecond layaway on the window edge and has had to drop off
onto the path.*

*There he is lying on the path moaning about his broken ankle
and I'm wondering how to get him away from there without ruining
his ankle for life and Mrs. Armthwaite knowing, when out comes
she looking very flustered.*

*"Here comes the storm"' I said to Batesie, turning the notices
upside down.*

In crime fiction, inventing an amateur sleuth who can then
be used over and again is common practice, and to an extent
these characters become the alter egos of their creators, going
where they go and sharing their tastes and personal quirks.
Gwen Moffat's Melinda Pink is a kindly, middle-aged, semi-
retired climber and writer, and devoted conservationist, who
first took shape in 1973 and is still going strong. Moffat's
plots are inventive, having the ring of authenticity that is the
result of dedicated homework. Miss Pink will sidle up to a
parked sports car and measure whether or not a body would
fit into its boot; her butcher advises on the grislier intricacies
of dismembering corpses. Moffat shows flair, too, in the way

the bodies are disposed of. One she composted with the grass clippings in a hippy commune. The stories are well paced and sufficiently mind-bending to keep you alert and guessing to the end, but although Gwen Moffat's books retain their links with climbing, it is probably true to say that her readership is now drawn largely from the non-climbing public. Certainly few of her more recent novels have been reviewed by the climbing press.

Futuristic writing is particularly popular with short story writers. Mostly they are concerned with the way climbing might be conducted in the next century, what form new climbing aids could take (like heated chalk bags), or what effects might be felt through the imposition of outside control. There have been a number of when-the-bomb-drops stories: Martyn Berry in *Last Climb* has two men scaling Cloggy as atomic rockets land all over Britain; Dermot Somers in *Nightfall* places his climbers on the Eigerwand when Armageddon strikes.

Then there is space travel. Kim Stanley Robinson's *Green Mars* describes an expedition to Olympus Mons, the tallest mountain in the solar system. A convincing alternative 'world' is created for Mars, but it is a world that has been tampered with, greened by the Earth scientists and populated with a bewildering array of mongrel species created by the very best bird- and mammal-designers. Throughout the expedition, the hero, Roger - who preferred the planet the red way it was when he first saw it as a young man - cannot shift a weight of depression, and that is the nub of his isolation. Only too well he remembers the endless, windswept desert, and the brilliant golden light - and it is this ability to remember back nearly three hundred years that sets him apart from his fellows. Less than one per cent of the antique population share the gift (or curse) of powerful, long-term recollection. The leader of Roger's expedition is a woman he loved way back when he was a canyon guide and she a young city girl on one of his treks. She has no memory of this, of course, but there is still some of the old magic there, and this warmth of affection, coupled with the fact that on the summit of Olympus Mons, beyond reach of the new atmosphere, he finds traces of old Mars, gives Roger the strength to face a few more hundred years!

A Climbing Expedition provides a very satisfactory framework for a story. Not only does it provide action and give direction to the narrative in the form of a quest, it is also a particularly good vehicle for exploring psychological interplay. As in the ever-popular desert island or airplane-crash scenarios, the cast and characters are well 'contained', and the only outside influences that creep in - apart from the odd monk or sherpa - are in the form of emotional baggage that the characters bring with them.

Greg Child's *In Another Tongue* is interesting for offering an alternative view. The tragic events that claimed thirteen lives on K2 in the summer of 1986 are seen from the perspective of the Balti porters who watched and waited below. Barry Collins in his powerful one-man play *The Ice Chimney* sought to recreate the last tortured hours of Maurice Wilson on Everest. Mallory and Irvine have crept into a surprising number of stories: Guy Waterman's *The Bronx Plumber* concerns a visionary workman who has Mallory moments while mending a leaky toilet; Jeff Long's *In Gentle Combat with the Cold Wind* is a spooky tale of a climber picking up a hitch-hiker, who turns out to be the ghost of Irvine; *Mother Goddess of the World*, also by Kim Stanley Robinson, tells of a modern expedition that goes to Everest to look for Mallory and Irvine.

Expeditions also serve in the Awakening-of-Consciousness Department. I will hand over to Rosie for an outline of *Déva* by Michael Tobias - Tobias, the Obscure...

Someone said to me recently, "You've done well if you've managed to read Déva." It's that sort of book: wordily and idealistically 'heavy'. It is, after all, published under the literature/philosophy category. I don't doubt that it's art, but it takes a very dubious form of it sometimes.

It starts with a lot of physical masturbation and you wonder after a bit if that isn't self-parody of the intellectual masturbation to follow. But it does have a plot! And that is the quest by alpinist pilgrims for ineffable wisdom. They find it, to a greater or lesser extent, in a remote Himalayan 'Garden of Eden' peopled by a handful of holy mystics - horny holy mystics, it must be said.

In places, you wonder if Tobias is just waffling deep and meaningful American gobbledygook or if you're just an out-and-out Philistine, and in the end you suspect both might be true! Some extracts seem to be just lists of words - academic and philosophical name-dropping. Try this for size:

Spirit? A combination, of intuition, reptilian ego, slimy, mud-caked volition. All earthbound. I was celebrating a limbo of myself. Rhapsodic with an animal parody so vivid, so alluring... Jeffers in Big Sur, Lawrence in Taos, Neruda on the beach in Malaysia, Kazantzakis in Murmansk, Shelley on the Mer de Glass, Lermontov in Tiflis, Basho in the far North of Japan, Sappho at the white cliffs of Lefkas (off which she jumped - Katapontismos -), Claude Gelee in the Campagna, Hukosai before Mount Fuji... with all my western enumerata, I felt firmly, squeamishly linked to a tradition of the hypnotic, the suggestive...

... it doesn't read much better in context, either.

In short, Tobias never uses one metaphor where ten will do, but again there is a hint of self-parody in Chapter Sixteen when he says:

My metaphors were failing me.

As I said, though, it does have a plot, and the narrative itself is highly entertaining and descriptive, and certainly doesn't shrink from parody of the people and ideas it promotes. It is worth getting past the wordy sections to access this.

Those of you who have read Bernard Amy's short story *The Greatest Climber in the World* would recognise a possible basis for this novel. Still, in the end, who has the last laugh? The reader? The author? The narrator? Or Déva? And how many climbers have sneaked off after reading it to spend hours staring at lichen and becoming one with the rock?

A novel which places its central character on a Himalayan expedition, yet to a large extent concerns itself with events that have taken place beforehand (the emotional baggage we spoke about) is Elizabeth Arthur's controversial *Beyond the Mountain*.

Some sources suggest that the inspiration for this comes from Arlene Blum and the Women's Annapurna expedition. Certainly it uses an all-female expedition as its focus, and one cannot deny that the central character is called Artemis.

The said Artemis reflects during the course of the expedition upon the tragic deaths of her husband and brother in an avalanche. She remembers many scenes and incidents with both characters, and traces through the tortuous paths of her relationships with them both. She was so close to her brother as to almost cross the acceptable bounds of sibling love, and had a passionate and stormy time with her husband, whom she is contemplating leaving when the accident happens. Her experiences in the course of the expedition are cleansing and painful by turn, but she is finally able to work the guilt, pain and doubt out of her system in a long and vicious storm high on the mountain. Only after this is she able to relate properly to the other women.

As can be expected from a sport so long participated in by more men than women, there are times in climbing fiction when female characters get pretty poor treatment. This does not necessarily mean that all their authors agree with such treatment. In places this is used only to convey the attitude of another character, not to condone the acts or descriptions themselves. But there are certainly a few examples that elicit winces or make your blood boil. On the whole, though, the sexes are becoming less stereotyped in more recent fiction, and Tim Ahern in his latest piece in *Ascent*, called *Headwall*, has presented the case of a young gay dancer who turns to climbing and does extremely well at it, much to the outrage of some heteros who failed where he's now succeeded.

Some years ago, in the middle of winter, a plane carrying a cargo of smuggled marijuana crashed into a lake in the High Sierras. Climbers were first upon the scene. By the time the official agencies caught up, the frozen lake was pockmarked with chainsaw holes and there was little left to find. (That year a lot of smart new climbing gear appeared on the rocks around Yosemite Valley......)

Sounds like fiction? Yes - but true. However, the event has provided the stimulus for two quite exceptional novels. First is Jeff Long's *Angels of Light*. This really is a climbers' novel. Its rough language and drug references, as well as its assumption that no jargon needs describing, will automatically place it beyond the reach of 'mainstream' readers - very much to their loss. Three reviewers saw it as a modern-day Western, and it is easy to see why: the Camp Four bums around whom the story is based are outlaws. There are deep and unquestioned loyalties between them, action is fast, and the retribution violent. You'll go a long way to find climbing description as vivid as this:

By the movements of Tucker's head, John could tell the crack was oddly shaped. Freeing one hand from the crack, Tucker rapidly pawed through the clinking hardware, spreading the bunched metal and slings with a small slap to see what there was. That innocuous slap, its impatience, further confirmed what John had guessed: Tucker was too wiped to waste muscle on anything but a sure fit, and the crack wasn't going to allow a sure fit. Tucker powered himself farther on, running the rope out another three feet in search of some crack that would take his protection. He pawed the rack and fished a piece loose, one of the large tubes. He unclipped it and tried to stuff it into the crack. The movement of his hands was slightly too fast, a bad sign. Nerves. A moment later his right knee twitched, no more than a hint of sewing machine leg, but still a hint. He was getting scared.

John spared a glance at the belay anchor. Three solid nuts, one slotted to take an upward pull. If - when- Tucker fell, John was going to get yanked up into the wall. The anchor would hold. John saw that he could catch the fall. But Tucker was going to smash against the wall like a watermelon on a cord. John moved tight against the anchor, bracing for the pull. He was spellbound.

Tucker kept trying, all his effort devoted to inserting the tube and covering his ass. When nothing worked, he did something John had never seen in all his days as a climber. Instead of clipping the piece back on the rack, he simply tossed the useless tube over his shoulder, just cast it away. The tube dropped through the air. Not once did it skip off the lower wall. The overhang was profound and the metal disappeared without a sound. Tucker thrust his hand into the rack again, unclipped the largest spring cam, tried it once, twice, then tossed it, too, into the void. Forty dollars.

"No," wailed Tucker, and he tried to scoot his hands deeper into the crack. He was too tired to rest, and if he rested he'd only get more tired. His hands started slipping. John expelled all his air, clamped his hands tight on the ropes.

Tucker fell.

The other story inspired by the airplane crash is *Vortex*, a powerful first novel from the Canadian writer, David Harris. This has not yet been published, but will make its debut in our anthology. (*Advertisement!*)

To develop the smuggling theme, Harris has shifted his main action to the North Cascade Mountains on the US/Canadian border: two climbers discover a crashed light aircraft on Mount Redoubt with a contraband cargo and an injured survivor. By rescuing the man, they get sucked into the deadly business of drug-running, and the story is told both from their point of view, and that of the San Francisco cop who is trying to bust the drugs ring. Swift cutting between these two fields of activity and the containment of the story almost completely within dialogue and action (i.e., few descriptive or ruminative passages) make for very slick, film-like editing - and no doubt it was always in the author's mind that this might eventually transfer to the screen. That is not to suggest that the writing is not skilful - it is: compact and clean. The characters are strong and believable, you want to know what happens to them and, although this is a very long book, the sense of menace is maintained to the very last line.

But the point really to make about this story is that although it is about climbers, and includes climbing episodes, it is climbing set into a wider context - in the same way that Dick Francis explores all around the racing world without overloading his thrillers with actual race descriptions. This would seem a very positive way forward for mountain fiction - if it is to reach wider acceptance.

Two things have happened recently that really excite us as 'state of the art' climbing fiction. One is the publication and recognition of Harrison's controversial *Climbers*, the other is the Fringe performance of a musical called *E5 6b* at the Edinburgh Festival. *Climbers* will be discussed later this afternoon, and you will hear a reading from it, so suffice it to say we think it's brilliant. *E5 6b* is a musical play around the exploits of a group of girls who go to the Lake District to climb Footless Crow and there meet and clash with two Yorkshire lads of similar intent. The cast were Lower Sixth Form students - fourteen girls and one boy. It was intriguingly billed in the Festival programme as 'unsuitable for children', but received a Fringe First Award. You can see it at the Wakefield Theatre Royal in January.

It's very frustrating having had to condense such a large

and wonderful subject as climbing fiction into a 45-minute talk. We just couldn't cover everything. There's so much to say, so many themes and ideas yet to explore, but most of all, so much to read. Don't dismiss climbing fiction until you've given it a very good try. Hopefully no-one would dismiss all fiction because the first thing they ever read was a *Janet and John* first-year reader book, would they? So if you hear someone who says they've tried a little bit and do not like it, suggest that maybe they just tried the wrong little bit for them.

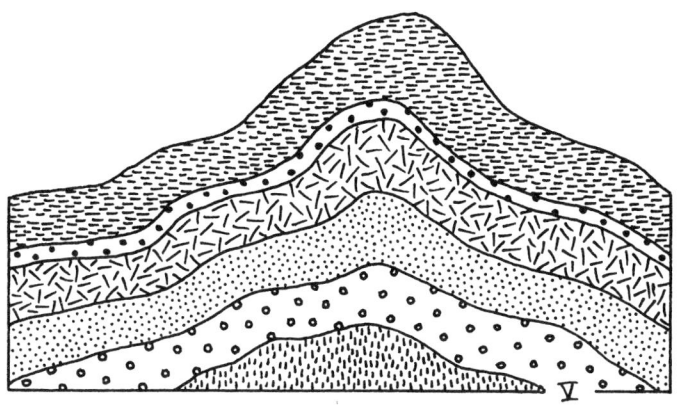

Midges

by Geoff Dutton

Midges have been much maligned. They not only protect us, provide an unsleeping Air Umbrella for our precious West Highland scenery: they can also help us to a First Ascent - or to understand what a First Ascent is really about. They are great teachers of ethics. As we discovered to our cost. Although we made that First Ascent - the Best-Seller of its day - with the help of midges, we were ashamed of ourselves, the Apprentice and I; we still are.

Yet, as a Munro is a Munro, so a First Ascent is a First Ascent, and nowadays nobody is perfect; moreover, the germ, so to speak, of this biological weapon emanated from the Doctor, hitherto so upright a man. He was not in the climbing team - the grade was too high - he was Base for the expedition; Base indeed. But he ensured our success; if it can be called a success when the vanquished, however disreputable, trudge off with the moral victory.

Enough of snivelling. To the story. It is a lesson for all climbers. It should be told. For, as the Doctor observed by the Primus that evening, peering into his glass through a penumbra of equally thirsty uncountables: "Too much competition - *poogh* - tends to obscure the - *poogh* - essential Spirit."

The Apprentice had to cross to Harris for that first ascent. His fellow-Weasels were Alpineering and rivals were athirst. So I joined him; the crux coming last, I could at worst be hauled over it. The Doctor was there to cook, and watch the fun.

The weather steamed close and cloudy, after weeks of cold rain. We waded over a sopping hill, and the great cliff of

Sròn a' Mheanbh-Chuileag rose imperturbably before us. Our eyes scurried nervously about it. No one was there. We would be the first! Straight up the centre unrolled the only possible line, Leac Mhòr, the Great Slab, that unclimbed new discovery everyone was raving about. It had been attempted only the week before by a couple of teams but, as the Apprentice pointed out, they came from Glasgow. They had, nevertheless, pioneered as far as the crux. *That* appeared impossible - it jerked outwards above us like a vast flight of stone steps seen upside down from underneath.

"Great," declared the Apprentice, a little hoarsely.

We splashed down to the river gravel for a meal. Our domestic help began to make jammy pieces and set up the tent. The Apprentice and I, adhesive from sweat and apprehension, stripped and plunged into a fine bellowing pool, frothy with spate.

"Don't!" called the Doctor. "It's dangerous!"

We looked at each other. We had all of us forded and swum (often by accident) much fiercer water than this. The Doctor had now turned not only cook but nursemaid. Nonsense. Perfectly safe.

"The midges!" he shouted. "They'll get you when you come out."

So what? We two were going up the Slab, not festering round the tent like him.

As we munched our pieces, vastly refreshed, and insulated by the Doctor's unseen rucksack from infinite bog, we ridiculed his prognosis. Ah, but immersion, he averred, removed the body's protective layer of oils. "You mean dirt?" suggested the Apprentice, through his crumbs. "Exactly!" It appeared that the accumulated greases of the skin impeded midgy mandibles. They found it difficult to sook. Washed, we would be a naked lunch to unnumberable multitudes of Chironomidae. This place in this weather would generate the most ravenous midges within the whole lengthy jurisdiction of An Comhairle nan Eilean. The Doctor had already identified them as the two worst of the whole bloodsucking bunch, *Culicoides heliophilus* and *Culicoides impunctatus*. So there.

A few of the brutes had already appeared that morning. They bit us even in our then well-enough-larded state. As the old man at the last croft had remarked, "The midges is no very *good* the day." So we rubbed in more midge-repellent and hurried across to the climb, the Doctor remaining entrenched behind turned-up collar, pipe smoke and Natural Oils.

I do not want to remember the rest of that day. Instead of climbing out of midges, we climbed into them. The Sròn was the west end of a high boggy tableland, its top and sides dribbled with bog; it stood in a bog. So, from bottom, sides and top midges screamed out at us, radars blaring, rockets firing. Faces, hair, necks, ears, eyes, backs of hands, wrists, crawled with a million engines, tracers incessantly stung and flashed. Torture of infinite needles. Jab, jab, jab. Hell, hell, hell; more hell...

I gave up half-way, blind and one-handed. The Apprentice lasted a little longer, banging in a runner at the crux. But he ran out of oaths, and midges swarmed into the vacated territory. We spun down, coiled ropes and vanished. Flies were nothing to this.

At the tent, we dived into bags, head and all. The Doctor, puffing valiantly, made supper. Midge-netting kept most outside, and those within - chastened by St. Bruno - congregated along the ridge-seams and were periodically incinerated by a brandished Primus. Numbers gradually decreased. We uncovered heads, warily.

"Midges no very good the day," observed our companion genially, poking the pot. He remained unchastised, for cooks are the Sacred Fools of climbing, licensed jesters, dear to the belly. And he had warned us.

That night, sleep was fitful; we were iridescent with bites, and refugees wandered wakefully about our hair. The Apprentice tossed, in a rage of frustration. First ascent... first ascent... and last chance.

We rose late, to a midgeless morning. But the steamy weather promised another yesterday. However, the Doctor had not been idle. He produced two midge-helmets for us: his spare stockings, with slits for eyes. "And you can wear your own spare socks as gloves, the ends pierced for fingers." That, and the remaining midge cream, would see us up to - maybe over - the crux, now the way there was familiar. We blessed him as he stirred the porridge, twinkling grand-maternally.

The Apprentice crawled out, stood up and gazed happily at the Sròn. Then his eyes popped. He groaned, swore, stamped, slapped thighs and cursed again. We all peered out.

Below the crag stood People. We were forestalled. Who?

"No, no: Oh NO!" wailed the Apprentice. "It's *them!*"

"Who's Them?" asked the Doctor, beginning to regret his slit stockings.

"Wee Dander," sobbed the Apprentice, "*and* Greetin Jimmie; *and* The Porpus." He named three legendary figures. "And there's Else and Big Ian to look after them..."

We were suitably silent. Wee Dander was one of those youthful prodigies who - for a few years - climb apparently everything with unstopping ease and no little scorn. More than that, he would never write up his routes, never bother to record them. He had no use for journals or guide-books, or other people. He was pure Oral Tradition, pure Hero, sheer Me; free as the wind. Hateful, no doubt; but enviable in many ways. His companions tied themselves always second and third on a rope that was invariably the best you could buy, like the rest of his kit - which he never did buy; the three of them, aided by Else and Big Ian, took whatever they needed from any unoccupied tent or car they came across. Hateful. Dangerously enviable.

They saw us and ambled over as we swallowed our now tasteless porridge. Wee Dander was indeed wee, a laddie, in tatty shirt and shorts, with an open expressionless very pale face and uncannily penetrating blue eyes; any age between twelve and seventeen. He bent over and picked a piece of bacon from the pan the Doctor was frying and nibbled it carefully. Then he picked a couple more pieces and threw them to his companions behind. All three masticated in silence.

We looked them over, refusing to speak first. Greetin Jimmie was a long skeletal youth in grubby denims and greasy shirt; his equally oleaginous hair sprawled to a thin pimply face, dreepy red nose and sparse fringe of unappetising gingery beard - or he may not have shaved that week (it was indeed difficult to imagine him shaving). A dismal enough streak, from knocky knees to watery eyes. The Porpus - round and polished as the playful Cetacean - bulged from relatively clean sark and shorts; he grinned even while chewing, small pink nose and ears oscillating independently. He rolled an enormous boulder across and sat on it; it was one the Doctor and I had failed to move when pitching the tent.

Before Wee Dander could appropriate more breakfast the Doctor smartly tossed the rest to us. Our guest was then moved to communicate.

"Saw yer runner. Been up, eh?" A hard, clear, raw-fish accent.

The Apprentice, wrestling with honesty, said he'd had a look and come down early, but would be up the day right enough.

"Like hell." (Pause) "But thanks fer the runner; nae use here - 'll dae fine fer the Ben next week, though." (Pause) "Well; we'll jist awa up. See ya."

And he sauntered off back to the cliff. Greetin Jimmie nodded morosely at us and followed his leader. The Porpus, still managing the odd chew, beamed and waved a flipper. He clanked away uphill; they were particularly well-equipped that morning, having passed a Mountain Adventure camp the day before.

They paused at our pool. The Porpus gesticulated. He wished to gambol therein. Wee Dander scowled; and was moving away when the Doctor, to our astonishment, leapt up and shouted.

"Hi! Don't go in! It's dangerous..."

What the devil? We looked at him bewildered; then at the three. But the Doctor knew his man. Wee Dander stopped dead. His eyes unslung their Kalashnikovs. *He* was not going to be head-mastered by any what-ho! tweed-brandishing establishmentarian.

He stripped off and dived, right into the considerable whirlie under the waterfall; and stayed down a long while to prove his point. The Porpus rolled and splashed, gleaming epidermally, while Jimmie, even dirtier with his clothes off, waded in slowly, rubbing long thin shanks bitterly and fading gradually to a pale shrimp-pink.

The Apprentice smiled for the first time in twenty-four hours. That, of course, is why we climb with the Doctor. A practical man, so *good* with People.

We took it easy. We watched them rope up; we saw Big Ian and Else unfold some sort of encampment on the bog beneath the cliff. We kitted ourselves out, packing midge-helmets and socks carefully, and used up all the midge cream so we needn't tell a lie later. The Doctor stayed to guard the tent. We strolled across in the gathering fug, regarding emergent midges almost benignly. Of course we were a little dirtier now, more naturally repellent...

Wee Dander proved a marvellous climber. He was already entering the crux. He would easily get over, he contemptuously pocketed the Apprentice's sling, he flowed with a lovely movement, elastic as rubber. Greetin Jimmie stalked after him like a vertical pond-skater; multilimbed, and impeccably adept at ropework. The Porpus, whose job was never to peel but to hold the others when they did, scuttled like a crab. It was a great team to watch. We felt ourselves almost wishing them success.

Then they began to jerk, increasingly. Early Warnings had sounded, the defenders were busy. Progress slowed, became intermittent. The rope twitched, agonisingly; coiled, uncoiled, gave forth sobs and cries. It was not so nice to watch. A beautiful animal was being done to death. The leader crouched between moves, slapped bare thighs and neck, his second agitated beneath a cloud, the third man beat bongo-drums about his waist-band, jangling in disarray.

We came up to Else, a plump vaguely belligerent Amazon, and Big Ian, even larger and grinning hugely. "Bloody midges," he remarked, rubbing with vigour. What went on above was not of great concern to him. Else swore low and continuously, rummaging in an ample knee-length jersey, well adapted to supermarkets.

A great crash above us, and we all fled. Wee Dander, blinded by midgery, had peeled on the final step. Greetin Jimmie, enmeshed in his web, shot up - still scratching - to a sentry box. The Porpus, smacking his backside, sat down in space and held them all; a large sling of Mountain Adventure cutlery had meanwhile slipped off his tray and nearly brained us.

It was a curious sight; three in tension at various angles, writhing and scratching like St. Vitus. Somehow, Wee Dander fought back up, Jimmie slithered down to his stance, The Porpus swam to the surface. But all magic was gone. The lower pair, fisting eyes, faces and limbs in a frenzy, implored their leader to come down. Wee Dander tried again. And again; wiping his forehead - milling with millions - blindly against the cold Precambrian. Terrifying. At the very profile of the last step we watched him slip, slip, recover; slip, recover.

Then he abseiled down. And yes; we were sorry.

They stood beside us, two of them rubbing and cursing. Wee Dander, his pale face bloodstained, crawling with tormentors, looked straight at us. His teeth had bitten his lips white.

"Any... midge... cream...?" It must have cost him.

We had used all ours up, the Apprentice explained. He displayed the flattened tube. He did not look at me, nor I at him. Silence.

"Aye," said Wee Dander.

Else and Big Ian had packed up the tents. They all moved off, hunched and muffled, pummelling zipped anoraks, Wee Dander leading. He slowed, the others overtook him. He stopped, looked back and spun something towards us.
"Yer runner," he said.
And went on.

We deserved it.

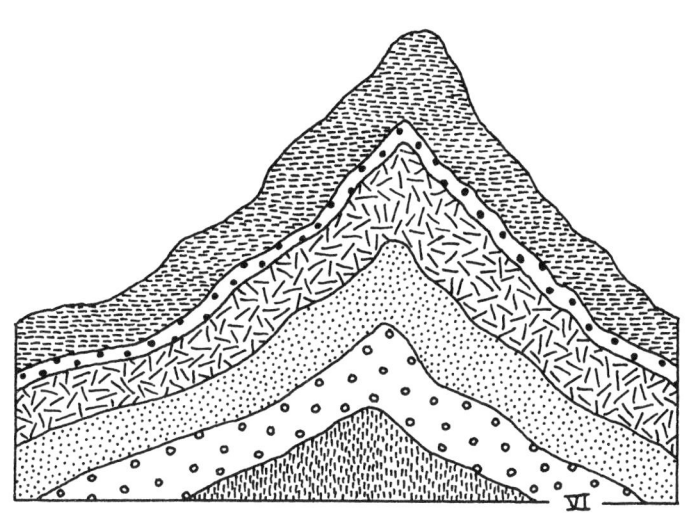

The Eleven Metre Crack

by Bob Cooper

The crack holds coldness
which pours down your arm.
Your hand, tight scraped red,
no longer feels pain.

Your last runner runs
scuttling down the rope.
Your stretched leg aches.

There is no turning back.
Each move is now doubt;
you must trust yourself.
The air is tense with waiting.

Boardman Tasker Memorial Award for Mountain Literature Chairman of the Judges' Speech

by Geoff Dutton

We found this year's submissions very interesting indeed - from the variety of topics treated, and from the neck and neck finish of the two finalists - whose respective approaches could hardly be further apart.

Now, to comply with the condition of award, outstanding literary merit was the sole criterion. Not the quality of the publisher's presentation, not the binding, the print or the illustrations. But the writing. I must stress it is not the subject of the writing, but the Treatment of it, the Actual Writing, which counts in this award. Even a textbook of technique, for example, can be of outstanding literary merit - as Geoffrey Young's *Mountain Craft* makes clear. In fact, new subjects about the mountains and climbing are very refreshing to meet.

This year, as well as pleasantly-varied Expedition books, we saw a lovingly-detailed history of the famous Pinnacle Club - one of the few gallantly surviving clubs requiring biological, as well as climbing, qualifications; a breathlessly authentic account of a dedicated fell-runner's - or racer's - addiction (no more to be dismissed than the similar compulsions to tick off eight-thousanders, three- thousanders, or an unclimbed E6); and a remarkably comprehensive textbook on Scottish winter mountaineering by Martin Moran, a real *tour de force* illustrated by lively anecdotes. And some good guide-books, of which we could specially mention that of Tim Noble - *Great VS Climbs of the Lake District* - which is rather more than a guide-book: by its uncontrived flashes of actual incidents it really does convey the tang of the mountain, the climb and the climbers. Another book we particularly liked was *Soldiers and Sherpas* by ex-SAS man Brummie Stokes, which we found - surprisingly perhaps - disarmingly frank, fresh and breezy.

The two finalists, by unanimous agreement of the judges, were *Everest - Kangshung Face* by Stephen Venables and *Climbers* by M. John Harrison. I shall refer to these books by their authors' names; but obviously the book itself and not the author or his achievement (5 times former winner of the Ben Nevis Race or not) was the only consideration. We were looking for outstanding contributions to literature, and we found two contenders here. Outstanding in quite different ways. Venables' book is beautifully planned, written in a clear, calm style, his keenly perceptive comments are courteous and modest. It builds up to an exciting climax, and steps down to a satisfying relief. It conveys the pleasure - the joy - of what seems to have been a truly happy expedition, and the tension focuses uncomplicatedly on the climb itself. Rarely has the irresistibly glorious foolishness of Summit Fever been so well captured, nor its wry aftermath so engagingly described. It is an expedition book of the highest calibre, joining the increasingly select few at the top of the bunch.

If Venables' book is outstanding, like a great peak rising among other great peaks, Harrison's book is outstanding as a single, provocative and abrasive pinnacle above a hitherto largely featureless wasteland. In the first place, it is a Novel. We all have ghastly memories of some climbing novels. Ambitions, rivalries, beautiful girls, dastardly guides and heroic clients (or dastardly clients and heroic guides), impossible precipices and avalanches, Laws of Gravity defied or repealed at the author's whim. And writing, down at the same base-camp level of tabloid indigestion. We were pleasantly surprised to find, in this book, fiction used to extend realism, not to escape from it. Women treated like other human beings. And writing lean, clear and compelling, beautifully crafted, no word unnecessary, each one tuned to the rhythm of the sentence, always sensitive and exploratory;

biting and unforgettable descriptions, echoing with unstated overtones; and ever in the background, a tightly zipped-up compassion.

We found the book difficult to put down, despite the somewhat vertiginous absence of plot, and the substitution for it of a shifting fankle of time-strands, through which a spectrum, almost, of eerily familiar but largely undifferentiated characters perform - exactly as we know they *do*.

And they perform in and around gritstone quarries, pubs, climbing walls, mountain sports shops; against the background of a North of England polluted topographically and socially almost to caricature. Almost, but not quite. The morose and fascinating distortions not only of climbers but of their wives, mothers, families; of tourists, bikers, cavers, dropouts and entrepreneurs - these distortions are always pulled back in time, held on a tight rope. The good rock remains under our hands and yet, the sun breaks through the hailstorm. Just!

Because of this control, we find ourselves accepting, for example, the tiresome contemporary litter of expletives - scattered usually with irony - and the sometimes too tortuous obscurity: the author is on a quite new route, he is feeling for unseen holds. As he gets up, he takes us up with him, shaking and complaining maybe, but excited no end.

He took up all three Judges. All three stood at the top, excited and arguing. All agreed this route broke new ground in climbing literature. And all of us, standing at the edge of the derelict quarry, with the sodium lights coming on all about beneath us, and the smell of cold chips and stale beer breathing up in the evening fog - all of us looked back at the pure white of the Kangshung Face, and its blue summit sky; and thought again of Venables' splendidly uncomplicated achievement.

So it was a damned difficult decision. It provided memorable discussion, during which all the problems - why we climb, why we do not, why it is there, why it is somewhere else as well - were raised and settled to our own satisfaction. But the more difficult question - which book to award the Award - stayed to the very last.

Finally, one of us reluctantly chose the relative security of the Kangshung Face, Cauliflower Towers and all; the other two, sympathising but maybe gripped by Summit Fever and believing that an imaginative work that could provoke such discussion was really what the Boardman Tasker Award is about, opted for *Climbers*. And all three of us were happy with that final decision.

So this year the Boardman Tasker Award is to the book *Climbers*.

I would like, in finishing, to quote one illustration of the very many poetic insights of the book. This illustration might well sum up the effect of reading and re-reading it (it gets more satisfying with each reading - new balances are discovered). The illustration is of the untying of a grimy knot in an old rope, exposing "from the nest of convolutions" the preserved and hidden colours - pink, yellow, green and orange - "releasing the light that was caught up in the knot".

Reading this book releases light that was tied up where you might least expect it; among the bleakest and seemingly most depressing of scenes and people. It releases the joy and satisfaction, not this time of a great summit, but of a single unexpected and logical move on an otherwise repellent slab above a dirty car park; of discovering the quirks of kindliness and dignity that break out from the most coarse and apparently anarchic of companions.

You cannot ignore this book. You will disagree, like us, with much of it. It will provoke you to fury or delight; even maybe to thought. It throws climbers, dirty and dishevelled, into the big, dirty and dishevelled world around them. And that is a great service to both parties.

Sean's Story

by Terry Storry

The coroner announced a recess, and the motion of people standing all around shook the Irishman out of his reverie. The court emptied into the sunshine and he wandered with the rest over to a neighbouring bar. As he sat down he caught the tail end of a conversation going on at the next table.

"La condition sine qua non est un temps froide, faute de quoi la course peut devenir dangereuse."

The speaker was one of the Guides who had been on the rescue, and leaning back in his chair he caught sight of the Irishman. He gestured to him and moved across to his table.

"Salut mon ami," the Guide said. "I think maybe we are, how you say, going round in circles in there," he gestured towards the courtroom. "Mais, c'est bizarre. This is the second time it happen."

"What do you mean; je ne comprehend pas?" the Irishman leant forward frowning in concentration.

"I explain," he said continuing in his heavily accented English. "Until four years ago this girl she climbs with an English. I guide them in the beginning, so always later they call at the bureau for the weather and to say "ciao". Then the English he dies on the mountain. I am on that rescue as well. The boy, he goes to climb the Couloir Mettrier by himself; the girl she is not feeling well, and is waiting at the camping. But he is not coming back. Some Allemands in the couloir see him wave and go on to the Sialouze. No one else travel this way, and it does not freeze well this night, so it is easy to follow the tracks on to a broken bridge over the crevasse. Chance is good for this boy - the crevasse it close 10 metres under. He must still walk for we are finding more steps. The crevasse becomes more open and just there he has cut steps almost to the top. Merde c'est encroyable, I am following these steps with the crampons and the corde and it is hard. And it is three metres from the summit and no more steps. It is overhang - not possible without crampons. He must fall. Below it is more than 200 metres; we have not enough rope to look. But what is the use of it anyway?"

The guide sipped his drink, and seemed to have finished what he was going to say. Then almost as an after-thought he concluded: "I'm telling the girl at the camping, but she seems not sad. She only asks to know where he goes down. And now she also dies on the mountain; it is strange, no?"

He placed his empty glass on the table, rose, and in the ubiquitous Gallic gesture of *that's life* raised his palms upwards.

* * *

Years later Sean could still conjure up the guilty pleasure he felt that night when he put his arms round the girl, the two of them pressed together in a crowded Alpine hut. Because of their situation every action was elongated by caution, every movement slowed to silence. Their body talk was shy and fumbling, but after a while their senses developed a momentum of their own. Tears came to his eyes and laughter to his lips, but no sound did they make, strangers in a room full of strangers. That was how it was at 7,000ft, a moment frozen in time and, like the snow outside, dissolved into nothing by the morning sun; a moment never to be repeated but always to be remembered.

Sean remembered even less than usual about that Alpine start but as he stumbled to the door he glanced back at the bunks. She sat amongst the sleeping forms watching him go. Her face filled his mind, and he was grateful that soon the business of finding their route up the moraine in the small circle of his head-torch absorbed all his attention.

He and his client went to the top of the Pelvoux in good time. Nothing on the steep icy slopes or loose rock traverses seemed to worry Sean that day. Perhaps he was over-relaxed from the night before and it occurred to him as he descended back to the glacier that the anxiety and subsequent release from tension he experienced in climbing might be a substitute for sex. So preoccupied was he with this conceited and extempore theory that he failed to notice the bunched group on the glacier waving their ice-axes, until his client pointed them out.

As he approached it became clear that someone had fallen down a crevasse. A rope disappeared down a dark slit in the snow. It was loosely wrapped round an ice-axe some way back from the edge of the hole. Two people lay prone, looking into the darkness, held on ropes by those further back. Sean recognised a few faces from the hut and they in turn recognised him saying "Guide, Guide," and pointing down into the crevasse.

Burying his axe in the snow he clove hitched his rope to the shaft and abseiled down into the cold, dark world below. She was sitting at the bottom almost naturally. It was only after he unclipped from the rope that he noticed the injury to the back of her head. The terrible business of hauling her out of the crevasse took an age, but even so he thought she might survive. All the while she stared at him deep in shock with no sign of recognition. Then just before she was winched into the helicopter, she reached out for his hand and stroked it two or three times, just as his mother would do after waking him from some childhood nightmare.

* * *

I hardly knew the Irishman at all, but was caught up in the tail end of that rescue on the Pelvoux. The Gendarmerie asked me to attend the inquest, and I introduced myself to him in the cafe during the recess - shortly after that one-sided conversation with the Guide. He was nervous and distracted, but became more relaxed after talk of mountains and routes we had both climbed. When he knew I too worked as a guide, he even talked a little about the Pelvoux accident. We exchanged addresses before walking back to the courtroom, and promised to stay in touch.

I only heard from him twice, a couple of postcards from the Alps, Switzerland I think. Then there was a gap of about 10 years until two months ago when I received a letter from his solicitor, the executor of his will. The letter told of a provision in his will that, in the event of his death, I should receive a diary (enclosed) and two letters. One letter was from the Irishman asking me to use his diary to write the story of the accident.

"...I know you sometimes write for climbing magazines and you know the background to my story. I am too much of a coward to write it myself, but I steel feel guilty about not producing her letter at the inquest (I found it in the pocket of her duvet). It probably wouldn't have made any difference but somehow I feel it is important that people should know. Isn't it a shame that life has to be lived forwards, but can only be understood backwards."

So I have done as he asked. And here is the other letter written by the girl to an address in London. I have translated from the French.

* * *

Dear Pete,

I wrote to you some time ago at the college but you obviously didn't get the letter - it must have arrived after you left for the States. Anyway I expect it's lurking in a pigeon hole somewhere.

Things have changed rather dramatically at this end. Gaston has got a job with his company in Fes (Morocco), so we are moving there at the end of September. I have very mixed feelings about this, but feel I must go along with his plans to make everything seem natural. Perhaps it will all work out for the best if it helps him to forget about you, but the thought of being so far away is frightening.

We are coming to the end of our second week in Ailefroide. It hasn't changed much, still less crowded than Chamonix and the weather, as usual, is perfect. But I have spent the whole time feeling nostalgic, and giving more thought to you than is good for my peace of mind. I never imagined that four years could pass so slowly. The strain of pretending to Gaston is unbearable, particularly when we are here.

What makes it worse is that I keep comparing Gaston to you on the mountains. He is so careless, you wouldn't believe it. He hardly ever gets the rope out unless I ask, and on glaciers, which he knows freaks me out, he walks just behind me with lots of slack rope. Sometimes he doesn't bother to tie on. I don't know enough to convince him that this is unsafe, and he is always saying things like, "well it never bothered Pete, did it?" I keep telling him that you died on your last solo trip, but I have a terrible feeling that he might have found out. Do you think that's possible? Perhaps you should change your name again - you know how many connections he has in England.

I am writing this in the Pelvoux hut. I know it's dangerous but Gaston has gone to bed and I can post it on our way into the camp-ground. There is an Irishman here who looks very much like you. I feel like talking things over with someone. The strain of keeping it all to myself is terrible. Do you think we have done the right thing after all. Perhaps Gaston won't accept the settlement, or try to keep the children. Can we meet again before I make the final break? I know it's hard for you, but it would help me a lot. Perhaps you could come climbing in Morocco and I could arrange to get away at the same time. The Atlas Mountains are only down the road, and there are no crevasses there. Love Simone.

Mind Games

by Ian Vickers

Whenever I try a hard route, I imagine that the first ascensionist is there with me, taunting my every move; this takes my mind off the fear and presents the challenge in a different and competitive way. I remember my first real challenge in which I tried out my method, it was on Joe Brown's *Vector*, E2 5c, at Tremadog.

The challenge was laid down for me by Keith Dawson whilst I was browsing through his crag shop in Accrington. I was just 13 years old and full of myself, when he told me that the youngest person to climb *Vector* was only 14.

"There's a real challenge for you," he said. The challenge became absolute and so I began to read all the available articles and books, first about Joe Brown and then about *Vector* itself. I dreamt about its every move. The description from the guide was word perfect in my brain and I trained all winter until I was able to lead E2s comfortably on my home crags in Lancashire.

In February, the weather was extremely mild, so I persuaded my father and Dave Cronshaw to take me to Tremadog for the weekend. We slept in Eric Jones's barn and, on the Saturday, I led *Merlin Direct*, HVS 5a, and *Extraction*, E2 5c. We finished the day with a few classic VSs and then I asked to have a look at *Vector*. It was so incredibly inviting that I could feel my pulse racing as we stood there staring at the famous Ochre Slab. Even though there were still wet streaks below it, I knew I just had to go for it. I imagined Brown swinging across the roof on the first ascent, as all the way back to the cafe I babbled on to Dave about it. He had done it numerous times, but he still enthused about its quality, a true Classic. Eventually, he smiled: "I can see we won't get any peace until you've done it," he said. "If it's fine tomorrow, we can have a look."

"Can I lead the Slab?" was all I could reply. He nodded and I went off to bed feeling more than a little excited.

I woke at 7am covered in sweat, I dreamt I had failed, falling through an endless space and Joe Brown was standing there smiling down at me as I lay on the ground, battered and bruised. "Not good enough yet," he said, grabbing my arm and raising me to my feet. Looking across the road to the crag, I found that the wet streaks were drying up.

It was a clear morning, cold and crisp. The jackdaws heckled me as I ran through the trees to the foot of the route. Bouldering about the lower wall I felt really good, this was definitely the time to go for it, so I ran back and dragged them out of their pits and into the cafe for breakfast.

Time seemed to drag on and on, and then we set off. We geared up at the car and before I realised it, Dave was on the first stance. I joined him, no time to turn chicken, the gear was passed across to me and I was on my way to the famous spike runner and the approach to the hanging Ochre Slab itself. I cursed them, releasing my pent-up feelings as I bridged up to its foot. In with a runner and a quick pull on to the slab and clip the tat on the old peg.

Move up and stitch the crack with gear, move across, panic, brain racing, slow down brain, stay cool, legs stop shaking. Words of encouragement float up, the jackdaws mock me again, Brown's face flits across my mind smiling: "Well what do you think of it?" he whispers.

I lick my dry lips. "Desperate," I croak. Bang in a Friend, always guaranteed to steady the nerves.

"We didn't have those when I was a lad," he laughingly taunts.

Up to the peg, clip, chalk up. "What's that you're using?" says Brown as he drifts across the cave.

"Chalk," I gasp as I try to climb across.

"Didn't need that either," he taunts again.

I can't reach the holds, back to the peg. I look down to Dave and call out: "I'll have to belay here, Dave, I can't reach the holds."

"Rubbish," floats up the reply, "it's easy now, you've done the crux, get your act together and go for it." I chalk up again, Brown is in the cave laughing, his picture floats about taunting me to cross. "Come on, more chalk, it's easy, think about the challenge."

Sweating, heart pumping and legs shaking I swing out and across. Smear? Smear? Stick feet, stick; clip. "Okay Dave I'm there," I yell, feeling totally drained as I complete clipping the other pegs. Brown is in the corner, his image fading in and out of my steamed-up glasses.

"Not bad for a young one, the next bit's the best." He disappears, probably waiting for me at the foot of the famous groove.

Dave joins me, takes the gear and disappears up and across to the overhang. What a fantastic position this is. Like staring out of a space station window, across the whole universe. A head appears. "Hutch up mate and make room for a little 'un, that Slab's fantastic, really pushy." He clips in and settles down. Dave shouts:

"Taking in," and I leave the safety of my little world to be confronted by Brown once again. "Well, what are you going to do about that one?"

"Bloody Friends," I reply, "it's totally jammed."

"I used a peg there, wonder where it went to?" he says.

I fiddle about with the cams and it comes free. "Got it," I say, but he's gone again.

"You're not bringing a young lass up there are you?" a voice drifts down from above.

"That lass is a lad and he just brought me up the crux," smiles Cronshaw as I slip over on to the ledge.

The bloke smiles, "Sorry," he says looking really embarrassed, "it must be the blonde hair."

Brown titters in the background, "No, it's the tights, definitely the tights, you big Nancy," he says to me as he drifts off. I lead up to the top where he's sitting there cross-legged grinning from ear to ear.

"Well, Brown, what do you think, eh? Youngest ascent or what?" I punch the air.

"Could be but what about the Friends, the chalk, the boots?" and then he rolls over howling with laughter.

"Those tights, they really kill me, more like a clown than a climber. See you around." He disappears again and I wipe my glasses. Great bloke, super route: was he really there, or was it just a figment of my imagination? Thanks anyway Joe, the route's a true classic, can't wait to meet you in the flesh as they say.

Climbing at Heptonstall Quarry

by Graham Mort

The will of the spidering men
Has split the rock:
Gritstone sweats out their palm-grease,
The sun clambers over a grey arête of cloud.

Water globules seep from the cracks,
Wobble past their sweating shoulders to
Smash on jackdaw-shit debris below.

These men are climbing into the rock,
Jamming themselves into honey-coloured, warm,
Unleavened stone with groaning insteps.

Their minds have gone dark,
Narrowed by sheer upward motion.
Rock surforms elbows, knuckles, fingertips:
All around golden faces have sheared off,
Clean and empty.

The future has no finger holds
Yet the men rise upwards, upwards, upwards
Into the lip of the overhang
Into the shadows that grip their hands and pull.

Report of the Fourth International Festival of Mountaineering Literature

by Kevin Borman

A nine-hour bash with as wordy a title as this sounded as if it might be a daunting experience after which one would be relieved to rush off for a pint or two. Those attending for the first time perhaps worried that they would be trapped for a day in the confines of Bretton Hall when they could have been enjoying themselves on their local crag. Organiser Terry Gifford, however, stressed the informal nature of the event and his intention that the programme he had put together should be enjoyable.

Chris Bonington saw the day off to an excellent start with his perceptive reflections about how he gradually came to make his living from 'communicating' about mountaineering. His honest insights about writing without hurting climbing companions unnecessarily while still giving an accurate picture of the climbing experience impressed the audience and caused experienced Bonington-watchers to suggest that they had never heard him speak better.

With a wry smile Kev Howett thanked Chris for warming up the audience and read a piece which he had still been working on earlier that morning, centred on the holistic experience of new routeing in Glen Nevis. Once the audience had penetrated Kev's Sunderland accent they were riveted. Ken Wilson prompted lively discussion with his question to Kev: "Will it be possible to write like that about sport climbing?"

Lunch produced the major snag of the day when, much to the chagrin of Messrs Simpson and Haszko, the bar ran out of beer after 34 minutes.

On his first visit to Britain and lecturing for the first time in English, Waclaw Sonelski, editor of the Polish climbing magazine *Bularz*, provided an intriguing historical overview of Polish climbing. With only 3,000 active climbers in Poland and at most only 10 active writers among them, he wondered whether anyone would retrospectively tell the true story of the hassles Polish climbing had to contend with under the Communist regime. Thought-provoking stuff and I for one was glad to have had my horizons broadened by what Waclaw had to say.

Lucy Rees' brief was to say something about the deliberations of the Boardman Tasker judges, Robin Hodgkin, Rob Collister and herself. Frankly she seemed unprepared and, at one point, even said that she had been out of touch with climbing and its literature for years. A strange choice as judge perhaps, and with Rob Collister absent for most of the judging process, Lucy gave this listener at least the distinct impression of having acceded to the stronger opinions of Robin Hodgkin.

A lacklustre extract from the winning book, Victor Saunders' *Elusive Summits,*was read very well by Ian Smith. The open discussion which Supremo Gifford had invited at the beginning of the day came much to the fore, with general agreement by those present that a) choosing a 'winner' from among different types of climbing books will always ultimately be a subjective decision and b) ranking the short-listed books which do not win serves no purpose and should be avoided.

Just when the afternoon might have been flagging, Dermot Somers took the stage and announced that, as he did not wish to be 'safe', he would not be reading from his highly-acclaimed Boardman-Tasker short-listed *Mountains and Other Ghosts*. Instead he proposed to read from a long manuscript which had been dormant for several years but which he had ruthlessly cut during his three-hour ferry journey the previous morning from 100 pages to something that could be read out in 45 minutes. *Dru North Face* was stunning. There was self-deprecating humour, there was richly-textured description, there was the fresh imagery at which Celtic writers excel. The audience was gobsmacked. Perhaps their enthusiastic applause conveyed their opinion about the iniquities of literary prizes.

The best way to follow that was with a change of scene. We removed to a small gallery where the work of Lakes-based painter Julian Cooper was exhibited. The large format of Julian's work added powerfully to his images: a strong charcoal study of Stanage's Flying Buttress, an eerie landscape from Scafell to the distant obscenity of Windscale, and a fine picture of the crags at Wharncliffe created specially for the festival. The change of pace and stimulus at this stage of the day is one which Director Gifford has got off to a tee. Things had improved at the bar too. This time it was 37 minutes before the beer ran out.

Mike Harding, seasoned professional entertainer, admitted to a bout of nerves as he prepared for an experimental venture during his slot in which he had been given free rein. He read a selection of his poems about the Dales (from a forthcoming book). That was the experimental bit, to be followed by slides from *Death Valley Health Center: Travels in America* (from another forthcoming book). Only when he showed slides of his experiences in Nepal did his contribution have a high-mountain flavour, but Mike's idiosyncratic commentary and superb sense of timing ensured that the audience was won over.

At the end of his stint Mike announced the winner of the Festival/*High* Writing Competition, which you may read elsewhere in this issue. The author, Andy Anderson from Merseyside, listened as his entry was read, and is rumoured to be still grinning from ear to ear.

By now you will have twigged that the festival is no dry academic symposium, but a celebration. In fact the mention of Literature in its title does it a disservice; it's far wider than that. This year it was a Mountaineering Arts Festival. To prove the point Rosie Smith and Celia Bull, rather bizarrely-clad, performed two new songs, assisted by Dave Greenald (piano) and special co-opted vocalist Dermot Somers, to widespread acclaim.

Finally the audience repaired to yet another studio to be hugely entertained by the first hour from a work in progress entitled *E5 6c*. Directed by Mark Greenop, this tale of two Brits climbing in Europe is performed by sixth-form students from Hemsworth High School. The full production will be ready for Buxton and will be compulsory viewing. Don't miss the early scene with the hanging bivvy...

Looking back, it would be fair to say that a couple of the speakers who had very worthwhile things to say would have benefited from having their contributions delivered by more fluent readers, but we left surfeited with good things and several sceptics to whom I spoke were full of praise for the event. No pun intended, but we came away on a high. Only one question remains. Will Impresario Gifford be able to produce a 1991 festival to match the high quality and fascinating diversity of this one?

A Tale of Spendthrift Innocence

by Dermot Somers

I'll begin with a bang, and save the whympering for later. We were near the violent summit of the Dru, Tom Curtis and I, trying to bury ourselves alive on a ledge. The midnight wind was acrid with sulphur. Hail pelleted against the anoraks wrapped around our sleeping-bags. Lightning flailed and the slender mountain jolted like a whipping-post.

Shall I introduce Tom first, or the Dru?

Tom, I think. The Dru has been there forty million years and knows how to wait.

Tom was twenty-one then, and not expecting to get much older. With five alpine seasons including climbs like the Walker Spur, the Frêney Pillar and the North Face of the Eiger he was probably the best of the very young British alpinists at the time.

Stocky and bespectacled, with a tangle of fine, fair curls he had plenty of other ambitions. He wanted to find and liberate the joke trapped in everything; he wanted to expose the exploitation of the Third World; and he wanted a permanent sun-tan for his social image.

Earlier in the week, relaxing in Grindelwald, Tom surveyed himself with a happy gush of satisfaction.

"Brown legs, North Face of the Eiger......... I've had a bloody good holiday!"

The ledge was agonisingly inadequate. Two bodies in a single grave. Before the storm struck we spread the sodden ropes under us. We slid our feet into the rucksacks and pulled them up - up to the knee in my case. I insulted Tom's stature, insinuating that he could pull his up as far as the shoulders. The axes hummed like chinese-fiddles in the electric air. Wet hail built up in mounds upon our huddled forms. It slid down between us and melted into our bags. Cold encroached with the insidious certitude of disease. The intense wait for incineration was a slow death in itself. We couldn't challenge the lightning, but we must defeat the horror.

"It's not enough, you know ..." Tom pronounced, hiccups of effort in his voice, "... to boycott instant coffee because the makers sell baby-food to the Third World. Do you know how much tea-pickers earn so that you can drink tea for next to nothing in Ireland?"

The wind stalled. A sense of violent revelation. The air chilled and tightened. The axes hummed their unearthly requiem.

"It's coming again!" I warned, "Keep talking, Tom. How much do they earn?"

"The tin-industry is even worse," Tom's voice vibrated with conviction and electricity, "In Bolivia..."

A roaring hiss. A flash hit the summit. The explosion blocked the ears with pain. Electricity seared down the cracks. A hundred and fifty feet below the summit the charge hit our niche, the gap in the spark-plug. It picked us up like puppets, heads, legs, arms, jerking and twitching. Fuses buzzed in the nerve-circuit.

"Next time," I thought, dazed with survival, "It must be next time. We can't get away with this..."

Tom was on the outside of the ledge and getting the worst of everything. He was still kicking and twitching after my strings had been dropped. I thought he was overdoing it to get more space.

"Jesus Christ..." I swore and prayed simultaneously. My voice wobbled, as if worked by elastic bands.

"Are you okay, Tom?"

"I think so," he quavered. "Do people survive this kind of thing?"

"Electric shocks are good for you," I assured him bracingly, "They tone up the nervous system."

The Executioner peered down into the death-chamber at his two victims strapped to the electric chair of the Dru. He ground his teeth with chagrin, looked surreptitiously around. There were no constitutional lawyers at 10,000 feet to demand a technical reprieve.

"Go Again!" he thundered, and threw the switch.

The temperature swooped. The air was a cold, dead skin. Nerves stretched in the body like barbed wire, the scurrying mind caged in the skull trying to bale out through the window-slits. As the tension tightened again towards crescendo my hair stood entirely on end.

Rip Van Winkle was caught out in a lightning storm. His hair and beard went white with shock, and when he staggered down next day he was twenty years older.

Tom was cursing out of a mixture of hysteria and hilarity, blaming the statue for the inferno. Some of the alpine peaks have a little storm-scarred Virgin on the summit to aggravate the pagan elements. He swore the thing was attracting the lightning and conducting it on to us. His language had the crackle of blasphemy in the tense air. I felt the primitive pull of old superstitions in my blood.

"Not now, Tom! Not now. Don't talk like that just now," I advised.

Long years of indoctrination had left scars on me that reappeared when extremity pinched the skin. Nothing too embarrassing, no rosaries or that, just... a Catholic sense of voodoo.

I cast around for an explanation of my unease for Tom, who was actually brought up in the same sorcery, though there is nothing in England to approach the claustrophobia of the Irish version.

"It's..... ah...... it's Bad Magic," I offered lamely.

The Dru itself is a gigantic lightning-rod anyway, and a massive statue in its own right.

Hundreds of miles from the Alps there is a particular little town in the south of France, clay-red roofs, mediaeval walls and tiled towers, olive trees on the stony hillsides, cicadas in the dry light.

Overlooking that town is an ancient statue of a saint. Neither cast nor sculpted it was built up of bricks and stones and then plastered over crudely to create a column of a body with a rudimentary head on top.

It has weathered to the textures of its rough components - broken bricks gaping out of the belly, fleshy strips of plaster stuck to the shoulders and the sides, the face entirely eaten away. It is a terrifying depiction of corruption and decay.

The Dru, about 3,000 feet high, has that kind of shape and compulsive presence, but its meaning is radically opposite. Overlooking Chamonix, it is the archetypal column; a monolith, an obelisk, a roundtower, a cathedral spire, depending on the angle of view, comprising all the symbols of human aspiration. Difficult to say whether it is phallicism or a sense of architecture that attracts, but the great column of the Dru has been a seminal source of mountaineering progress.

The rock is granite, but the colour and texture vary with the aspect. The North Face is cold and austere, ribbed, cracked and grooved. The rock contrasts darkly with the eye of the Niche, a hooded icefield in the centre of the face. The West Face, with its southerly pillar named for Walter Bonatti who spent six days and nights, solo, on its first ascent, is a sheer, smooth wall from base to summit, made all the more elegant by the rougher rock on both sides.

...

The first time I saw the Dru from the squalor of a climbers' campsite I thought it achieved an impossible perfection of form, and something like the magic of myth.

The Sword in the Stone. Only a king could rip the sabre out of the rock.

Bonatti proved that like every jutting handle in history it was not a sword at all, but a challenge to the imagination. I was impressionable that year, and determined to be impressed. An hour earlier, alighting from the train at dawn,

I was transfixed by the serration of granite peaks sawing the sky above the town. That high horizon, I learned gradually, could act like the jawbone of some insatiable carnivore, but for the time being I was all elation and spendthrift innocence. I watched the Aiguille du Midi engrave its precision on the sky with the point of a needle. During the day I discovered from a cheap postcard that the exquisite peak of the Midi was a concrete pillar built on top as part of the telepherique station. I felt embarrassed, caught out in a Three-Card-Trick on the first visit to town.

But the Dru didn't deal in illusions.

If an imaginary architect had to design the ideal mountain the result would be some kind of Dru; inspiring in appearance; accessible, though not without effort; classic climbs on a number of faces; the potential to challenge new generations; finally, it should be possible to escape from the mountain in bad weather, though not so easily as to diminish the commitment required.

Very few mountains qualify under all these conditions, though they may be none the worse for that. Some boast an excess of one quality, which can be a virtue in itself.

The Eiger, for example, offers a poor exchange-rate between life and death, but it pays a higher dividend on success. The Matterhorn - to stick with the public mountains - is all aesthetics from afar, and whoever makes the mistake of probing its instability will only succeed in kicking holes in that perfection.

Mont Blanc, I suspect, is more than one mountain. The great faces of its Freney, Brouillard, and Brenva aspects simply happen to share one broad summit. I calculate with a little geometry that if Mont Blanc were twenty thousand feet high instead of fifteen, all the good routes could finish direct on a pinpoint. There'd be problems of course; those walking-routes via the Grands Mulets and the Dome de Gouter might overhang in their upper sections...

It must be obvious by now that I'm reluctant to rescue those twitching wretches from the summit of the Dru. Curtis will be alright of course, he was born to survive; but shouldn't I do the decent thing by my alter ego, zoom in on the Dru, typewriter clattering like a chopper and pluck that lanky insomniac off the ledge? Deus ex machina.

But this is an irresistible chance to conduct an experiment, an advance on those infamous cruelty-tests when people were instructed to give massive electric shocks to other individuals, with medical assurance that it was for the victims' own good. The torturers were the subject of the Real experiment since the patients were only miming pain, there was no current, and the object was to see how much pain people would inflict, under instruction, against all the evidence of agony. Now - can I bring myself to extend that storm, step up the voltage, intensify the whip-flash, and make a True Hell of that bivouac halfway between earth and heaven?

The excuse is there; it's often done in mountain-writing, exaggeration of extremity to increase the drama. As easy as tilting a photo to increase the angle of ice.

Back at the experiment the wires are heating up nicely now, spitting sparks, and I must admit there is a strange temptation to step up the pressure on the unfortunate characters on the ledge. An obscure desire to Make Something Happen. It is, of course, a futile urge to shock one of them into some glorious statement, a timeless speech from the dock, a fist brandished in the face of fate.

Something, in short, I didn't have the courage to shout when I had my chance up there to challenge Death.

But after all, survival is more important than heroics, and finally, after two hours of torture I had yielded up no secrets other than a feeble sense of irreligion, and the politics of the left. The storm had appointments with other souls. It packed its black bag of truncheons, wires and batteries, and moved on to the next cell.

They will sleep till dawn, exhausted by trauma and the second bivouac of the climb. And there is time to abseil down the dangling puppet-strings, back to the real beginning.

The weather that month was perfect for the North Face. A cynic would have smelled an ambush. Long days of heat treatment caressed the rock, massaging the ice out of the deep wrinkles high on the face. The mountain sweated under the strident cosmetics of the sun. It was like a thawed-out film star back in fashion. Scores of people came courting. Half Belfast was up there. Eddie Cooper, Dawson Stelfox, Ian Rea, all found the face in carefree mood, autographing guide-books, having its grapes peeled...

A clean, translucent dawn - that suggestion of a polished glass sky - when we left Snell's Field, stumbling heavy-loaded towards Argentiere. The sulky statue brooding on the skyline didn't look in the least like a mountain anyone was about the climb. Along the road I fought that trudging lethargy, as if trapped on a milk-train of sleeping villas, dewy orchards and shuttered bars. The real morning streamed past me in its urgent air; light, colour, excitement speeding by on another track. I felt the illusion of sliding into reverse... Tom was leaving me behind too with the reproachful air of one who has never quite learnt to be angry. I tilted forward on my toes and kicked a gaping hole in my lassitude.

The climb began at the base of a broad gully, 300 feet high. A long stripe of fresh snow bedded the groove, rock-ribs showing through. A lip of ice barred entry. It faded out on a brief rock-bulge. Tom hacked a few moves upwards, dispensed with the axe and pulled up on rock, crampons scraping and hooking. Water flowed as the fresh snow melted. The moves were unexpectedly hard. I locked my hand between ice and rock and groped uneasily for a hold.

Scrabbling overhead, a flurry of small stones, introduced company. Three bedraggled climbers had bivouacked overnight on a ledge-system to make an early start, and were outraged by nocturnal snow. They were going down, they informed us in shivering French, and formed a low opinion of our judgement when we continued up. But we, after all, had spent both a dry night and a cable fare.

As other groups of refugees plunged down past us it was obvious that a general exodus was underway. We were pleased with this thinning out of the queue.

There was no longer any impression of the inaccessible magnificence of the Dru. It was simply another mountain-shaped cliff. After partnership on the Walker Spur, the Frêney Pillar and the Eiger our procedures were automatic; brief immersion in a lead, and then while Tom climbed I contemplated savagery and civilisation as proposed by the wild Aiguilles and the teeming valley below.

The roofs of Chamonix glowed with miniaturised perfection in the depths of the daily world. The sinuous river and the gleaming motorway flowed together through the long, tight valley. I swung a size 11 boot out over the void and casually obscured a vast area of civilisation. I experimented thoughtfully, stamping out the town of Chamonix, and then with a quick jab of the heel I stubbed out Snell's Field. Paying out the rope to Tom, who was involved with a steep and intimate crack, I wished I was down there, sitting in a warm bar in front of *un grand cafe au lait*, dunking the flaking subtlety of a croissant, with the climb wrapped up in a neat cassette of memory, playing away quietly behind the eyes and ears.

Half an hour later, I was balanced in a steep, wet groove, the minutes leaping off the face like rats, wishing I had an extension-ladder. I was supported by one boot braced with an air of strained credibility against a rib of wet rock. The flared groove contained a malevolent core of old ice. It left just enough space for a fist and a boot. I scrounged and grudged painfully up the groove, my back lodged against one gurgling wall and a sodden knee genuflecting piously against the other. At the top I hauled onto a flooded ledge, soaked, scraped and enraged.

Ladders were in my mind, because the situation recalled a filthy day spent painting gutters on a Dublin school. Water and dirt had turned the paint to a greasy sludge. You save time on a long ladder by bouncing it at the top so that it jerks along the wall and gives a wider reach, while the bottom remains in the same position. Tilt too far and the ladder will slip, of course, but if there is a gutter or a windowsill to hang on to you can lean to a ridiculous extent. I had reached the angle of absurdity, clinging to the gutter and painting away, when the wind whipped the ladder out from under me. As it went I grabbed the lip of the gutter and hand-traversed along it until I got my knees on a windowsill. Water poured down my sleeves and trickled inquisitively into my armpits, while the window was opened out against me from within by an entertained audience.

I stood dripping on the stance above the icicle and the wind skinned me like a knife-thrower's model. The weather was going downhill. Chamonix exuded a desperate nostalgia as mist erased it like a lapse of fond memory.

I'm tempted again to cut through the murk of mixed motives and spare my man the embarrassment of cowardly feelings. But I can't afford another shift of focus - since mountain, and chapter, are already littered with stranded doppelgangers, spitting images awaiting deliverance from ledges, windowsills, and waterfalls.

In any case, as I write this in an old cottage in Wicklow I'm no better off than any of them... It's pouring rain outside, and the roof is sieving it mournfully into buckets in the kitchen. The vast, cranky fireplace has its priorities obstinately reversed; all the heat goes up the chimney and all the smoke comes into the living-room.

Regularly, I have to stand at the back door for air and relief, sprayed by rain and wreathed in smoke. There is no comfort here at all for the man on the mountain, shrouded in mist and spat upon by the elements.

There was an airlock in the plumbing too and earwigs were living in the taps. I coupled up an aqualung to the sink and gave the system a blast at 2,000lbs per square inch. It cleared the blockage, and the earwigs, but now there's an inch of rusty water on the bathroom floor.

Yes, and the rent is due. I wish I was back on the mountain.

It might take my mind off things. Meanwhile, the fellow shivering on the ledge wishes He was back here! People are never satisfied.

Mont Blanc and the higher Aiguilles were still clear of the weather and Tom was fully in favour of going on. That, I pointed out severely, was suitable sentiment for an effervescent youth who had climbed the icicle with a rope above him. But I was less optimistic. The effects of last night's storm would be worse the higher we climbed. And how could we trust a forecast which had already betrayed us once? With all the hard climbing still above there was no guarantee of the summit that day. Still... I wanted to go on too... Tom's great ability and enthusiasm, and the deviousness I had developed with age, fitted us for this route in almost any condition.

Onward Then! We turned heroic eyes once more upon the heights, and blinked blindly into the mist. We were not alone.

A pair of voices, one faint, the other frantic, had been yodelling above us for some time. Burrowing vertically between fog and rock I arrived below a blocky wall just as a large rump and rucksack disappeared overhead. French climbers dress to a high standard of elegance, but this rump was clad in a rough boiler-suit. The rucksack bulged prodigiously, and was saddled like a hiker's backpack with a roll of canary-yellow Karrimat. The scene had the mock-serious quality of a cartoon; hapless hitchhiker takes a wrong turn in the fog, the road gets steeper and steeper, until he is hanging by a finger from an overhang, still thumbing hopefully. I pursued him and he lurched upwards, blunt boots scrabbling, the voice hissing desperately for a tight rope.

"Avale! Avale! Merde! AVAAAALE!"

The slack rope jerked suddenly, a lasso coming tight on a bullock, and he was hauled bucking and kicking over the horizon.

I was intrigued, as by a circus-act when a bucket-footed

clown wobbles on a tight rope, but the pitch ahead demanded full concentration. It was steep, with massive ice-bedded flakes sticking out at eccentric angles. Some of the bigger blocks made minor overhangs.

A hundred feet higher I reached a flat ledge, hooked my fingers over the rim of the cartoon-frame, and squeezed into the picture beside the portly boiler-suit. I saw his slimline partner silhouetted above us, entirely unburdened by any sack at all. The mystery cleared. The dungaree-man was carrying the lot; two sets of bivvy-gear, double rain-gear, all the food. And since the leader was wearing a light pair of rock-shoes, his heavy boots, crampons and ice-axe must also be in the bag.

The man in the boiler-suit welcomed company with a broad, red-faced beam.

"Est-ce que vous avez fait bivouac sur les terrasses la-bas?" I enquired amiably.

A flash of teeth.

"We haf bifouack on ze terrass las' night," he informed me.

My sympathy hardened to resentment instantly. If there is one linguistic conceit I cannot stand it is that continental habit of speaking English to foreigners no matter what the foreigner wants to speak.

In resorts like Chamonix and Zermatt the shops employ staff who can speak Anglo-American, and they are so anxious to prove their competence in threadbare slang that they will speak nothing else no matter how earnest your French or German may be. The hitchhiker was one of these.

'Where are you from?' he articulated proudly.

"Irlande," I gritted. "Je suis Irlandais!" with a pronounced accent on the 'Irl', since nine people out of ten hear 'Hollande' instead. If they grasp the Irish angle they differentiate between North and South, Catholic or Protestant, often accompanied by gunfire mime. We are characterised internationally by the twin terrors of violence and religion.

"Ah! I haf been many time in Amstairdame..."

"Est-ce qu'il y avait beaucoup de neige pendant la nuit?" I interrupted the autobiography.

"There was much snow," he assured me with satisfaction, as if that was in order and the place wouldn't have been the same without it.

I busied myself bringing Tom up, and soon the anglo-garrulous Jacques was winched creaking and panting off the ledge like a fat pantomime-fairy with yellow, rubber wings.

"We'll have to pass them," I warned Tom as he prepared to lead through, "I'll be damned if I'm going to listen to pidgin English from here to the top of the Dru."

A lot of British climbers would have taken this as a reflection on their own conversation, but Tom let it go.

The rock was continuously sheer and difficult now, a grainy grey-green granite with clean corners and cracks, and there was no chance of passing the pair ahead. Jacques and I worked out a stubborn compromise; he practised his foul English, and I responded in what I hope was slightly less atrocious French. Tom led our rope with panache up the severely exposed Lambert Crack, a thin slit in a solid wall, hounding Jacques' heels, and I stepped up the pressure on the next pitch. Unfortunately Jacques' partner wasn't always responsive to his panted needs, "Avale, imbecile! AVALE!" and at times a dribble of slack rope gathered on his paunch, while he hung by his fingertips and hissed for tension.

Finally we seized our chance to pass when the route branched in the uncertain mist. I jumped into one of those evil grooves that appear to have been built upside down, and emerged somewhere along the lower edge of the Niche. Visibility was down to twenty feet and the thick snow cover blended with the mist to rob the eye of focus. Progress in that haunted half-light was arrested by huge warts and carbuncles of rock rheumy with ice. We were lost. A voice mewed piteously out in the mist. He wasn't talking English now, I thought spitefully. Tom was brilliant on this kind of terrain. Being lost suited him; he could pick the hardest way ahead and pretend it was the only way to go.

The guide-book had nothing to offer. I shoved it down my jumper and sent Tom out into the unknown with the air of Columbus throwing pigeons at the New World. He ducked beneath an overhanging bulge, and was gone.

I was left with the frail rope, the sling that bound me to a flake, and the shapes that came and went in the pale fog. The mountain was no more substantial than a pillar of cloud and snow scoured by the wind. Hunched within myself I brooded. The human body has reflexes that are common to all creatures, and a mountaineer on a windswept stance bears a marked resemblance to a hen on a windy day, clucking disconsolately, the head withdrawn, elbows clamped against the ribs like scrawny wings, alternate legs doubled up under the body. Every now and then the querulous head extends a squawking enquiry into the outside world.

Eventually Tom called and I thawed into movement. I'd love to have left an egg on the foothold in a salute to the surreal. Instead - I lost the guide-book. Ducking under the bulge I saw it swoop into the obscurity, covers spread like wings. It was lucky we had maintained diplomatic relations with the French! Guide-books, I realised, were above language-barriers. I listened ardently for Jacques' voice in the mist. Beyond the ice, at the base of the pillar, there was a sloping terrace, broad enough for a few uncomfortable bodies. The wind screeched into a higher register and a spatter of hail raked the ledge. The weather was hardening, breaking up into pellets of its own solidity. The day's climbing was over, and we settled into an amicable ambush for the French.

"'Allo! Can you 'elp me please?"

Thus, we had been warned in Catholic myth, the voices of damned souls cry for release from Hell, and must be kicked in the teeth by the righteous.

"Ici," we yelled, "Ici! A droite!"

Jacques stumped out of the mist like a refugee from purgatory, and cramponed across the ice.

"Ou est le sac, Jacques?" I quipped, wondering if the pack

had joined our guide-book at the foot of the Dru, and if it had, was their book in it?

"Henri 'as ze sack now." Jacques beamed with the satisfaction of justice done. He squatted on the tiny portion of ledge we had allowed for their occupation, and anchored himself with extraordinary thoroughness. No danger of him being pulled off his perch.

"Henri 'as no..." he pointed at his feet in explanation.

"No crampons?" We were surprised at such an oversight.

"No boots," Jacques corrected calmly.

"No Boots!!!?" We gaped at each other in amazement. No boots on the North Face of the Dru, on a second bivouac, before second storm...

"'E 'ave only 'is..."

"Fires," we filled in automatically, still stunned. No crampons, no boots. How was he going to tackle the icy cracks and chimneys above? Worse still, how would he descend the crevasse-ridden Charpoua Glacier on the other side? Were we being cast as guardian-angels when we were looking for guides ourselves? The blind leading the blind. We were going to need a description in Braille.

As Jacques began to take in the rope, bawling instructions at Henri, an impossible suspicion struck me. Jacques was advising Henri to climb down first and traverse lower across the rock. That could only mean...

"Est-ce qu'il a un piolet?" I asked faintly.

"'E 'ave no axe," Jacques sighed, as if he too was beginning to find Henri's nakedness a little trying.

Invisible offstage, Henri swore that he'd be damned if he would descend any of the frightful rubbish he had just climbed. He insisted he could traverse the ice in his rockboots. Jacques was adamant that he couldn't do anything of the sort without ice-tools. He promised Henri that when he fell off his body would swoop in a great bruising arc across the Niche and smash at high speed into the side of the pillar a hundred feet below us.

I knew this scene from somewhere else. The dialogue and

the characters were absurdly familiar; any moment now the mist would sweep aside like a cinema-curtain and something wildly incongruous would come trundling up the ice... not a hen, or a hitchhiker... A Grand Piano!

That was it, Laurel and Hardy mullocking that piano up the thousand steps all over again. There was something simultaneously disastrous and invincible about this pair - the rubber bones of roughhouse comedy. I felt that if Henri took his 100-foot swing and pancaked onto a rock he would simply raise his little bowler-hat of a helmet, measure the lump on his head, stalk up the rope and punch Jacques on the nose, who would promptly somersault a hundred feet down the West Face only to spring back like a Jacques-in-the-box, and... I settled down to enjoy myself, and then Tom spoiled it all. He put on his crampons, took both our ice-axes, and disappeared into the mist to rescue Henri.

Henri and Jacques, it transpired, had embarked on the North Face of the Dru under the impression that it was a straightforward Piola rock-climb. They knew nothing of the complex descent. Henri was a good rockclimber, and Jacques wasn't bad on ice, so here they were. They had light sleeping-bags, already soaked from the previous night. They had no stove, and very little food, but they gave off a fine sense of tolerance for their shortcomings.

The final touch of distinction came with a pair of old-fashioned cycling-capes which buttoned around the neck, and covered the sleeping-bags in condensation. We gave them tea, and studied their route-description. It was a French pamphlet especially notable for the number of synonyms it offered for the word 'fissure'. Everyone knows the North Face of the Dru is composed of slits, slots, fissures, cracks, grooves, chimneys, and off-widths, but according to this pamphlet it was a full chapter from Roget's Thesaurus.

It snowed intermittently through the long night but the weather cleared before dawn. Fresh, shining snow amplified the lucid brilliance of the light. The Vallot Hut, a gleaming trinket, winked on the shoulder of Mont Blanc. Chamonix had sunk to an immeasurable depth below the huge headland of the mountain. Lightly hazed in blue mist, the tiny, clustered town - pale pebbles and mica flashes of light - was no more than stony shingle at the bottom of a deep pool. It had sunk beneath us while we tunnelled up into the cloud, and now it was submerged in a slow, fluid light, the current of the hours flowing in at the high end of the valley, meandering through towns and tents, washing wasted time and silted light down and out into the lowlands.

The first cable-car spidered down from the Midi, alpinists descending from the Vallée Blanche. If they considered the iced confection of the Dru they quietly congratulated themselves on gliding down to hot coffees, warm tents, and dry clothes.

I felt the resentment of the bound against the free. There was an ice-pitch ahead to avoid the snow-plastered pillar. We must bring Laurel and Hardy with us, not only for humanitarian reasons, but to share their guide. I chopped and kicked up the ice, warming the blood with a flurry of action, and suddenly, in that vast purity of shining altitude, the resentment burst into a flare of exultation. Breakfast sugar in the bloodstream of course, but it had a spiritual thrust far above biochemistry.

I could have rung hosannas and echoes from the great belfry of the Niche. Belayed, I hauled in the innocent climbing-rope summoning the faithful to a celebration... As a small altar-boy it was my job to ring an old church bell with a rope that hung down the gable into the gothic porch. A few brazen clangs were sufficient, but one splendid morning I got carried away by the mighty clamour I was arousing and the way the rope hauled me high into the echoing air with every ring and then hurled me back to earth again. I could no more stop than I could resist the temptation to pull a fairground swing-boat high enough to flip full-circle over the bar, human contents stuck to the upended seats like that mystery of upside-down water in a whirling, arm's-length bucket...

The valve for a fit of jubilation is a song at full volume, and I cracked the crystal air with Ewan McColl's great anthem of hard labour, 'Kilroy Was Here'.

"Who was here when they handed out the heavy jobs? Jobs with the hammer, the pick and the shovel..."

I substituted crampons for the shovel under the circumstances. Tom came groping up the rough, easy-angled ice.

"Who was here in the furrowed field stooped over? Pain shapes a question in bone and muscle..."

He had the slack of the French rope in tow, and I brought them up while Tom jumped into the golden cracks overhead. Crafty Jacques held on to the route-description for an exercise in translation. Every time I asked he translated laboriously with the hangdog hesitancy of a pupil who hasn't learned his vocabulary, but is determined to bluff it out.

"Take ze fissure... ze craque? on ze right...no, ze left, I tink..."

'*%£@Donnez-x£%moi,' I snarled at last, and grabbed the page.

Snow, ice and error slowed progress to a crawl. There was a tedium to the terrain now, which is best left undescribed, or catalogued in weary syllables; long, dull, slow, wet, cold, steep...

There is a hole through a thin ridge a couple of hundred feel below the summit, often exaggerated as a tunnel. Crawling through the little hatch I emerged on the Quartz Ledges, on the other side of the mountain. Tom's shoulders and rucksack jammed. For a moment his curly, grinning head protruded, outlined in north light from behind, and he seemed to wear the rim of the hole like the frame of a baroque portrait. In a little niche on the Quartz Ledges there were a couple of characters sound asleep, smouldering with sulphurous dreams. We kicked them back to the start of the chapter, and settled down in their places under a sky pregnant with apocalypse.

'LES HAUTES ALPES; Spectacle en Son et Lumière.' Performance began at dark, muted pyrotechnics in the distance, spotlights warming up, flickering across the walls and ramparts of this Acropolis among mountain-ranges. Tympanic voices rumbled the ritual responses among the ruined temples of the Aiguilles. Lightning outlined quivering horizons. The storm drew in its acolytes towards the great central altar, and the focus concentrated on Mont Blanc, the very Parthenon itself, the ice-marbled temple of the Alps. A subtle crown of lightning glowed behind the peak.

The scene was prepared for some unearthly set-piece now, a Tableau Vivant to generate the temple-goddess, Athene, who sprang by parthenogenesis from the cleft skull of Zeus... But within the burning chamber of the storm an infernal metamorphosis occurred. The spotlights, arc lights, footlights, and floodlights forked around the laboratory, and, instead of Athene, the mountain gave birth to a fire-and-ice Medusa, with lightning snake-locks to turn observers, if not to stone, at least to ash.

"By the way, congratulations!" interrupted Tom.

"Congratulations?! For what?"

He broke into an excited sports-commentary: "Mr. Dermot O'Murphy, first Oirishman to climb the Six North Faces..."

- Ah yes, I thought, shivering in my bag, - THIS Is Your Life! And isn't it wonderful? The magnificent menace of the *son et lumière* spilled over the edge of the stage..... The occupying Turks stored ammunition on the Acropolis, and in 1645 lightning struck the powder. Then they placed their guns in the shattered walls..... Massive eruptions ripped through the orchestra-pit, drums and cellos burst like balloons. Flash-fires raged in the front seats. The audience fled up the aisles, out the exits, into the teleferiques. Modern theatre is okay, but who wants audience-participation in a Greek tragedy? Going home with your eyes poked out.

The flames were racing through the balconies now, and

licking up into the gods.

The sports-commentator came on again -

"The award was conferred posthumously on O'Murphy..."

* * *

At daylight we began the descent.

Jacques and Henri, further along the ledges, were having a lie-in, so we left them there in their cycling-capes and bowler-helmets. Another fine mess...

The abseils went smoothly, stitches of rope unravelling, and soon we were on the knife-edge of the Flammes de Pierre. The blazing sun stripped the sheets of snow off the rocks like the bed-linen of an unwelcome guest.

We left the hungry ice behind, shuffled down weary paths, and then the endless gravel to the Mer de Glace. I loathed the mountains, and every atom in them. After every hundred yards of jarring descent I collapsed on a rock, cursing the gratuitous idiocy of mountaineering, the pangs of hunger, thirst, and pain.

Tom pinned down a mirage and filled a mug. Life held nothing more exquisite than the icy treble of water in the throat against the pounding bass of the blood.

And still the Mer de Glace to ford, threading a path across the ice in a maddening labyrinth of crevasses. Then up and up, up the far side to Montenvers, boots dragging, sweat dripping, and the last train missed.

Hunger drove us on to the empty station. On the platform, above the sweeping ice, in spite of the disapproving Dru and the outraged Jorasses, we plunged headfirst into the garbage-bins. Buried to the waist, Tom rooted out six tins of pate, four cartons of yoghurt, and a hard-boiled egg. The egg was unshelled and delicately dusted with Gauloise-ash. Thoughtfully picking orange-peel out of a salvaged cheese-roll, I gazed around me at the savage splendour.

Satisfaction resurged as pain subsided. I savoured again the old pieties... on top of the world... purity and peace... at one with nature... bird's-eye view... lords of creation... because it is there... trackless wastes... untrodden summits...

I wiped the cigarette-ash off the finest egg that was ever laid, and bit into it pensively. That humpy hulk of a mountain over there behind the Dru, the 4,000 metre Verte, we hadn't climbed that yet. What about the Nant Blanc Face, then over the top, and down that huge snow-gully, see it there raking down from the summit - the WHYMPER Couloir, to finish the season with a bang.

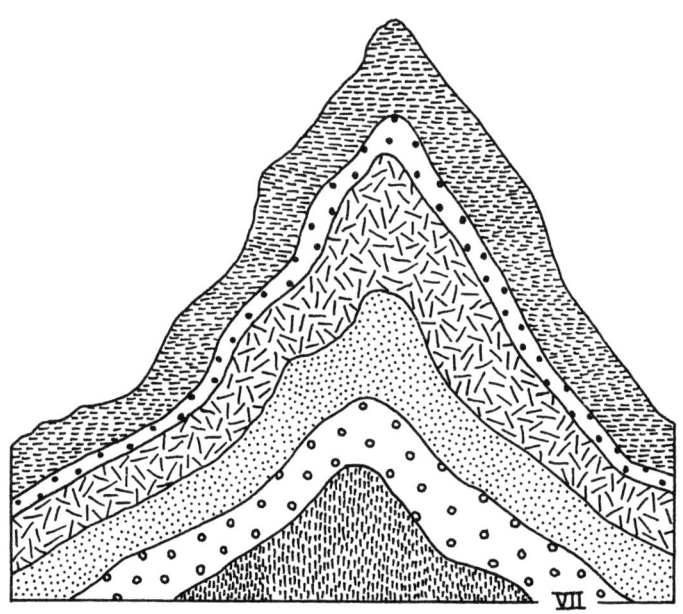

What Book Am I?

Words by Celia Bull and Rosie Smith
Sung to the tune of "Hey Big Spender"

The minute you peel back my page,
You can see I am a book of distinction -
A real blockbuster!
Climb with me, if you dare,
Even from the comfort of your own armchair.
So take a good look at my face:
Gaze in wonder at the features that you see.
What book am I?
Come and take a read with me.

My opening chapters will tell
Of the men who boldly tried to establish
A real hard passage:
Started off in 'thirty-five -
In three years only two contenders got off alive.
So maybe I'll give you more clues:
Two successful climbers came from Germany.
What book am I?
Come and balance me on your knee.

Do you think you can guess, guess, guess
If I say "Swallow's Nest, Nest, Nest?"
"Take a climb up my ice-hose!
Take a climb up my ice-hose!"
So I guess you've got the point,
Come and traverse with the gods and you will see:
I'm White Spider! Climb mein Eiger!
Hey, White Spider!
Slip between the sheets with me.

The Literary Song

Words by Celia Bull and Rosie Smith
Sung to the tune of Tom Lehrer's 'The Elements'

There's Reinhold Messner, Colin Kirkus, Lucy Rees and
Guido Rey
And Wilfrid Noyce, Menlove Edwards, Edward Whymper
and Dennis Gray,
Pete Boardman and Joe Tasker, Audrey Salkeld, H.D.F.
Kitto,
Bonatti, Borthwick, Birkett, Brown, John Long and W.
George Lowe.
There's Bonington and Child and Childs and Shipton and
N. Jack Soper
And Adam Smith and Gwen Moffat and Bill Peascod and
Steve Roper,
Anne Sauvy, Anderl Heckmair, Arthur Roth and Reginald
Farrer,
Tobias, Tullis, Holzel, Maurice Herzog and Heinrich Harrer

There's Wynthrop Young and Joe Simpson, George Ingle
Finch, Sir Arnold Lunn,
Maria Coffey, Rébuffat, Sir Jack Longland and there's Paul
Nunn
And Showell Styles and Dougal Haston, Jim Curran and
Gillian Kent
And Richmond, Link and Bourdillon, John Hunt, Frank
Smythe and Pat Ament.

There's Murray, Newby, John Noel, MacInnes and Claude
Ewing Rusk
And Humble, Howard-Bury, Charles S. Houston and Sir
Douglas Busk,

And Tilman, Gillman, Drasdo, Coxhead, Salter and Patricia
Barr
And George Pokorny, Roger Hubank, Mike Harrison and
Glyn Carr
Jeff Lowe, Tom Patey, Bowman, Mason, Pilley, Perrin and
John Ball
Trevanian, George Abraham, John Muir, Jeff Long and
Lincoln Hall
And James Ramsay Ullman, Tony Hiebeler and Paul
Sydney Powell
And Diemberger and Chris Brasher and Hillary and Galen
Rowell

There's Wilson, Newman, Venables and Saunders and
Norman Croucher
And Fanshawe, Milburn, Scott Russell and Irving, W.
Poucher
And Wilson Kendall, Charlie Clarke, Nea Morin and Annie
Peck
And Freshfield, Firsoff, Ed Douglas, Walt Unsworth, Buhl
and Allen Steck

These are the only writers' names
That fit onto this song sheet
So if you want to find out more
You'd better consult with Jill Neate

Climbing Language

by Tony Lopez

1

On narrow ridges
Fear sharpens attention
Strengthens the grip.

Extended rock problems
Call into being
Virtues otherwise absent.

Endurance and resolve
Meet stone resistance
Personal limits are
Tried and put to use.

To check a partner's fall
When roped together on the ridge
You jump off the other side.

2

A short but
Tricky descent
Onto the pinnacles

Watch where you
Put each foot
Take your time.

I'm taking in. That's me.
I've had enough of climbing.
Don't make me laugh, you said.

This is what is known as
'A section of sustained interest'.

3
'Snow and ice is different'
Forget finesse
Just hang on and haul up.

Chiaroscuro

by Kevin Howett

Badgers are emerging from their sleepy dens to change their soiled winter bedding and entice startled young cubs into new adventures. Beatrix Potter foxes hunt the tussock grass for voles, standing on their hind legs, listening for movement with their foghorn ears and leaping like springbok antelopes for their unfortunate prey. Courting birds dart from tree to tree, fighting for their territories as they are overwhelmed by the changes of the season; the contrast of slumber and play, ice and rock.

Like a rain-soaked shawl lowering around my shoulders, Glen Nevis cools, slowly giving off its heat as it prepares for a crisp Spring night.

The air is unbelievably clean. The simple act of breathing it in seems so refreshing. This is not a second-hand version that has been exhaled by countless halitosis sufferers or their nicotine-smelling cousins. I know I'm the first person ever to have inhaled this unadulterated mixture of clean, lip-smacking gases.

I desperately want to refresh my numbed and dried-out mind by gulping it down in great savoury mouthfuls of overindulgence, to let it replenish every stagnant pool of gas lying in millions of alveoli, then let it slowly trickle from my nostrils like spent cigarette smoke. Instead I feel as though I'm drowning in it.

Crouching down at the stream's pebble dashed fringe with hands cupped, I squat precariously on the balls of cramped and tired feet. Rocking unsteadily on the uneven ground, I dip my warm, bloodied fingers into the water.

It sparkles between my finger tips with the clarity of champagne, fermented higher in the hillside from a thousand delicate ice crystals, awakening the hairs on my arms and neck with its memories of a dying winter, its cold caresses inundating the lacerations in a painful tidal wave.

With lips pursed as if awaiting a special, sexy gift, I suck up any water which remains in my makeshift beaker in a long, noisy slurp. It tastes of cold mountain rocks, of the hard materials of the earth - granites, rhyolites and andesites, schists and gneiss.

Its roughness sticks in my throat, to choke me in staccato gulps, retching and spluttering it back out to mingle with long, sticky strings of saliva; the waters and placenta of the parturition of spring, of rock to reality

Distracted by these vivid sensations and the memory of their infliction on the crag behind me, I stumble on a tangled clump of heather and wince as broken ribs protesting at being briefly forgotten drop me to the floor.

I lie there, utterly spent and wondering why this world of climbing that wraps me in its multicoloured dream coat, always seem to hurt so much?

* * *

That morning the glen had been noticeably empty of human activity save for myself and Andy.

He had sat on the ground staring anxiously up the flapping ropes attending to their movements with an exaggerated care. It was almost as if he was trying to convince me that even if all the paraphernalia of gear strung out on the rock between us should fail, then his unwavering attention alone would hold a fall.

Ninety feet above him I'd sweated profusely despite the cool air as I'd contemplated the increasing likelihood of testing his theory.

Tiny mica-schist wrinkles pushed deep indentations into my finger ends. It hurt like hell because my fingers were bruised to the bone after being stuffed into jagged slots too small for them, scraping knuckles against cheese grater rock to expose deep, tender, white flesh and oozing blood from under each nail where torn slithers of flesh splintered from their roots after too much strain.

The overly steep difficulties of the lower groove had seemed to relent and just a short stretch lay between me and the sanctuary of the tussled clumps of sweet-smelling grasses that straggled over the edge.

Convinced of victory, I'd confirmed it with a presumptuous shout of elation. So what a shock when, that small, insignificant finish had simply shrugged me off its back. And not just once, but twice I had sent screaming echoes down the glen as I hurtled out of control through thirty feet of space, to put to the test what I'd considered as a totally unreliable collection of protection.

To my relief, I'd twice been pulled out of this free fall by the parachute of gear and Andy's wishful thinking, but near the end of each fall, I was flung violently chest first at the rock to tear muscles and damage ribs and send nauseous semiconscious pains ringing round my head.

Twice Andy had lowered me down to recover and each time it had seemed beyond reason to go back up, to court disaster with one of the most marginal RP2 placements I'd ever bothered to use. Only this had stopped me while all its neighbours had hurled themselves into the air.

But by now I had sacrificed too much to back down and I'd become doubly determined not to be cheated of the route. But with the searing pain from my ribs that cut the breath from my mouth each time I moved or inhaled, I was fully aware of the inevitable result or the much more serious outcome should that RP rip from its precarious hold.

So, I had ignored the odds against me and chanced one more attempt. Back at the high point with mounting fear and rapidly ebbing strength, I'd started shuffling about with indecision over which hand or foot should claim the only two available holds; stalling to put off the commitment; of deciding to go and deciding to stay all in one hurried thought.

Monkey hanging (not the unbelievable sort of thing they used to get up to ages ago in Hartlepool but a resting technique stolen from the winter) had allowed me the briefest rest but each time my shoulders tired and my fingers began to uncurl.

Sticky-soled feet which had smeared automatically only a few minutes before had started skidding out of control. Legs that had suffered only the odd flirtatious quiver degenerated into aggressive spasms as they became pumped up with the by-products of exhaustion.

Fear, not the blind ignorant kind, but accumulated and reasoned, was rapidly taking over just as alcohol smothers a ship builder on the floor of a disco.

In this confusion of indecision and ebbing strength, I could no longer give a damn about the badgers or the foxes, or the beauty of the Caledonian woods scattered below me, or even the glistening screes of Sgurr a'Mhaim hovering in the lupin-blue sky.

I could hear the thundering of the spring meltwater crashing through the gorge below and the hollow echoing croaks of ravens circling overhead, but really they couldn't have been less important. All that mattered was to get it right. Like a baby learning to walk for the first time, I had to put one foot in front of the other and not topple over.

Andy braced himself against the cliff face as if he had some doubts about the outcome and had decided to get out of the drop zone.

.....I could see him fidgeting with the twin ropes, sliding them back and forth through the Sticht plate with uncertain, nervous fingers. I kicked my toes into the very front of my slippers in a nervous response.

..... I could hear him breathing louder and louder, exhaling hurriedly in order to grasp the next breath as fast as possible and I had felt stabs of pain from my ribs in harmony with his every breath.

..... His palms were sweating. He'd wiped them on his thigh and I'd struggled a hand free of the rock, erratically searched behind me for the chalk bag and plunged it in.

..... I'd felt his heartbeat vibrate up the ropes and pound in my temples to blot out all other sounds; I'd fidgeted with the little lumps of chalk which rattled about in the bottom of the bag before abandoning flurries of white powder that drifted about me in the still air.

..... Wearing his shoulders like a cape, he'd looked up with his eyes half hidden by concerned wrinkles of Tarpay skin. He'd opened his mouth and held his tongue gently between his teeth, had taken one deep breath and began to speak:

"Watch me," I'd shouted, and the woods had fallen silent.

* * *

The birds sat quietly on the top branches, nervously waiting. The ravens had deserted the sky to crouch coldly on the broken buttresses of Meall Cumhann, ruffling their cape-like feathers and hunching their shoulders around large threatening beaks, waiting for carrion. The river had fallen silent, freezing stationary over its cataracts.

Enveloped in a dream I had released my hand from the last vestige of safety and grasped a succession of inadequate dimples and stood on imperceptible ripples to finally slap wildly over the bulge and flap with sweating palms, onto a sloping shelf.

I had walked my fingers one by one, like a caterpillar of digits, over the surface, reaching further and further for the holds that would pull me to the top.

Frantically they had searched through the wrinkles of the schist and the precarious balance of the move until, all hope dwindling, they lunged into the air in one last desperate bid.......

....."Noooooo!" screamed back the air with a stranger's echo bounced from the distant tops.......

.....The stillness of the glen below me had shattered in an explosion of birds, flapping their way deafeningly into the sky in startled flight. The roar of water had grown deafening in the gorge below and the noise of the river had become the rush of air past my face as I'd hurtled in an agony of fear towards the ground, my own scream echoing from my open mouth, an emptiness filling my stomach, and the dream had shattered over me in a sticky sweat

* * * * *

The sun begins to dip behind Stob Ban and I shake the last droplets of water from my hands. Andy watches me quietly from his crouch by the river and smiles. He finishes drinking and shoulders both our sacks, half turning to walk away down the path but at the last second sharing my gaze with one last glimpse back to the crag.

Laughter floods between us as we remember how that RP had held; how the next frenzied attempt had me plunge ten fingers into the sweet-smelling grass where I had laid listening to a racing heart telling me for sure what I always knew; that no other place existed where the contrast of beauty and pain, fear and elation, share such an intoxicating balance than in this mystical land of Caledonia.

I shout loudly into the air to savour the sound of the glen, then turn and run with Andy and the pain and the elation down the track.

Stranger! If e'er thine ardent step hath traced
The northern realms of ancient Caledon,
where the proud queen of wilderness hath placed,
by lake and cataract, her lonely throne;
sublime but sad delight thy soul hath known,
Listing where from the cliffs the torrents thrown
Mingle their echoes with the eagles cry,
and with the sounding lake and the moaning sky.
Sir Walter Scott

[A description of the first ascent of Chiaroscuro E7 6b Glen Nevis by K. Howett and A. Nelson, 1988.]

Diff in the Afternoon

by Andy Anderson

The mountain which is Birchen runs almost due North to South along a spur of the English central massif. In the eternal snows just below the summit a Herdwick sheep stands, belly-deep, forever frozen in a ruminative posture. The left eye-socket is empty, pillaged long ago by a raven, venturing high above its normal scavenging contour. The right eye stares, oblivious to the sunlight lasering from the ice crystals, down toward the distant cities of the plain. When the snow thaws a little in midsummer, it can be seen that one foreleg also is missing from the carcass. Local peasants know the spot as Nelson's Monument.

I came often to Birchen that year, mostly alone, sometimes in the company of other aficionados. I was young, but intending to write seriously about serious issues. I thus needed to discover the meaning of life, and the reason for death. Such issues are examined, in public, every Sunday afternoon in summer on Birchen and other similar mountains. The men conducting the examinations, existing in the narrow margin between comfortable life and violent death, are the Rockstars: Los Soloistes.

I watched his dresser assist him into the fluorescent tights, easing clinging nylon past thin muscle-knotted calves. Unusually, the peon was a girl, slim but awkward and angular, gypsy-black hair cropped short in the fashion favoured by the young men of that period. He was youthful, perhaps 19 summers. A novillero, from the new condition of his kit and the scarcity of scars on the pale skin he exposed. And unsuccessful, judging from the total absence of sponsors' logos and camp-followers; and with a girl for a body-servant. I had observed them for some weeks at Birchen and the other mountains of the range, progressing as far as an exchange of desultory conversation at appropriate moments. By that time I even knew their names: Kevin and Tracey.

He finished lacing the slippers to his satisfaction and stood erect, wiping off the soles against Lycra-clad calves. From her kneeling position she held out the Whillans belt, hands outstretched with palms uppermost, making a ritual offering of the act. Normally he would have buckled on the belt, followed by a bandolier linking the meagre hardware they possessed. But today he rejected the harness with a dismissive gesture. "I obscenity upon the Whillans," he muttered, and turned to face the mountain, armed only with raw courage and a chalk bag. Today, he was to perform as El Soloiste.

The climb which his destiny had selected for Kevin's novillada was *Sail Buttress*. Nose to tail, 45ft of Derbyshire gritstone towered above him. Hard, Very Difficult. He spat from a dry mouth and wished that his pigtail had been long enough to braid like the professionals, rather than left to protrude from its elastic band like one end of a bottle brush. An expectant hush settled over the arena as the trumpet fanfare died away. (The holiday-makers with the ghetto blaster had moved on to the next crag.) He crossed himself, dipping the chalk bag, and began to climb.

The first moves were laboured and graceless, thuggery in motion, his nervousness obvious. He missed the intimate clutch of the Whillans, the reassurance of a top rope. His apprehensions spread, echoing away from the rock face, dreading a greasing of rain from the cobalt sky, a sudden squall of wind from the midsummer calm. Even the Great Ones, he knew, feared unexpected wind, which could disturb the Soloiste's delicate balance, often with fatal results.

But the holds were there, he began to piece moves together; gradually a rhythm developed. By the time he had reached the crux his dreams of emulating Joselito, Little Joe, whom some knew as The Human Fly, dominated his consciousness again. He, too, would be a Great One. He had the cojones; abandoning the Whillans belt had ensured that.

Should you take it upon yourself to climb to that bleak, inhospitable spot, you will observe that the crux of *Sail Buttress* is a large, overhanging Roman nose of rock. A man must mantelshelf up, over a large block, on to a sloping ledge. There, if his nerve holds, he will reach high to his left to jam a horizontal crack before lunging into space to land a foothold on the very tip of the nose. When this man has placed a good runner, and an even better second, in position before committing himself, the move is exhilarating. For the Soloiste, it represents The Moment of Truth.

I watched him reach ineffectually for the foothold in three, four, five attempts, confidence visibly evaporating in the afternoon sunshine. He fitted the hand jam this way and that. Time ebbed away, spectators grew restless. Finally, as we knew it must, pride in his manhood overcame his fear. He jammed and swung into space but his lunge for the foothold lacked conviction. In slow motion, it seemed, he peeled away from the rockface, the audience caught its collective breath, and he accelerated down into oblivion.

Oblivion resided in the angular form of Tracey, waiting with upturned face at the foot of the climb. They met with the sound of fighting bulls when they clash head-on in the pastures of Andalucia, and crashed to earth in a flurry of whirling limbs and dust. As the cloud subsided, I overheard his murmured question: "Did the earth move for you, Little One?" She sat up and smiled a crooked smile, spitting out the front teeth loosened by the impact.

I went to offer my condolences, as an aficionado. I told him, in great detail, where the faults had occurred and why the jam had not held and what must be done next time to complete the move successfully. But the fire had gone out behind the dark eyes and his thoughts seemed elsewhere. Truly is it said that the brave blood is shed first. The girl, though, thanked me gravely with peasant courtesy. "Thod off," she lisped.

I never saw them again. Later, in the local bars where Los

Soloistes are sometimes glimpsed, the story circulated that
one star-filled midsummer night, in a sleeping bag bivouac
high on the mountain, she had throttled him with a length of
shock tape. Now only the mountain remains, with the
Herdwick carcass just below the summit. Nobody knows
how the sheep came to be there.

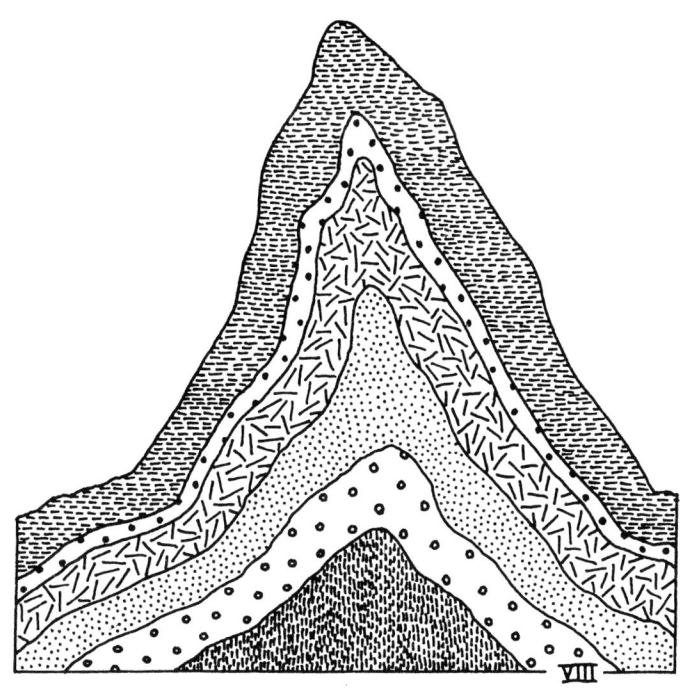

Marie Paradis, maidservant*
"Ficha moi dans une crevasse et alla ou vo voudra"

by Alison Fell

Ici on voit l'incroyable point
de l'Aiguille...

The gentlemen quiver their staves, wild
heads thrown back, their throats
bared to one another

Mont Blanc like a tablecloth flung
over a banquet, concealing the *cailles*,
hump of the *grosse dinde*,
the geometric gleam of spoons.

In the village they jostle at telescopes:
six sisters who know, now,
how she wanted to be somebody - Marie
the modest one, secret as glaciers.

In the tottering black they're laughing
and pinching, taunting her to the edge.
Memory. Her face curls back
from the debris of childhood: Papa
smothering in a crevasse of snowy

petticoats. She pants for water, gathering
her weight, filling her laced boots
with nails. Squatting like a *grosse dinde*
in her own steam and for what?

Down in the flatlands she was strong enough
and square, capable as thumbs.

Air streams past her face:
in the cold night the mountain
is a whisper-giant: her dreams tease her
she will kiss the stars.
La première femme d'Europe, perched
on her father's high white shoulder

On the summit her anger arches
like an arrow, sickening and falling

Let them spread their own napkins
on the folds of the snow, peel
the ham from its hot stones.

She will eat pared cheese hard
as a boot. *Ça suffit pour moi,*

say the red hands sullen in her muff.
Champagne at altitude explodes,
she knows it, vanishing like spin-

drift on the blank blue air.

(*The first woman to climb Mont Blanc. "Throw me down
a crevasse and go where you want to.")

All for Love

by Martin Owen

It all started in the Members Bar of the Drones Club, as these things tend to do. It was particularly crowded that afternoon with refugees from the Carlton Club, covered in plaster dust and generally cluttering up the place, and I had just collared a couple of large gins (to save the waiter's legs, you understand) when I spied the dreaded Tubby Glossop looking even more morose than usual.

"What ho, Tubby," I cried cheerfully, reluctantly parting with one of the gins, "you appear to be in need of a good party - a dose of the old Wooster Magic, if I may say so."

"You're not wrong, Bertie," quoth Tubby, knocking back the gin. "Fact is - I'm in love. It's Angela," - he paused dramatically - "but she doesn't know I exist. What am I to do to win her - it's driving me mad, Bertie, you must help me!"

I considered this shattering news. The Hon. Angela Spiffington, 'doyenne' of the University Climbing Club, and the most heart-stopping creature ever seen in a leotard was hardly in Tubby's league I would have thought.

I tried the tactful approach. "Surely she's not interested in you, Tubby," I joshed him gently, "you need to be leading 5c to get a place on her dance card, never mind a proper date - and struggling up V. Diffs as you do is hardly likely to catch her eye."

Tubby glared balefully at me. "You don't understand, Bertie," he said determinedly. "I am in love - and love knows no difficulties. All right, so I can't climb as well as Angela but I do have other qualities - it's simply getting her to see them."

I resisted the temptation to suggest offering the lovely Angela a magnifying glass, and decided to concentrate on the problem at hand.

"It strikes me, Tubby old thing, that this is a problem well within my wide experience of life. I shall cogitate and come up with a Plan."

Tubby looked anxious. I continued, "I shall ask Jeeves to help." Tubby's brow cleared. "That's all right then," he said with satisfaction, and we parted promising to meet on the morrow.

Since the plan I intended to devise would involve a foray into the jolly old mountains, I thought I'd better get properly kitted out, and so a stroll along The Strand took me into one of those climbing-type shops, where a very helpful young chappie togged me up with all the latest gear. He even threw in a rucksack for Jeeves to carry it all in.

That evening I put the problem to Jeeves. "It strikes me, Sir," he said, as he did something geometric with the cutlery, "that Mr. Glossop needs to impress the lady with something other than his climbing ability."

"You're right there, Jeeves," I guffawed, "poor old Tubby isn't built for climbing in any case and as to ability - he has enough trouble getting up in the morning."

"Quite so, Sir," said Jeeves, giving me one of his looks, "may I suggest that if Mr. Glossop were to be involved in something like a rescue, perhaps of a dramatic kind, in front of the Lady Angela, then she might be so impressed by his bravery and skill as to overlook his lack of climbing talent."

"Brilliant, Jeeves," I acknowledged, "but how is such a thing to be arranged?"

"Well, Sir," he continued, removing an infinitesimal speck of dust from a wine glass, "your own climbing ability is not, shall I say, of an exceptionally high standard. Suppose you, Sir, were to place yourself in an ostensibly hazardous situation and then allow Mr. Glossop to save you, your delighted expressions of gratitude and awe at Mr. Glossop's courage might well do the trick."

"Jeeves," I said, with pride, "you are a gem," and went immediately to phone Tubby and tell him of my plan.

The day dawned bright and early, Jeeves and I having driven to the rendezvous car park beneath the crag and encountered an anxious Glossop.

"I've found out which climb Angela is doing today," he said, indicating what looked like an impossible line of smooth vertical wall, "and luckily there is a Mild Severe right next to it which will do for us."

"Righto, Tubby," I said, "you go and lurk at the top with your abseil rope, and when I am in an appropriate position I will squeak loudly. You then leap down, rescue me, and Bingo, an impressed and smitten Angela will fall at your feet."

"I hope you're right," said a grim-faced Glossop, stomping off, chocks jingling.

"Now then, Jeeves," I said, "we'd better get dressed up. You did pack all my new kit, didn't you?"

"Not quite, Sir," replied Jeeves, looking shifty.

"What do you mean?" I cried, and dived into the rucksack. "Where are my new pink Huecos, my Ron Hill tracksters and my High T-shirt as worn by Andy Pollitt?"

"A gentleman, Sir," said Jeeves firmly, "does not wear pink shoes, and certainly not figure-hugging clothing. I have taken the liberty of packing something more appropriate."

"But Jeeves..." I gasped in horror, as I pulled out the moleskin breeches, check shirt, woolly socks and nailed boots, which Jeeves had put in, "nailed boots! How can I possibly climb with this old-fashioned equipment?"

"If it was good enough for Mr. Mallory and Mr. Irving, Sir," replied my man with his most severe expression, "it should be good enough for you. My father, Sir, was Butler to those heroic gentlemen on their ill-fated Everest expedition, and was devastated when they failed to return - he had made a soufflé especially to celebrate their success."

I have to say that old Jeeves has the ability to make a chap feel jolly ashamed of himself sometimes, so, without further ado, I got kitted up and set off up this fearsome-looking route. "All for love," I told myself bitterly as I thrutched over a bulge and into a recess where I belayed and hoiked up a surprisingly athletic Jeeves.

"On the next pitch, Sir," whispered my man, "you will find the crux. I took the precaution of placing a strategic peg earlier, to which you may attach yourself safely, while pretending to be at a full run-out with no protection. If you then call Mr. Glossop loudly, he will descend and rescue you."

"Good," I said, "but we'd better check that the delightful Angela is within sight," and leaned round to see if I could spot the best-known posterior profile on the mountain.

"Coo-ee, Angela," I cried, which earned us a vaguely contemptuous wave as she majestically swanned over some horrendous overhang, and, happy that she would be able to see our triumph, I set off for the crux.

By the time I got to Jeeves' peg, I was pretty bushed, I can tell you, and it didn't take much acting ability to hang on and bleat loudly for Glossop (or anybody) to come and save me. I vaguely caught sight of a pink bottom zooming up the next climb, but then began to concentrate on not actually falling off, which would have rather defeated the object of the exercise!

Anyway, within a few minutes, a rope's end dropped past my nose, to be followed by the sound of feet on the rock and the smell of perfume. "Perfume?" I thought, "what on earth?" and then, to my horror, a well-known female voice crying, "Don't worry Bertie, I'm coming."

"Angela!" I cried aghast, quickly unclipping from the peg so she wouldn't spot the subterfuge. Within seconds I was seized by some charming, if muscular, arms, turned upside down, strapped into some extraordinary arrangement of slings and left dangling like a fly in a web while Angela whisked upwards out of sight. A short time later I was hoisted unceremoniously to the top to find a grinning Angela and a glowering Glossop who refused to speak to me. It was a matter of moments to bring up Jeeves who, for the first time I can remember, actually goggled.

"It's quite simple really," explained Angela later, as we sat in the pub. "I had just finished my solo route when I heard you yell, so I wandered over. When I discovered that Tubby didn't understand what prusiking was I knew I should have to intervene." Tubby glowered even more.

Angela placed her hand on my arm. "Do you know, Bertie," she enquired looking speculatively at my moleskin trousers, "I've been looking for a new climbing partner, someone who needs to develop their skill, and who has a nice car and a man who can help hump all my kit. I think you will do nicely," she smiled, and actually kissed me on the cheek.

"Get the drinks in, Jeeves," I croaked, "- and a large one for Mr. Glossop."

"Quite so, Sir," was the reply.

Climbing under Communism

by Waclaw Sonelski
translated by Danuta Holata

While preparing for this presentation, I did some investigation into the Polish-English exchange of climbing writing. The outcome was pitiful. To the best of my knowledge, only one Polish text has been translated into English. It's titled *Stefano We Shall Come Tomorrow* and was published in 1962. It is a short story about a rescue operation on the Eiger; it's author, Adam Skoczylas, was undeniably one of our most talented mountain writers.

The situation the other way round isn't any better. Our pre-war reading public got the Polish translation of Smythe's *Camp Six*, then in 1956 we had *Ascent of Everest*, and 30 years later, Bonington's *Everest, the Hard Way*. This year, Curran's book about the K2 disaster in '86 has come out. I don't think such a state of affairs needs much comment.

You expect me to talk about Polish climbing literature, I presume. But this won't be the focus of my lecture. It wouldn't be fair if I didn't first present a fuller picture of Polish mountaineering in general. Its image - according to the European and American climbing press - is sort of monotonous: Kukuczka, Rutkiewicz, Kurtyka... That's very one-sided! Or just boring! In order to appreciate the literary production of Polish climbers, you can't ignore the historical traditions, social, economic and even political background.

So let me tell you about it, about us - Polish climbers.

The way we are is the way we climb and - ultimately - the way we write about it. This is a trivial statement - but I don't think it really refers to Polish mountaineering. The reason is that since its beginning, Polish climbing has seldom been climbing for its own sake. Instead, it has been burdened with other, more or less lofty, functions. Moreover, in the past it was sometimes difficult to draw a line between climbing and its literary image, to determine where real life became literature. It's the case of myth overpowering the reality.

Today, climbing in Poland (unlike in Great Britain) isn't practised by a large number of people. There are no more than three thousand active climbers, but the number of armchair mountaineers is surprisingly high. Let me prove it: a book on a Himalayan expedition has on average a circulation of 30 thousand; as far as I know, Jim Curran's book has been much more popular in Poland than in England; my latest rock-climbing manual has sold, despite its sky-high price, nearly 14 thousand copies.

Amazingly, the general public have only a vague idea of what rock-climbing is about. The word 'climber' is almost solely associated with 'mountaineer' - armed with pitons, crampons and ice-axes. Yet, since 99 percent of what has been written in Polish about climbing concerns alpine climbing and mountaineering, then the result is hardly surprising. Small wonder if in Poland it's much easier to buy a book about climbing than to meet a real climber in action.

Polish climbing came into being while Alpinism was reaching its Golden Age. In the nineteenth century Poland was off the map, partitioned among the three empires. The Tatras - our only mountains of some sporting and climbing potential - lay in the Austro-Hungarian Empire. At the beginning of the last century, Zakopane, where it all started, was a small and filthy village at the foot of the unexplored Tatras. The mountains were an attraction and Zakopane quickly grew into a fashionable holiday spot. It was frequented by the elite of Polish society: writers, scientists, politicians, artists, from all the three partitions. Thanks to the liberal policy of the Habsburg monarchy, Zakopane enjoyed an independent cultural life. Therefore, it soon became the spiritual capital of Poles on holiday.

This situation consequently led to the disproportionate growth of the Tatras' fame. Their role in the national culture was overdone, inflated by poets, writers and journalists. The Tatras were all but worshipped and regarded as a symbol of national greatness. They were seen as a sanctuary for the national spirit, a storehouse of patriotic virtues and became, as one poet put it, 'the altars of independence'.

I don't think I've heard of a similar exaltation of mountains in any other European culture.

This elevated attitude partially descended upon Tatra highlanders, native dwellers of the region, as well as upon Tatra climbers. The Tatra ascentionists found themselves on a pedestal and their climbing activity was burdened with all manner of national and artistic virtues. They were credited with values totally beyond the understanding of our contemporary climbers.

So, from the beginning, climbing in the Tatras was over-intellectual, whilst activity itself was pursued by a mere hundred climbers. The ethos of the noble knight was only too readily ascribed to them. But from another point of view, this image of the Tatra climber had grotesque undertones. Climbers themselves were eyed with suspicion and often referred to as would-be suicides, slightly mentally unbalanced. And so it is today! Isn't it funny that our contemporary Don Quixote seems to be a climber with an ice-axe instead of a lance?

At the turn of the century, Polish mountain literature was dominated by two genres: the expedition (or travel) narrative, and the more or less sublime Romantic poems. Climbing literature proper didn't appear before the 1930s.

At that time, its most distinctive and representative form took shape. This form - bujdalka - isn't strictly speaking a literary genre and escapes precise definition. The word itself comes from climbing slang and is openly ironic. The name suggests some kind of spoof that can't be taken seriously. A bujdalka-story is a short narrative about climbing, but never about a huge expedition. The realistic description of full, technical route particulars and the author-climber's experiences during the climb come to the fore. I'm sure you know exactly what kind of writing I mean. After all, it's probably universal and has been created in all climbing communities.

In their early days, Bujdalka-stories were published almost exclusively in the Polish Alpine Club magazine, *Taternik* (meaning Tatra climber). Consequently, these climbing narratives were addressed to and read by a relatively small number of climbers. However, it was the authors' ambition to follow literary principles to the nth degree.

Some of these old stories, written by climbers of true literary talent, or by climbing writers, are still considered masterpieces of non-fiction. As far as their literary merits are concerned, they have lost nothing over the decades.

Climbing motifs were also eagerly exploited by popular literature: books for boy scouts, detective stories, thrillers, even erotic novels. 'Sheer drops' and 'yawning chasms' have always been impressive, and if 'an intrepid climber' was suspended in their midst, the picture was complete.

Surely enough, practical realities were more often than not brushed aside with a carefree wave of the hand, relying on the readers' ignorance. Let me give you an apt example from a pre-war novel pompously entitled *White Eagle*. The book did boast a tremendous success: two alpinists, agents of the Polish and Soviet enemy intelligence services, take two full days (and plenty of energy) to climb a shortish cliff in the Tatras. Let me point out that in their days and those weather conditions, the hardest route on the crag took... two hours.

After the last war, our country was subjected to the delights of caring Soviet democracy. Its best years, 1949 - 55, were the absolute rule of Stalinism. The Alpine Club was dissolved, then incorporated into a mass tourist organisation. Climbers were classified and certificated, their ideological consciousness and social usefulness checked. Only collective summit ascents, with the placing of the red flag on top 'in the honour of Comrade Stalin', could be done. Solo climbing was of course banned as 'a sign of bourgeois idealism'. What's worse, the Tatra playground was severely limited to two valleys, since the state boundary ridges were under strict military guard. Happy-go-lucky climbing without permits carried the risk of a warning shot. There's a grand story about how it happened to Andrzej Zawada - who was fortunately spared to become a famous expedition leader. Needless to say, no climbing trips abroad were allowed. So in a nut shell, the early 1950s were a gloomy time for climbing. Was its literature equally murky?

In those years communist propagandists established clear patterns of literature: its style, heroes and message. The most enchanting theme was of a young and buxom girl on a tractor, a patriotic song on her lips and a linen wrap on her head. There was only one obligatory style of writing: social realism.

Polish climbers, however, didn't stop admiring the old demigods of mountaineering, like Mallory or Buhl. They still wanted to continue the pre-war style of writing, but censorship was total. The results were often ridiculous: a climbing guide-book had to praise the achievements of Soviet alpinism; a monography on Tatra vegetation had to describe Lenin's adventures in the Tatras. With such stories, authors managed to 'bribe' the censors.

Polish mountaineering saw better days after the Stalinist breakdown. The Alpine Club was revived and its members permitted to visit the Alps. The reading public at large demanded travel books, adventure stories and exotic narratives. Books of Alpine stories became very popular.

One of them was written by Jan Dlugosz, an outstanding all-round climber. In one story he describes his participation in the first ascent of the Central Pillar of Freney by Chris Bonington's party in 1961. Dlugosz was a perfect story-teller and his book is still considered a great literary achievement. I read it ages ago but still remember, for instance, that Don Whillans hated mushrooms.

To help make up for the silent years, several books on

Alpine and Himalayan history, and a couple of excellent expedition books, came out. And that was all! There was no fiction; no-one dared to write climbing memoirs or autobiography, and last, but not least, satire or humorous writing was almost non-existent (although, occasionally, *Taternik* did publish a light-hearted story). Yes, there's no dodging the fact that Polish mountaineering was a serious, if not grave, affair. To laugh at climbing was considered a sacrilege similar to laughing at warfare. But on the other hand, the climbing community was notorious for its unique sense of humour, fanciful hoaxes and hilarious evenings in mountain huts. It's most regrettable that the legendary humour of that generation went almost unrecorded in literature.

Young people of the 1950s and 60s used to escape to the mountains to get away from the Orwellian absurdities of their life in the lowlands. At altitude, the tight grip of the real socialist state felt less oppressive and life could be lived according to simpler and brighter rules. For many frustrated young people, it was climbing that constituted the essence of existence. Their ambitions, dreams and satisfactions found fulfilment in the hills, while the plains offered only the hypocrisy of the communist regime. At the same time, climbers were gradually estranged from the rest of the society. Certainly, the climbing community had always been a kind of elitist group. But in the 50s this elitism was sanctioned by The Tatra National Park regulations. They stated that free access to mountain wilderness was granted only to certificated climbers, while all other hill-walkers had to keep to marked trails. Fairly soon, the climbing community became an isolated and isolating group. They knew one another well and, from the outside, it seemed hermetically sealed.

The 1970s brought about a radical change in the state of climbing affairs. Polish mountaineering turned commercial, but in a particular way. Blessed by the authorities, mountaineering clubs transformed themselves into enterprises paying climbers to clean and paint industrial stacks and high constructions. This work earned really big money. All of a sudden, we could afford Himalayan expeditions, and didn't miss the opportunity. The Tatra and even the Alps were ignored, since anyone who knew one end of an ice-axe from the other rushed into Asia. No-one cared about old ideals because all their attention was focused on a rusted stack with a Himalayan peak shining in the background.

This wasn't without harm. Soon it wasn't only climbing that money paid for. Many climbers earned a comfy living, and for some, the old membership card of a mountaineering club meant the possibility of getting gainful employment. Our climbing Don Quixote suddenly became a primitive workman, petty businessman or simply a crook, or a decorator painting over the old ideals.

You may think that such a stormy, critical period would yield equally crucial writing. Climbers faced plenty of revaluations both in their sport and in their life-style, and sensitive writers should have been challenged or inspired. But alas, no. Literature failed to record it.

In fact, the ever-growing number of expeditions also meant more and more expedition books. As a rule, each mountaineering expedition was followed by an unofficial account. In many respects, this situation resembled that in the British mountain writing of the 1920s and 30s. At first readers cherished every book about our Himalayan feats, but familiarity brought boredom. Nepalese villages lost their exotic appeal, frost-bitten fingers and struggling for breath found no pity and an 8000 metre bivouac was all but commonplace. The pages were impatiently turned over in a vain search for some substantial values. Even the literary standard of the books was barely acceptable.

Why were those expedition books so utterly boring? The previous concept of 'the real life can only be in the hills' did not quite apply here. The whole concept of expeditions; human passions and ambitions, money, professional competition and the rat-race were the very essence of life. So why couldn't it breed at least readable stuff?

Herman Melville once said that grand literature needs a grand subject. As far as size goes, the Himalaya fulfil that condition. Yet Polish epics of high altitude blizzards and avalanches found no truthful literary record. I don't think the lack of talent on the part of the writers was the only cause.

At this point let me refer to my own experiences in this field.

I took part in two Himalayan expeditions: the western face of Makalu and Dhaulagiri in winter. They were unforgettable adventures, but first and foremost, they were all-embracing and deep-reaching personal experiences. Each time I came back from Asia, I felt much older, wiser, and still more soured. Despite the constant insistence of my friends, I haven't written about my Asian travels. Why? Because I knew it would be bad literature, false and insincere.

The true picture of a Polish expedition used to be trimmed by communist censors. They would gently edit out the fact that all Himalayan trips were largely paid for with money earned by smuggling goods and illicit trading, hide the common practice of bribing officials at all levels, both home and abroad and conceal the Nelsonian eye that was turned towards financial machinations, false papers and accounts. Such hideous practices concerned 90% of all Polish expeditions.

Moreover, I couldn't honestly present my fellow climbers and write about their characters and behaviour on a Himalayan testing ground. The solidarity of the climbing community forced me to keep silent. The myth of the impeccable purity of the Himalayan Don Quixote had to be preserved at all costs. If I turned out to be a talkative Sancho Panza, I would lose a lot of colleagues and probably have no-one to go with for another expedition.

This was the pressure of self-censorship. It prevented the truth and I didn't wish to lie about those most traumatic experiences of my life. Poles in general are afraid, or ashamed, of writing about their personal affairs; and so was our expedition literature: self-censored, bland, inoffensive and hypocritical.

Yet not everything about climbing was like this. In the mid 1970s, a small book entitled *Obsession* came out. Its author was a famous mountain rescuer, mountaineer, writer, literary critic and is at the moment still a vice-minister of culture! A reviewer of this collection of short stories said: 'Over the last 100 years, mountains have been associated in common consciousness with spiritual sublimation..' It has been dogmatically believed that a human being becomes a better person in the hills; since they tear away all masks from a human face, what is left must be good because it's authentic. The author of *Obsession* turned it upside down. Mountains evoke the worst elements in our personality and release all pent-up resentment. From the hollow men of Eliot's' poem, 'straw and tow are showing'. The characters from the book suffer from an obsession which is usually an inferiority complex.

I think very highly of this book. It is probably the first breach in the common silence, an attack on the myth which is beautiful, but only a myth. Thus in *Obsession* literature tries to destroy a literary, but outdated, creation.

At the same time, these short stories are a graceful pinnacle in literature and an intellectually satisfying piece of writing. The contrast with the mediocre scree at its base is striking!

I have here touched on another weak point of Polish mountain writing: the scarcity of essays. Mountain sports seem to be absent from any broader, not necessarily literary, considerations. Most competent climbing writers treat with disdain any writing which doesn't describe climbing action. On the other hand, all climbing sports are by and large regarded as a kind of game whose rules are severe. Since the entire situation is contrived, I won't give it another mention.

This overview of Polish climbing literature, very impressionistic and perhaps a bit too personal, spans 100 years. This century has not produced any masterpieces, but, please note, all this came from a community of 100 members in the 1920s to about 3000 now. I suppose the statistics of climbing literary production per capita would put Poland on top of the world list for productivity.

But what of the artistic value of this literature? Definitely not exceptional, but on the whole, quite attractive. With the exception of the 1930s, it has never become purely commercial. On the contrary, writing about climbing endeavours is considered a moral duty towards the community of fellow-climbers. The same reason may also account for the lack of biographies or autobiographies. For example, we don't have a single book about the late Jerzy Kukuczka. A paradox perhaps, but the blame falls largely on sluggish publishers and low royalties. Literature is not good business in Poland.

If you asked me about the most prominent feature of Polish climbing literature, I'd have to say that it is more concerned with the climber than the climbing. The climber's figure, his national characteristics, complexes and problems obscure the mountains, even the biggest ones. When a moment in history lends its grandeur to a climber, the literature reaches a high point; the eras that suppress the individual produce worthless literature.

Last year, the communist regime kindly deserted us. It also closed an epoch in Polish mountaineering. That epoch was made by people who are now in their forties and fifties. They had been brought up in times when the romantic and noble climbing hero was alive and well, and proved that the essence of life could only be found in the mountains. The image of that epoch and its generation will be derived from literature. Will anyone make an effort to present the true picture of those bygone days? Will I dare?

The Case of the Vanishing Hangers

by Dave Gregory

Holmes was bored. He fiddled incessantly. My only peace was when he leaned against the window and scrutinised the street. Even then I got no respite.

"Watson, your opinion on this gentleman?"

"Short, young, well-dressed, vigorous, paunchy, once much fitter, pale, uncertain of his whereabouts..."

"Yes, yes, that is obvious, but his profession?"

"A jockey would be leaner, more tanned, less well-clothed. Once a rowing cox, perhaps. No, not enough of a gentleman. Pale, a billiards marker?"

"Come, come, Watson. What billiards marker would be so well-dressed?"

"I referred to snooker, Holmes. It is very popular. The better men earn princely sums. Even a lady makes a living at the sport."

"You read a poor class of newspaper, Watson, and you are wide of the mark. He has not the bowlegs of a riding man, nor the seedy air of the snooker hall. Obviously a member of the legislature, undoubtedly an MP, even in the government, and he has found our door. At last, Watson, an end to this infernal boredom."

"Quickly, Holmes, before he comes, how did you know?"

"I have been expecting him all morning. Here, read this note."

And he roared at having hoodwinked me.

Holmes was in a fever to hear his story. It appeared that some of the young bloods, denied their summer sport by the dismal weather of the last few Alpine seasons, had taken to scaling crags at home. Not just in the Lakes or North Wales, but on small, steep faces in the Midlands. Two schools of escalade had developed. One safeguarded themselves by temporarily placing in fissures small pieces of metal in which a wire loop was set. This impedimenta could be removed by the following members of the party and the face left unaltered. The second school drilled holes in the rock and inserted the socket for a screw. From this screw hung a hanger, a metal plate with a hole into which climbers could fix a clip through which ran their rope.

Holmes was becoming restless.

"A moment, Mr. Holmes, I am almost finished. As Minister of Sport I am gratified by the development of any sport, particularly if it does not lead to drunken riots. You can have no idea how humiliating it is to attend international meetings knowing that one is held responsible for our loutish drunkards. The British Mountaineering Council has reported that someone is stealing these hangers. Not a matter to involve the government or yourself, eh Mr. Holmes?"

I could not resist appearing more knowledgeable than the great detective.

"You are afraid of the habit's spreading to hotter climes, Minister?"

"How did you know, Watson?"

I choked back 'elementary, my dear Holmes' and answered that my cousin Reginald's boy had gone to Spain at Easter to follow this very activity.

"You have it, Dr. Watson. Our football supporters have been well-behaved recently and I had hopes of our ceasing to be the pariahs of Europe. We hope to hold the Olympic Games in Britain. The Committee informs me that Spain, Italy and France intend to make similar applications. These countries have many rock faces on which hangers are left. If our thieves descend on Europe, just think of the ammunition it would give our rivals. They would point out that every British sport has its hooligans. It would only need The Prince to imbibe a little too deeply at Ascot and we should never hold an international event again."

"We are, then, to apprehend the thieves, discreetly?"

"Your country will not be ungrateful, gentlemen."

The telephone summoned Reginald's boy, Arthur Watson. The three of us alighted at Millers Dale, we two attired for a walking tour but Arthur more flamboyant in coloured trousers and an iridescent knapsack. "This is," he informed us, "the valley of which Ruskin so despaired. You see across the river one of the faces from which hangers have already been stolen and further along is one as yet unrifled. We can cross by the stepping stones a little further along."

The ground below the hangerless face was of black mud, dry and, despite the rank growth nearer the river, devoid of vegetation. "Covered in footprints though it is Watson, we shall discover nothing from them if all climbers wear slippers like Arthur's."

At the left-hand end of the crag the mud was less trampled and Holmes followed with joy a trail of large foot marks bearing a distinctive tread, with a rough groove by them which led into the river.

"What of this, Watson?" he cried.

"One of the ledges hereabouts is, according to Arthur's guide-book, called Pterodactyl Terrace," I offered. "This could be the mark of the beast's dragging tail."

Holmes was not in a playful mood.

"One is inclined to forget," he remarked to Arthur, "that medical men were once medical students. Has your pterodactyl marked that arrow upon the face?"

"It may," broke in Arthur, "merely mark where one of the newer climbs goes."

And indeed it marked the only line of shiny alloy plates left upon the whole of the crag.

Holmes insisted that we return immediately to the Angler's Rest where he monopolised Arthur, the guide-book and the telephone. Lengthy contact with the Mountaineering Council's office in Manchester completed, he reappeared rubbing his hands.

"Our thief has worked systematically up the Dale. The hangers we saw will be his next target. It is Thursday. The depredations are discovered each Saturday. Arthur says that no-one could remove them in the dark. Ergo the thief will go for the hangers above our arrow at first light. We must sleep a few hours and be on watch betimes. You, Arthur, must borrow something a little more sober from the landlord. Our tweeds will be camouflage enough under that giant rhubarb. I trust, Watson, that you have your service revolver. Any number of pterodactyls might lurk in that undergrowth."

It was still dark when we hid among the butterbur and not dawn when a light came along the path. I confess to a sense of fear when the flicker on the rock indicated that the torch was being held some six feet above the floor. What size of brute was this? However, as the bearer approached it was evident that he wore the torch upon his head, as might a miner. Opposite the crag he slipped off the sack he carried and changed into waders to cross the river, relying for support on a ski-stick. At the arrow on the face, he turned to walk back into the river, finding and pulling from it a large plastic bag. He undid the neck and drew therefrom a small metal ladder which he extended to some twice his own height and leaned against the face.

He exchanged the waders for rock boots and donning a belted harness climbed the ladder and fastened the end of a rope into a clip on the first hanger. He went further up the ladder until he could fit the hook on the end of a long metal rod into the hole of the second hanger. He made short work of the ascent, frequently dispensing with the hook, trailing the rope behind him through a succession of links on the hangers until he disappeared into the trees.

"We've lost him."

"No," said Arthur, "He will slide down the rope taking out the hangers as he comes. I am sure I know him. He has represented the country at climbing events but is known for his antagonism to the bolted form of the sport."

Shortly the free end of the rope was thrown to reach the floor.

"We will surprise him," whispered Holmes, "as he nears the floor."

However when our culprit flicked the topmost of the hangers from him into the river, Holmes stepped forward.

"It will go better for you if you leave the rest, my man. We know who you are and we have your equipment."

When our northern monkey reached the floor I expected the handcuffs, but Holmes surprised me.

"Is it he?" he asked of Arthur.

"Definitely."

"Well, my young villain. If we report this you will never represent your country again. If this business stops we hold our peace, but if it starts again we shall expose you. What do you say to that?"

Our captive agreed but Holmes would have his pound of flesh.

"I will take charge of these," he said and, having quickly mastered the collapsing of the ladder and hooked pole, he pushed them both into the plastic bag and presented what he ever afterwards called Watson's Pterodactyl with his card.

"Send me a bill," he said and we parted.

Mr. Moynihan was pleased to hear of the end of the thefts and although the future Olympic Games were given to Greece, Arthur, Holmes and I received an acceptable envelope of tickets for the Games before.

Watson's Pterodactyl took the silver. A Frog took the gold.

Living Room

by David Hughes

Those rare occasions when you did come here
to drink and plan our trips, it scarcely changed:
old chairs, those lush distorted plants, the sheer
amount of books and posters I've got ranged
around my walls. You used to take the piss
about my first editions and the Pepys
across the top shelf, yet you'd rarely miss
approving of the newest. Now I keep
the sort of shrine that would have made you laugh:
the pictures I was taking on the steep
ice-slope before you fell; that Arctic half-
light photograph of you which makes me weep;
those portraits of the group which measure how
you're always absent, always present now.

Report of the Fifth International Festival of Mountaineering Literature

by Andy Popp

Now five years old, the International Festival of Mountaineering Literature, organised by Terry Gifford and held at Bretton Hall in Yorkshire, can justifiably consider itself to be an established, if as yet minor, fixture on the climbing calendar. Certainly the event has displayed greater tenacity than either the more populist Kendal Film Festival of yore or today's supposed big wow, competition climbing, which has still to gain a firm foot in this country. Is this success symptomatic though of an underlying strength in mountaineering literature or the product of a vociferous but desperately enclaved minority?

What is not at question here is either the quality of the event or the commitment of the ebullient Gifford and the contributors he recruits. As a first-time visitor to the Festival I found this year's programme to be stimulating, occasionally provocative and, above all else, entertaining. Featured, amongst others, were a gentle and wry Harold Drasdo on the specifics and the metaphysics of falling (examining the past without nostalgia and interpretations with intelligence), sardonic humour from Curran and an unexpectedly theatrical Steve Ashton, history from Anne Sauvy and readings from the recent Boardman Tasker award winners, including a tentative but engaging performance from Alison Fell. There was poetry, about which Gifford was needlessly defensive, discussion and the announcement of the winner of the latest *High* writing competition: sly fun from Bristolian Moira Viggers.

What the Festival did not do though was to address directly

either its own role in and relevance to British climbing or the health of climbing and its literature. Perhaps the latter was assumed. Certainly the festival is thriving and we have seen in recent months much activity on the publishing front, particularly of fiction new and old. However at points, most noticeably in a question from Ken Wilson to Anne Sauvy, an ill-defined suggestion that the course of the sport must dictate the fortunes of its literature seemed to be being broached. As he certainly despairs of the modern sport, does it follow that Wilson, and perhaps others, are equally pessimistic about the writing? In conversation Wilson proposed interesting societal theories as to why the sport is changing and went on to suggest that the apparent boom in publishing is based upon tiny print runs and perilous margins. So might all this frenetic activity be of both limited appeal and impact? Certainly attendance at the festival is small and chummy, though far from exclusively male or unwelcoming. There also seemed to be an occasional inability to open up beyond stereotypes to embrace the new or unfamiliar. *On the Edge* itself was characterised by Curran as being written in a language unintelligible to all but anorexic teenagers, a glib and unthinking assessment of a magazine with a proven interest in publishing fiction and the speculative, much of it from new names in climbing writing. Similarly, most climbers I know in Sheffield showed scant interest in the event. Many of them were out on the crag that Saturday. This makes me consider Paul Nunn's paper, which described a climbing culture from the fifties and the sixties that, whilst articulate, had little time for the act of writing; it was, he said, essentially artisanal and oral instead, the keepers of a credo that placed doing first. There seemed to be much in this, both as an historical evaluation and a philosophy.

In reality there should be no conflict here, and to be fair there was little sign of one at Bretton Hall, just the odd intimation. It is important though that there should be no divorce between doing climbing and writing about it. As proof, the pedigree of the day's contributors as activists was (largely) hard to fault. Any dislocation apparent at the moment may simply be caused by a natural delay as new directions in climbing find an authentic voice of their own.

Prove me right.

On Falling Off

by Harold Drasdo

The climber's attitude towards the fall is decidedly ambivalent. In fact this ambivalence is so strong that, occasionally, it has been encoded in his institutions, the climbing clubs.

The nineteen-fifties saw the appearance of many new clubs. For some, the technical entry qualifications were set higher than ever before. By contrast, the Dublin-based Newton Club asked only a single accomplishment, two seconds of free fall. That seems a curious threshold and it's a reasonable guess that it must have been the minimum flight achieved amongst the founding fathers.

The Newton Club faced an irritating problem. It could appoint President, Treasurer and Secretary, and have no members, or it could have three members and no officers. The club was determined to be recognised and it showed extreme ingenuity in keeping up appearances. But no new candidates came forward and it was torn between its wish to maintain a high standard and its boredom with the same old stories.

Inevitably, the rule was relaxed. Totalling-up was allowed. The striking of rocks, or other climbers in passing, no longer disqualified. Splashdowns into sea, river, lake and Irish bog were recognised. Slides were still ruled out but skiers who'd tumbled over natural precipices were invited to apply. The club had a motto: "G". And it had its own tie, bearing, it hardly needs saying, the simple device of an apple.

Typically, climbers treat matters of gravity with levity. For a number of years the Cromlech Club awarded its Iron Cross to the member achieving the longest fall in the year under review. The decoration held an ambiguous prestige, sharing the status of the yellow jersey of the *Tour de France* and that of the dunce's cap. It was an honour everyone wished to have held but for which no-one wanted to compete.

An obvious platform for any reflections on falling would be the use of one's own credentials. But if I were to copy out my C.L. - curriculum lapsus - in careful detail, and if I were to add to it those falls of second and third parties in which I was involved, I could hardly spare a glance at people, times, scene and consequences. Instead, then, I'll select just a few falls with strong sentimental associations.

I fell off inaugurally on Yorkshire gritstone in the winter of 1950. Not important, but it was a beginning. In old army boots I was attempting the first ascent of Short Circuit in Ilkley Quarry. As I was completing the last move something happened. My intelligent second sat down, I barely touched the quarry floor, and I didn't feel the least bit subdued.

A fall in Langdale off what is now the Pinch Finish of Jericho Wall was more stimulating. Pete Greenwood had taken a bold stance at the top of the flakes. He had a good footledge but the rock was impending and he couldn't stand in balance. A hanging stance was problematic before the day of the sit-harness and belay plate and he was paying out single-handed over his belay loop and across his waist. Dangerous. I went round the bulge and found myself precariously placed. The very steep slab was crusted everywhere with a dry grey lichen. I moved leftwards towards an easier position but felt the lichen crushing, rolling like grit beneath my toes. I was still very uncomfortable. I realised I hadn't much time and I looked at the choices. To reverse these difficult moves on the powdered footholds: dicey. To climb rapidly up to easier ground only ten feet above: brave. But before I had quite made up my mind a third possibility occurred to me, a back somersault, and I was hanging in mid-air and not even turning. I was looking across the valley at the juniper-covered slopes of Lingmoor, still catching the evening sunlight. Either the mountain or the observer was upside down.

Pete seemed upset. He was shouting swear-words at me. He went on and on. I was getting myself right way up and trying to work out what had happened. It was hard to believe but it was true. He'd had a moment of blind panic. Here was an insight. He could take these terrific falls and often his determination would only be strengthened. Now he'd seen it from the other end, from a bad stance, and it had shaken him. Gradually, though, the abuse began to falter and I could see that he was being visited by an idea. I'd got my weight off him by now. He grew two or three inches. Obviously, he licked the palm of his hand and sucked the web of his thumb. He rubbed his ribs. He eased his shoulders and squared them. He'd held me one-handed and he'd done the right thing. If he'd let me go and killed me he might have burned through his belay loop.

He was recovering fast. "You climb down," he says, "I'll give you a tight rope if you want." He was about back to normal. "Don't bother with runners for me," he says, "I'll drop the rope and solo down." We got back onto the ground. It was too late to do anything else. But, suddenly, each of us was perfectly satisfied with his role and his performance.

Remember Nietzsche: "Whatever does not kill us makes us strong." Remember Zweig: that tales of close calls constitute "the original definition of what is worth talking about." Man, you should've seen us! We strode down to the D.G. bar like giants.

Over the next couple of years, as leader, I fell off from time to time, always in one of two situations. The first of these suggests a good question but it hadn't been formulated at that date: "If you're so smart, Mr. Drasdo, how come you got your socks on outside your shoes?" Well, it was what I was taught. That the only way to get up the harder routes in the rain or in wet conditions was in stockings over plimsolls. I could list some impressive successes in that footgear. But gradually it became clear that the adhesion frontier of the stockinged foot isn't always well defined and occasionally I got washed away.

In the second circumstance I simply pulled off loose holds. We were often on new routes or on the earliest repetitions. It was in this situation, cartwheeling off Alph on Pavey Ark, that I first hurt myself. The following day I had to admit that my hand wouldn't work and to seek advice. The advice said I had a scaphoid fracture. For the first time, now, I read the small print and for a tedious ten weeks I carried a plaster cast around. The only happy discovery was that a wrist cast is extremely effective in wide cracks on gritstone, making a fist jam completely painless and marvellously secure. Embarrassingly, the cast eroded rapidly and needed rebuilding at intervals.

From that time onward, partly perhaps through changes in my circumstances, partly through those slight and unconscious shifts in the set of the mind, I seemed to stop falling and for years I thought that phase had ended. A slide at Chamonix added a small new perception. Is a slide a fall? The intellect rejects the application but the body keeps muttering that it felt like a fall. I'd come down about four hundred feet before stopping myself in an ice axe arrest. I was astonished by the effort this demanded and by the physical beating a variably frozen but apparently uniform snow-slope was able to administer.

Many years passed. If I were to describe my last and shortest fall it would be at greatest length since it proved the most consequential. It left me with two souvenirs, a slightly twisted finger and a rather beautiful three-and-three-quarter inch Smith-Peterson pin, retrieved eventually from my right neck of femur. I have it by me now. It has been recycled as a necklace.

In a supporting role I attended the falls of friends and I paid back a few debts. Out of this rain of bodies I have to declare that Peter Greenwood easily showed foremost for sheer bravura.

He really impressed me on Great Central on Dow. It was a clear sunny morning but the rock was wet and very chilly to the fingers. The infant Dennis Gray had led the first bit, I'd led the South America Crack and Pete was engaging the crux, Bandstand Wall. We were climbing in socks. It wasn't a long fall but he fell very slowly so, as he fell, he turned around, looked about him, made a subtle body swerve, spread and raised his arms to just above shoulder level, put his toes neatly together and finally settled on the very tip of a pointed, slippery, boulder-like projection on the edge of the ledge. We stared open-mouthed for a couple of seconds, then grabbed him. He stepped down, did a little jogging on the spot, dried his hands, blew on his fingers, set off again, did the move and fell off the next move. Having rehearsed the part he took it more quickly this time and, having rehearsed our parts, we seized him immediately. But I had the eerie feeling we weren't even needed. On the third attempt he went straight up.

I'll go through that again. I don't want it to be said that I exaggerate but is it possible to fall very slowly, or even slowly? Yes, it would appear so. There are three stipulations. First, that the fall is seen in line, so that there is less apparent movement in the time-lapse than for the fall viewed from the side. Second, that the faller is profiled against a neutral field, ordinarily the sky, so that there is no blur of background transits to emphasise velocity. Third, that the faller describes a slight arc. Then there is a moment like that in a clay pigeon shoot when the skeet, still having forward motion, seems for an instant actually to halt at the apparent limit of its trajectory. So, in a fall, the eye abstracts a single position. The faller is stilled in a dramatic gesture, giving an image of tremendous potency. It has halted ten thousand moving pictures. It has inspired the covers of a wallful of paperbacks.

Alright. But wasn't he just about to tumble over the second time? Well, maybe. Or he was just correcting his balance. Memory suppresses inconvenient detail. I want to say how it was but sometimes that means how it seemed. The impression was of an Olympic gymnast seen on television. The impact was strong since we'd never seen an Olympic gymnast because we'd never seen a television set.

We set off for the third or fourth ascent of Ivy Sepulchre. The description allowed two aid pegs but only one was in place. I was clipping in when Pete started barracking me. He'd just made his point on Kipling Groove and he was going to make it a trademark. The peg was clearly obstructing the vital hold so, inviting him to demonstrate, I came down. He went up and saw the problem but he wouldn't admit defeat. Instead, he faced into the grossly overhanging corner-crack, put left hand, right arm and foot inside, braced his left leg under the overhang and wrestled it Cumberland style. It seemed an unlikely solution but in two or three powerful moves he had head and shoulders above the overhang.

It looked as if he'd done it. But then he dislodged some chockstones from deep inside the crack and these began to stack up against his body. From time to time he'd dart his left hand down and scoop one out. Then he'd part his knees like a bomb bay and discharge a whole salvo but the crack kept on sending down reserves. Fifty feet below, in the centre of the target zone, attached by long slings to a tall sapling, Neville and I kept colliding in an amateurish attempt at maypole dancing. Finally it all got too much, he resigned his position and came whanging out in a hail of rocks.

Once I was quite relieved to see him fall. He was after the unrepeated Gimmer Girdle and he had a second but the second wouldn't go without a third. I was called in unwillingly, since I'd be descending last on the Grooves Traverse which none of us had seen and which was said to be hard. There he was, then, on the eleventh pitch and, watching from Gimmer Crack, I saw that he was struggling. Then he fell, was checked, and unbelievably started again, forty feet, eighty, a hundred and twenty and still going on, half jumping, then bouncing, tumbling from ledge to ledge at the foot of the crag. Two passing walkers hurried up to comfort him.

The middleman's hands were badly burned. Managing an awkward rope-length of slack I got up the rest of the Crack and helped him across and up. Then we descended Junipall Gully to rejoin Pete, who had hurt his ankle. He was in a foul mood. As I remember, he said nothing to the middleman, who stood a little off, head bowed, cuddling his hands. Instead, he rounded on me. He'd borrowed some of my line slings and now he said that they were dangerously long. As he'd been making a delicate move one of them had snagged and jammed under a tiny downward-pointing spike and he'd slipped in trying to free it. We helped him slowly down towards the valley and gradually a more tranquil temper overcame him. He began to speak thoughtfully about his future, which was not to include rock-climbing. It was to centre upon the Gaiety in Bradford where, apparently, he was already hugely admired for his virtuosity as a ballroom dancer.

I could see the point. He'd still be leading, there'd still be the savage competition and the trophies. Briefly, I imagined him in the Tango Finals. That would be something worth watching. And at the Gaiety, I supposed, the only recreational injury to be feared would be simply the broken heart.

Sometimes, in the fall, the element of epic or heroic is subsumed in the tragic, a category I defer. More often, in my experience, that element is undercut in comic deflation. I've even known seconds - maestros of the banana skin - who could turn small incident into large spectacle. I've already discussed iconography, allusion and the influence of patronage in Shirley Parfitt's large oil painting in the bar of the Dungeon Ghyll Hotel. Now - watch carefully - I'm going to stretch out a hand and I'm going to release the bearded central figure from the picture. Like that. He stands before us, blinking. Still a young man! Gently but firmly, I'll detach the pint glass from his fingers - he resists a little: there! - and I'll put it on one side. We'll let him keep his pipe, he won't go on the hill without it. Now I'm going to stand him at the foot of Godiva Groove on the north-west face of Gimmer.

We're only a few yards, in fact, from the ledges where, five years earlier, Pete landed up.

He was in high spirits that day. A beautiful morning, the rock bone dry. There's no real traversing on the climb but he had a local expert in front of him and a local expert behind him. Compulsively, he kept checking everything again and again: pipe, tobacco, matches, and the bowline and ten half hitches still securely tied.

We were about halfway up before he slipped. He'd been reporting any redundant slack in the rope ever since we started but he went down a few feet and then, just clear of the rock, he floated across to the left for fifteen or twenty feet. As he was swinging he made a quarter-turn - I saw his worried face - and then he just touched the rock with a saucy bumps-a-daisy. Instantly, amazing us, delighting us, he made a strange popping noise, gave out a dense puff of smoke, and burst into flames. And for twenty or thirty seconds he danced in the sky, bawling his head off and trying to stamp himself out.

There was an occasion on which I didn't show to advantage myself. Winter fifty-two or Spring fifty-three I was set on making an ascent of the then unclimbed Kilnsey Crag. It was an almost universal opinion at that time that limestone was dangerously unreliable. I knew this to be unfounded but we were anxious not to discredit the belief. It reserved an arena for aid climbing, an essential technique for some of the routes in the Western Alps and Dolomites on which our ambitions were set.

Kilnsey rises from the green floor of Wharfedale in a long grey bulging wall. It was finally climbed some years later after a determined siege by Ron Moseley. The film of *Moby Dick* had just been released and a friend in the team said to me that the cliff, festooned in siege ropes, tiny figures clinging to it or hammering away, brought the final scenes to mind. When I repeated the remark to Dave Nicol he cast Moseley as Ahab. That was right. There was no more obsessively driven climber operating in Britain in the fifties. But the whole image was appropriate. Everything about Kilnsey - the random drainage vents, the bitumen stains, the succulent, almost littoral character of the little plant life it holds, the swell of field surging against the cliff - everything suggests its marine origins as if the leviathan had freshly surfaced from the ocean and the waters had, only a moment ago, cascaded from its flanks.

The second visit provided the entertainment. I want you to see this clearly. I've picked the one line leading towards some sort of exit weakness because I'm worried about security on the smooth steep grass slope above the crag. Here, a vertical rebate in the wall gives a left-facing reveal a few feet wide. A peg crack runs up the middle of this reveal. We could climb it free but certainly there is some loose material and we're here to practise pegging. I suggest that my companion, Keith King, should take this pitch, since I've already led it on the earlier visit.

What happened was my fault really, though he shouldn't have done what he did. First, I'm not belayed. What can he do with me? Drag me across the field to the road and get me run over? Second, in view of the loose rock I've moved well off to the left. Third, since it's always fun to see someone struggling, I've moved a bit further left so that I can watch him without cricking my neck. So he works upward, remarking, as I had last time, that the pillar forming the right side of the crack gives a noticeable vibration. I'm close to the foot of the wall but looking straight at the facet. The rope runs almost horizontally from my hand, then rises vertically through the snaplinks.

In aid climbing, when the leader falls, the pegs strip from the top down. Except on this one known occasion, when they stripped from the bottom up. It was a contingency for which neither of us was remotely prepared.

In retrospect, the mechanics were simple. The idiot had pounded an absurdly thick peg into the top of the thin crack. The crack had expanded slightly and all the lower pegs were marginally eased. The other idiot was sitting dreaming in the position best calculated to exploit that weakness perfectly. Finally a moment came when he asked for tension. I set my heels against something and I gave him tension.

For the next few seconds we were really busy. He was into particle physics, I was into wave physics. He was dropping like a bomb but in a distinctly stop-go sort of fashion. Yes, in quanta. Much against my will, I was gliding across on an interception course in systematic undulations. First I was snatched into mid-air and then I was mysteriously released. I just managed to get my feet in front of me. But as the subsequent pegs pulled and as he disposed of each new increment of slack the angle of the rope increased, tending to lift me more directly. At the same time a pendulum motion was being initiated, working to lower me. And so it went on until, still only just above the ground, I hit him like a homing missile.

Keith King lives in Penrith. You can get his address from the local phone book. If you ever have an hour to kill in that town, look him up, hang around his corner, and see if you can spot him. I'll give you a clue. He is the old man with the head hacked out of oak burr. The torso and limbs are to match but it was only our heads that met, in a ringing concussive detonation. A flash of light lit the skies over Wharfedale. I think I let go the rope then. Apparently we woke at about the same time, possibly only seconds later, in a heap and groaning with shock and pain. Then, little by little, we found ourselves laughing. Until finally we were possessed by that debilitating laughter in which the one who's just about to control it restarts the one who had it under control.

While I'm at Kilnsey I'll finish this story. A bit at a time we climbed carefully onto our feet. We had sore heads. We had lumps. And his pride was hurt. He stood there, fists bunched, still swaying a little, and scowling up at the top peg from which the ropes still depended. We bounced on it. Solid. With a top rope who needs pegs? He went up and I followed. Then I continued up the groove, a few moves free, then pegging. There was a moment of surprise when I broke in my hand one of the small keyhole-shaped gadgets we'd bought cheaply to supplement our war surplus karabiners. They'd been sold as parachute hooks, a chilling thought. The groove arrived at a loosely imbricated bulge but here a horizontal crack ran left across the wall. I crossed it, wishing I had deep channels, and arrived at an exposed and narrow ledge. He joined me and I started to peg an insecure wall to the foot of the exit weakness.

Call me Starbuck. He was the one sane man on the Pequod, he was the first mate and the first of the three harpoon boat chiefs. He said: "I will have no man in my boat who is not afraid of a whale." It didn't work, nobody even listened. The crazies just piled aboard and he had to die with them.

Keith was no threat. Now don't misread me. He seemed to have no personal ambition, he was content to follow me around on my tick list. I'd take the harder pitches and he'd take the easier. But once or twice, when a description wasn't specific, he found himself faced with the crux. He'd complain but it wouldn't stop him. As a second he was brilliant. It was all a huge joke and he'd urge me on even when I was in extremity. Except that on a few significant occasions, when he thought I was getting the pair of us in over our heads, he fell silent.

He was saying nothing now. After the traverse he'd let me know that he'd shaken every peg out by hand and he'd said this in an unusually serious tone of voice and as he said it he fixed me with his eye. I explained that it didn't matter, the corner peg was solid and the rest had been locked in by our weight on the etriers. I was having second thoughts myself, though. I could see into the weakness now. It was vegetated but still so steep that it would have to be pegged to clean off the loose material safely. The time and effort required wasn't easy to judge. And I was deep in this calculation when a third factor intruded in the shape of Miss Elizabeth Duckworth, who was calling to us from the road. It was her fault, really, that we didn't make the first ascent of Kilnsey Crag.

Betty Duckworth was a fairly recent arrival at Wall End. The occasional visitor might have gained the impression that, like the fair Briseis, she was being passed from hand to hand through the tents of the allied camps. Actually, it was the other way round. She was on some sort of tour of inspection which found most of us wanting. I'd have considered her at some length here but I learn that she's now retired from her position as County Librarian for Cumbria, a post in which she might have wished to buy up many copies of this book. Even then, she was going places. We were hitch-hiking, she had a car. It was there on the road beneath us. In a half-hour we could be walking up to a sunny gritstone edge. Suddenly it seemed ill-mannered to leave her sitting waiting for the rest of this cold afternoon. I depegged back to the stance.

We still had to get off. I looked again at our anchors. All our pegs were crude lunch-hour apprentice jobs, copied not from specimens but from our explanations of the idea of the peg. They were ring pegs or offsets of heavy metal, a stupendous weight. I had in one short blade, not much to look at. But the other was the pride of my collection, a huge bowie-knife-shaped ring peg, a piece of sculpture really. With this, the inventor or artist had followed his impulses. It was made, he told me proudly, of stainless steel. I'd driven it hard into a little pocket. Keith was the heavier so he abseiled first from this dagger while I held him belayed from the other. He didn't like setting off and he didn't like the move into space, ten or fifteen feet down. And he'd no sooner left the rock and relaxed when there was a crack like a pistol shot and a little plate of rock had blown away from one side of the peg. Our eyes met. Nothing to be done. Standing uncomfortably upright I took as much of his weight as I could on the safety rope. Down he went, slowly and smoothly. I didn't like setting off either. But now Keith had swung on the peg so I took out the other and followed, making a countdown of height and injury as I descended. For one reason after another I never returned. Many years later I saw that the first Yorkshire Limestone guide had recorded our attempt: "their monster abseil peg is still in place."

Looking back at this short selection I imagine two extreme responses. The modern expert will say: we log up mileages like that every weekend. But I was remembering the hard fall. In all but one of these recollections we were tied on with a bowline round the waist. The first fall mentioned was on Italian hemp and all but one of the others were on the original, rather slippery, laid nylon, sometimes only half-weight in calibre. The falls were held by gloveless seconds with a waist or even a shoulder belay.

The non-climber, on the other hand, will say: all this sounds like lunacy, you're alive through luck, not judgement. That's true to a degree, as it is of all survivors and story-tellers. But it appears that we saw most of the risks and that our primitive safety systems worked remarkably well.

Beyond the particular, my knowledge of the fall is in three tenses. I look back at past falls and I say, that taught me a lesson, that amused me, that simply energised me. On the actual present experience of the fall I reserve the most acute observation I've come across to serve as a conclusion. For myself, I can find little to say. It was only the cliff that flashed before me, never my life. The mind, it seems, makes a mute but startled exclamation and the event is over. But I might be wrong. Maybe I gave myself no chance. Some principle of prudence grouped nearly all my falls within twenty to forty feet while the fearless Greenwood explored the full rope's length and its stretch as well.

There remains the future fall, the possible fall, and it is this that all climbing is importantly about. The body is programmed before every other emergency to attend to its balance, that is, to avert a fall. In fact, climbers hardly ever fall through loss of balance. They fall through loss of strength, loss of adhesion or loss of libido, aside from objective causes. But any preliminary signals of those threats activate the whole system. And it's when a fall is anticipated, and when this anticipation is long-drawn-out that the idea of the fall most strongly defines and declares itself. Far more alarming than any fall I ever had, I relive just one of these disturbing memories.

Decided to do Gallows Route on Buachaille Etive Mor. We were told it had been repeated only once, by the originator himself, John Cunningham. Was Cunningham any good? He'd arrived in Langdale and he and his partner couldn't follow Neville and myself up Perhaps Not in White Ghyll. True, there were extenuating circumstances but in climbing one doesn't make excuses for other people. We knew nothing about the Gallows but one of the Creagh Dhu had showed us where it stood.

At the stance before the big pitch I couldn't find a really good anchor. Never mind, get some runners on quickly. I crossed the initial traverse without hesitation but with some surprise. It had looked simple but I'd found myself making readjustments in mid-move. I knew I'd done it expensively and I ascribed that simply to my footgear. The standard black plimsoll had vanished from the market and the only alternative was the Bata baseball boot. At a glance these seemed attractive, disposing of the worry that a plimsoll might slip off the heel. In fact they had a welt and the glazed yellow sole seemed to give no real adhesion. At the resting place I couldn't find any protection for the first overhang. Feeling distinctly committed I went over it, not difficult. That got me to the second overhang. It was only a bulge really. There was still no protection. Wide awake now, and feeling oddly tired, I pulled over it and looked up the long groove above. The angle had relented but I couldn't see any obvious spike for a sling, any thin crack for a jammed knot, any big resting place. What do we do now?

Clausius said it: entropy is always increasing, call that the Second Law of Thermodynamics. Energy bleeds away, everything grinds to a halt and falls to bits. I knew exactly what to do. I got down from the bulge and rested briefly. Then I got down over the first overhang and rested a moment again. Beneath the sleeves of my anorak I could feel that I had the hard swelling of the forearm tensor muscles that's delicious at the end of an afternoon's bouldering but is bad news on a big mountain pitch. I set out to reverse the traverse, couldn't see how I'd done it, and knew suddenly with certainty that the next move was the terminus. Fast, ragged, I just got back to the resting place, third visit. I'd failed to get up and I'd failed to get down.

I looked back across at my brother. I said: I'm going to come off on this. He said: Better not. You've seen this belay. This stance doesn't help. We could both go. I said: When I come off I'll be as close as I can get. He looked unhappy. I turned away and for a long time I watched the Rannoch Moor, where nothing was happening. Until, surprising me, a strong impulse of determination, no, of glee welled up, actually wanting to fight it out.

Boltzmann said it: $S = K \log W$. Entropy is the product of the constant Boltzmann found and the logarithm of a particular statistical probability. All systems incorporate entropy. But even in the clockwork world of physics probability, not certainty, is the final word. So what about the world in which human factors enter? Nothing is certain. In the end, disorder rules. In the meantime, islands of stability or continuity, seeming like miracles, survive the storm. Maybe this was just part of a pattern. I was going to be scared stiff lots of times, I was going to nearly fall off lots of rock climbs lots of times. That turned out to be true.

Alright, I can hear you, I know. I'm just gutting the equations for the poems and junking the hard bits with the commercial value. But I wrote the note down years ago. This year, to my amusement, I meet the same thoughts again in James Gleick's book on Chaos theory. The use of the Second Law by writers is misguided, he says. And using the strategies and weapons of the writer he tries to put the sums into words and to write of systems in which order survives, patterns persist, at least on a temporary basis. Well, temporary is okay. Temporary will do for now. As a matter of fact, I never expected more. I set off on the traverse again and when I got to the far side I was still there. Cunningham!

Maniac! I lunged for the belay loop, something to hang on. Deliberately, Nev blocked me. Gasping, I had to hold onto his shoulders, looking the very picture of the man who's been there and back. I convalesced for a few minutes. Of course, there was always the possibility that Cunningham had made an abseil inspection. Some people did that. There were even people around who top-roped hard lines first. Still, not a bad climber, Cunningham. When I was able to talk properly I said that for now we'd go and do something else, and we'd get some first-hand information, and we'd come back another day to do this thing.

* * *

There is a Doctrine of the Fall. It says that we're spineless, we know what the grades are and we know what we're capable of and we just give in. It's attached to the Biblical account of the temptation of Eve and Adam by the serpent and it uses the fall as metaphor. This Christian teaching takes a really hard line. It tells us that our weakness is congenital, coming to us straight from Adam, and it harangues and rebukes us when we show evidence of this inherited characteristic.

Question: What is the longest survivor fall so far claimed?

Answer: Lucifer's stupendous plunge.

Objection: Not a proper fall. Didn't slip, did he? He was pushed.

He was too smart for his own good, he was carving out his own rat pack among the angels, he was stealing God's jokes, he was spoiling the penthouse party. God smiled at Lucifer - "How do you make God laugh?" asked Woody Allen - God smiled at Lucifer - "You tell him your future plans" - God smiled at Lucifer, asked for a moment of his time, laid a pally but very heavy hand on his shoulder, steered him away from the crowd, chatting amiably about one or two admin problems, worked him adroitly up to the brink, and gave him a nudge. He went down the shaft and finished up in the basement. Damn wings didn't work after all, they were just cosmetic. Or maybe they gave some drag, because in the authorised version of this tale he finished up unhurt. He changed his name to Satan, more militant than Lucifer, less pansy. Nursing an implacable hatred he works to disaffect the tenants of the lower floors.

At risk of being tiresome, I can't leave the main point alone. What is the crucial, most obvious difference between life on earth and life in heaven? It is this: that in heaven there is *no more falling*. The people have wings. Sceptical, facetious, I say they're a job lot of seconds, bought in Hollywood. But it's not so easy. The problem is that whether you believe the Cosmos was dreamed up in the mind of God or whether you assert that heaven was devised on the drawing boards of earth this bizarre design discrepancy still invites explanation.

It has to be said, too, that religious metaphors of the fall are strong and natural. Notice that they belong to a group of three, the elevation metaphor, the ladder metaphor, the fall metaphor. The elevation metaphor, whether used for spiritual or worldly purposes, deals with condition and works by opposition. We feel high or low, elated or depressed, we have scores of names for these states and stations.

The ladder adds dimensions of effort and aspiration, risk and failure, progress made and ground lost. Where there are mountains the mountain may substitute and where there are forests the world-tree may stand in but possibly the ladder has precedence. Perhaps it first comes strongly into Christian theology, and almost certainly it arrives in Christian art, when John Climacus borrowed Jacob's Ladder for use as a teaching aid. But, like my friend told you, the image isn't exclusively Christian. It's found in the Egyptian *Book of the Dead*. Amongst the Greeks it's found in Plato. Amongst the Latins it's found in Porphyry and Plotinus. Here is a research project: Establish the region and period of origin of the game of snakes and ladders. Check whether its pattern of colonisation relates to the spread of the Christian faith.

The fall metaphor dramatises an instant. Whether religious or secular it has a strong psychosomatic aptness. When we regret a moral choice it's in our heads that the judgement is made. But it's in our bodies that we get that sinking feeling.

There is a Freudian slip. It draws attention to the world of dreams. Expeditions of highly-qualified field scientists have made long treks through the landscapes of the night, trying to record and classify the action. Weird goings-on. But while they can't agree what it's all about they agree very closely on what they've seen. All these grownups nearly crying because they can't seem to get their vests on or tie their shoes or pack their bags or catch their buses: social-conditioning dreams. All these couples, gliding into each other's arms, sometimes suggesting possibilities, destinies even, that hadn't yet occurred to the daylight zombie. These are families of dreams. But when we get down to particular events all the ethnologists are in agreement: the most popular occupation in dreamland is falling.

This seems very odd. In this context I can't help noticing two other strange dreams. First, the levitation, floating or gliding dream. Second, the downhill-movement, sliding, skiing, surfing dream. The temptation to put the three together is strong. In an old terminology, that would give the falling dream as an anxiety dream, the levitation dream as a wish-fulfilment response to the same anxiety, and the downhill-movement dream as an intermediate type with the fall held somehow under control. Notice that the three dreams have some curious correspondences with the three metaphors. Don't make too much of it.

The question of why people should dream so much of falling is something else. I have an intuition, not supported by any enquiries, that climbers dream intensively about falling, perhaps with some referential detail, in the first phase of their intoxication, and that as time goes by they probably stop having falling dreams altogether. If this were so, it would be mildly interesting. What is really interesting is why the civilian population should report all these dreams of falling.

The computer-function theory of dreaming proposed by Christopher Evans is ingenious and persuasive. But it disappoints us by having nothing new to say about this central dream. It has to rely on earlier suggestions, as that the dream is triggered by small bodily sensations, a delayed heartbeat, a pause in respiration, a slight gastric movement in digestion, and so on.

The bolder explanations of the falling dream are two, perhaps only one. The first is that it is pre-human, going back to our remote ancestry in the tree-tops and to the subsequent struggle to stand upright without the use of hands. It's been shown that in infant baboons the principal innate fear is of falling and it's been asked whether the 'startle reflex' of human infants might not spring from the same origin. The second would be that falling dreams refer only to the dreamer's infant struggles to walk and that therefore they might be regarded as the first example of social-conditioning dreams.

It would be interesting to know more. Surveys of dreams have usually used college student populations or have simply solicited respondents from magazines and newspapers. Dreams have been recorded since the dawn of writing but it's unlikely that there have been any systematic studies outside Westernised societies. Do primitive peoples, brought up in low huts in treeless plains, dream about falling? Would a cripple, on his back from birth, have these dreams?

Humpty Dumpty fell. And Jack and Jill. And Alice. Even in nursery rhymes, even in children's stories, there's some meaning or some mystery about the fall. Icarus fell. It wasn't because 'the wax of his wings melted', don't believe it. I have in my possession a full transcript of the Chief Priest's remarks on the affair. Sometime, I'll tell you the whole story. For now, just say, they loaded a parable and shot him down. Rome fell. And Troy, and Mexico, and Singapore and Saigon. Cities, cultures, empires that took centuries to build are laid to rest by the little word. The ambitious modern novelist can't stop toying with the ancient theme: Albert Camus, *The Fall*; William Golding, *Free Fall*; Colin Thubron, *Falling*; Jim Harrison, *Legends of the Fall*. A fallen woman, falling in love again, morale will fall. The verb has conjugated itself and its freight right through the language, which is to say, right through the way we think.

In some aspects of contemporary rock-climbing the fear of falling seems to have been disciplined but that control is provisional and precarious. Just inside the back of the skull, just outside the oval of vision, the real fall is standing by. And before all the dreams and beneath all the symbolism and behind all the jokes the fall has some simple, deep, central, premonitory meaning. In this, the climber is expert, but it doesn't take a climber to see it. Iris Murdoch goes close to the heart of it in a few lines from *The Sea, The Sea*:

Falling, what the child fears, what the man dreads, is itself the image of death, of the defencelessness of the body, of its frailty and mortality, its absolute subjection to alien causes. Even in a harmless fall in the road there is a little moment of horror when the faller realizes that he cannot help himself; he has been taken over by a relentless mechanism and must continue with it to the end and be subject to the consequences. 'There is nothing more I can do.' How long, how infinitely expansible, a second is when it contains this thought, which is an effigy of death.

SCAFELL PIKE

by Chris Whitby

Half way, we questioned whether to go on
And then again, ten minutes from the top,
Much less in doubt than to reaffirm the need
Within was stronger than the hurtling sleet
That sliced our cheeks, froze lips and closed our eyes.
Bent double, old beggars under sacks indeed,
We pivoted our coming and our going
On outstretched fingers brushing ice-rimed cairn.
When steaming gently in the heated car
We asked once more why on earth we did this,
We knew our answers would not be the same.
For me, remembering turning back from other goals,
I know no better spur to my intent
Than because I am here.

Back Where I Belong

by Steve Ashton

"Un ticket aller simple pour Plan de l'Aiguille, s'il vous plait," I said, in perfect French.

The official behind the glass screen at the Midi télépherique station peeled off a ticket. "Here you are, buddy," he said, in perfect English.

How utterly astonishing! How could he possibly know I was English? Particularly since the last Englishman to board a 6am télépherique had been back in 1974 when, in his drunken stupor, he'd mistaken it for the bus back to Argentière.

Ahah, now I understand. The secret of the ticket vendor's technique was not *auditory* - my linguistic fluency had seen to that; nor was it *olfactory* - the glass screen would have prevented all but the most persistent of English odours from penetrating through to his nostrils. No, his special skill was *acute visual observation*. He had seen what I had just seen from the vantage point of the steps: that, myself being the sole exception, every single one of the four hundred throatily mumbling climbers queuing for the first cable car was wearing a *magenta headband*. Yes, these people were from *France*, while plainly I had come from that other planet called *England*.

My, but how the French have come on! In the fifteen years since I'd last been to Chamonix, what had become, I wondered, of those exuberant fellows with tassel-ended floppy hats? Those jolly chaps with long axes and broad smiles who would line up for the cannons of the Brenva Face like ducks at a shooting gallery? I suppose one by one they must have dropped down a crevasse somewhere, having been momentarily blinded by a wind-whipped tassel. I dare say they'll become a tourist curiosity one day as they start popping out of the glacier snouts, still clutching their alpenstocks and with those imbecilic grins frozen to their faces.

I removed my floppy hat, folding it into my back pocket, and began to mumble throatily at anyone who cared to listen.

* * *

In that cable car, rising pluckily like some lunar module from the barren dust of a grim and gloomy Chamonix, I counted - and in this number I immodestly include myself - seventy-one gallant mountaineers (the seventy-second person, it being unheard of for a Midi cable car to lift off with anything less than its maximum payload, was an inadequately dressed Japanese tourist who, I can only assume, had forgotten to adjust his watch on the airplane). Oh but what a happy band of brothers and sisters we were! What grand adventures awaited us! While the pitiable valley-dwellers slept in their miserable hovels down below, we were borne skywards in this tethered rocket towards a heavenly realm of rock and snow and ice. The entire NASA space budget for the twentieth century could not have purchased such splendour as this. Yet soon it would be ours, for just forty-seven francs.

At the halfway space station of Plan de l'Aiguille I was, for some inexplicable reason, the only person not to board the mother craft bound for the Aiguille du Midi (the Japanese tourist seemed to hesitate for a moment, as if belatedly aware of his inappropriate dress, though in the end even he thought it safest to go along with the crowd). Did these climbers bound for the Midi know something I did not? The previous night I had for sure been disturbed by the timpanic bursts of rain and hail striking the metal roof of my car. But today had dawned clear and cold, with the météo forecast pinned near the guides bureau promising *beau temps* until the middle of the next century. Surely these seventy mountaineers weren't all making for the snow arêtes of Mont Blanc du Tacul thinking that the rocks of the diminutive Aiguilles might be a trifle out of condition? Nah! Perish the thought.

I shouldered my pack and walked out into the dawn to face my mountain and my destiny.

* * *

Inauspiciously wheezing from oxygen starvation, I began to question the efficacy of the training schedule I'd followed since arriving in my new home in France. This had consisted of bronzing myself alongside topless *Mesdemoiselles* at a bathing lake by day, and drinking cheap wine alongside Gaulois-smoking *Messieurs* in a dark cafe by night, thereby alternately increasing and suppressing my heart rate. But was it enough? Had I neglected my atrophied muscles, my arthritic joints, my shrivelled lungs? By the time I'd stumbled just five hundred yards from the télépherique station it had become clear that I must rationalise my equipment before embarking on this five-hour *Peu Difficile voie normale* on the Aiguille des Pélerins. On a flat rock I emptied the contents of my rucksack and began to compile a mental inventory:

Fifty metres of 9mm rope, hopefully in one continuous length.

One ice-axe (rusty).

One ice-hammer (with wobbly pick).

One pair of crampons adjusted to fit a friend's pair of size four walking boots.

Four drive-in tubular titanium ice screws, one of which appeared still usable.

Four rock pegs consisting of two run-of-the-mill Kingpins; one *huge* Leeper (which may in fact be a segment of the corrugated roof from the factory where Leepers are made); and one rather masculine, and rather embarrassingly named, Long Dong.

The last surviving range of original Chouinard Hexentrics sizes one through eight not in a museum.

A nest of tape slings of unknown number and origin.

Fourteen karabiners bearing the original hallmarks of

Thomas Telford's Coalbrookdale iron foundry.

A second nest of tape slings of unknown number and origin which hopefully is not that at all but a sit-harness.

One chest-harness - wait! - one *magenta* chest harness, which, with a bit of modification...

One belay brake for the use of my non-existent climbing partner.

One safety helmet with badly corroded rivets resulting from inadequate rinsing after its last use on a Pembrokeshire sea cliff when the rate of elevation of my leader was somewhat less than that of the incoming tide.

Eight metres of sexily-coloured abseil cord, thin as fishing line, naively purchased the previous morning in a sports-cum-fashion store in Bourg-en-Bresse.

One sleeping bag that could do with a good wash to get the weight down a bit.

One *hugely* expensive Gore-Tex bivvy bag which I'd rather leave in its stuffsac and get piss-wet through than risk ripping on a sharp stone.

One padded jacket held together at the seams by two-foot long strips of insulating tape.

One spare pullover which wasn't needed but which I'd mistaken for a towel which, come to think of it, wasn't needed either.

One *hugely* expensive Gore-Tex jacket patched with Band-Aids after being thoughtlessly worn out-of-doors during rainy weather instead of being hung in a wardrobe as advised by the manufacturer's garment care booklet.

One Swiss army knife incorporating bottle opener, tin opener, corkscrew, large and small blades, screwdriver, and a thing which is probably more useful than all the rest but which I've never quite been able to pull out.

One large first-aid kit containing items... too numerous to mention.

One headtorch complete with two spare bulbs and... one, two, three, four, five... de, de, de, de.. fifteen - *fifteen?* spare batteries.

One recently purchased pair of sunglasses fitted with swivelling shades which, the hire-purchase sales executive assured me, were *de rigeur* for *les hautes montagnes*.

Three half-full tubes of sun cream.

One small tub of zinc and castor oil nappy rash cream for treatment of an intermittent testicular ailment on which I'd rather not elaborate but which may be attributed to poorly finished trouser seams.

One camera for recording the glorious moment when, should it arise, which seemed increasingly unlikely, I arrived on the summit.

Two spare films for recording the ensuing struggle to get back down again.

One crampon spanner - thank God for that!

One spare pair of socks in case the others get smelly or I don't like the colour.

One floppy hat of inestimable sentimental value which I'd *never* swap for a magenta headband, even if it *did* mean I'd never appear on the front cover of *Mountain* magazine.

Four pairs of gloves consisting of one pair of thermal inners, one pair of Dachstein mitts fitted with idiot loops, one pair of once-oiled but now desiccated overmitts, and one pair of fingerless gloves ideal for climbing cold rocks and economising on the winter fuel bills.

One map of the Chamonix Aiguilles.

One map not of the Chamonix Aiguilles.

One guide-book for the Chamonix Aiguilles.

One guide-book not for the Chamonix Aiguilles.

Three ballpens, the first of which writes quite well, the second of which doesn't write *quite* so well, and the third of which came free with Typhoo tea bags and doesn't seem to write at all.

Twenty sheets of A4 writing paper for jotting down ideas for the next novel as and when they arise.

One copy of a recent Boardman Tasker prize-winning novel to find out how it's done.

One copy of a not-so-recent, non-Boardman Tasker prize-winning novel to see how it really *should* be done.

One pocket edition of the *Collins English-French dictionary*.

One copy of the *Practise your French* puzzle book that arrived in the post the day before from my sister.

One copy of *Teach Yourself French - new edition* (not including the available cassette).

One notebook of personally collated useful French phrases such as: 'Yes I know they're a bit flash, but I find swivelling shades essential on routes of *Très Difficile* and above in *les hautes montagnes.*'

One passport in case of inadvertent descent into Italy, Switzerland or other unspecified European country.

One wallet containing a full deck of cheque and cash cards unacceptable in any bank or retail establishment in continental Europe.

One toothbrush.

One litre of natural mineral water which, despite the abundance of water hereabouts, I couldn't bring myself to abandon because it had cost me three francs twenty in the supermarket.

One stale *baguette*.

One tubby little rugby-football of a loaf which I'd the temerity to purchase from the Chamonix *boulangerie* in the crushing urgency of those last five minutes before it closes.

One ball of *nauseatingly* smelly cheese of a type which, I'm given to understand, is used in petanque, a game that combines aspects of both bowls and marbles and is played in village squares in the South of France by rustic gentlemen wearing nosepegs.

Three blocks of once-melted chocolate now reconstituted into an inseparable fifteen-layer lasagne of coagulated contents and wrappers.

One packet... one empty packet of Garibaldi biscuits.

One packet of biscuits with an even sillier name.

One heart of lettuce (rotten).

Two, or it could be three, tomatoes (squashed).

Three, or it could be four, not-as-hard-as-I-thought boiled

eggs (cracked).

One bunch of blackening bananas which I'd have been unwilling to count even had it been physically possible.

One - no, surely not - yes, yes it is, one kiwi fruit.

One packet of brightly coloured mixed things which is probably edible but may prove to be an economy refill for a bathroom freshener.

One very large, and doubtless very necessary, roll of toilet tissue.

And finally, yes finally:

One large - or do you think that qualifies as huge? - would gigantic be going too far? - anyway, one considerably sized melon.

So, it's no wonder I was well buggered walking the five hundred yards from the télépherique station, is it?

I filled a large cleft in the rock with unneeded equipment and inedible provisions and sprang up the remainder of the boulder moraine like a chamois chased by a gang of impoverished window cleaners.

* * *

According to the guide-book, my intended route was, and I quote, "an easy and popular" one, yet I found myself quite alone on the approach. I concluded that magenta must clash with the ruddy coloured rocks characteristic of this part of the Aiguilles.

I dumped my axe and crampons at the start of the proper climbing and began to ascend a so-called rock ramp. Now here's a riddle for you: "When is an easy and popular rock ramp not an easy and popular rock ramp?" Answer: "When it's an overhanging, verglassed chimney." Ha-ha!

Isn't it fascinating the way the human brain can rationalise a progressively worsening situation? At the start of the chimney I was terrified that my foot would slip, causing me to bang my knee. Oh I hate banging my knees. Whereas by the time I'd reached the chimney exit, I'd begun to fear that if my foot slipped then I'd plunge to my certain death over a thousand-foot precipice. On reflection this fear was unduly pessimistic; there was a fair chance that from the snow patch beneath the chimney I'd be deflected leftwards over a mere hundred-foot cliff, down a friendly-looking three hundred-foot ice-choked chasm, and then with any luck - and before I came to any serious injury - fetch up safely in a crevasse before the glacier tippled over an awesome icefall. It's all matter of degree, isn't it?

It must have been about this time that I began talking to myself. Well, not to myself exactly but to an invisible companion. Oh, she was bloody full of it! Admiring the dawn light profiling the slender crest of the Frendo Spur; delighting in the iced-bun prettiness of the snow which had concealed all the best handholds; and marvelling at the kaleidoscopic structure of the crystalline granite beneath my bleeding hands.

Wielding my fingers like fistfuls of ice-daggers, I completed a hundred consecutive mantelshelves onto sloping snowy ledges which she levitated herself, effortlessly, alongside.

"Float down for my ice-axe and crampons, will you dear?" I pleaded.

"Oh whatever do you want those for?" she said, hovering. The accomplished bitch.

* * *

Back on route, I took the opportunity of this momentary respite to slacken my boot laces, to let some air at my bruised and bloody ankles.

In the present commercial climate of anatomic design and user-friendliness, plastic mountaineering boots remain something of an archaic anomaly; an evolutionary throwback to the days of the eight-inch Murphy television set and the Philips Gadabout motor-assisted bicycle. My plastic boots, I suspect, owe their design to a technology project undertaken by the remedial class at Glockenspiel Kindergarten.

By the time I'd reached the south summit I had, in an effort to ease the agony, completely unfastened the laces of both inner and outer boots and had folded both tongues forward. I might just as well have been wearing a plastic bucket jammed on each foot. In fact plastic buckets would have been preferable because it would then have been easier to empty the melted snow from their interiors.

Anyway, it was here, on this spiky subsidiary top, that I made a discovery of buttock-clenching significance. If I wished to ascend to the main summit then I'd first have to reverse a nasty little crack that had been polished to a sheen by the scrabbling breeched knees of innumerable secured and worthy alpinists. I was not breeched. I was not secured. I was not even an alpinist worthy of the name. It was only twenty feet, but being shaded from the sun it was still verglassed. "Time for another dump," I thought (no, not that sort of dump, madam).

By this time I had equipment scattered all over the Chamonix Aiguilles. I wasn't even sure I could find it all again. If I was routed by storm I might have to abandon several hundred pounds worth of rusty equipment, squashed fruit and unread novels. But the lure of the summit overcame all my misgivings; I stowed my rucksack in a crack, slithered down the slippery fissure, and scrambled up to the top. If I died tomorrow then at least I would know that for one glorious day I had truly lived (actually, no, because if I was dead then I wouldn't be aware that for one glorious day I had truly lived... Oh well, what does it matter? It was only one of those glib statements one utters on mountain summits for lack of anything more intelligent to say.)

The descent? I won't bore you with that. Let me just say that the verglas had melted by this time, but then so had the snow, partially, so it was like down-climbing Point Five Gully in thaw conditions without an ice-axe. Ha, ha! No, it wasn't that bad. Zero Gully, perhaps. Either way, you can imagine my delight in eventually arriving upright on the low-angle snow slopes of the glacier as opposed to lying head-down at the bottom of a fifteen-foot-deep crater as I had so often anticipated.

Having earlier tightened my boots to facilitate step-kicking in the couloir, I now celebrated my successful descent by unlacing them again. Ah, that's better. Stomp, stomp, whooo... whoooooooosh! Phlughcrumph!

For a tenth of a second after my arrest on the sharp-edged boulder I felt no pain whatsoever. All those months of studious psycho-synthetic meditation, perfecting the art of disidentification with bodily discomforts, had finally paid off. Pain, after all, is merely a sensation. A tenth of a second. Then I felt as though my leg was being bitten off by a carnivorous donkey. Stubborn little bugger, he just wouldn't let go! That sensation lasted for five seconds, after which I abandoned my crumpled body and embarked on a fifteen-second out-of-body experience, touring Mont Blanc and all its major satellite peaks, gliding down into Chamonix for a cool beer, then tree-hopping up the valley side back to the glacier. No boots, no parapente, no telepherique. Never got a blister and it didn't cost a franc.

At this point, having returned to see how my earthly body was coping with its now inevitably rather limiting new existence, I unwisely re-entered the flesh just as the central nervous system was about to stage a 4th of July firework display... Pain spun in multi-coloured catherine wheels, rocketed skywards with sparks trailing, shook with ear-numbing explosions, and cascaded in the red-hot showers of erupting volcanoes. It hurt. Do you understand what I'm saying? It bloody hurt!

Not only was I alone on the mountain with a probable compound fracture of the femur, but I had neglected to subscribe to the BMC's overseas accident insurance. At least if I'd been killed my next-of-kin could have met the rescue fees out of the settlement from my conventional life cover. And what was worse, I had yet to retrieve the cache of French phrase books. How would I convince my would-be rescuers that I wished them to delay evacuation until after my death? They would insist on rescuing me there and then; on flying me speedily down to Chamonix in a helicopter. A helicopter! And then, while I was recuperating in hospital and scoffing the complimentary grapes, they would come for my money. My money!

Well, they were not going to get it. "Ssshhh," I told myself, taking control, "keep quiet and no-one will know you are here. It's only a few miles over house-sized boulders and interminable glacier moraine to the télépherique station. You can do a Simpson. Three days, four at the most, and you'll be laughing. There might even be a book in it somewhere."

I was bitterly disappointed when I found I could stand up without difficulty. True, I had a bruise the size of half a grapefruit on my thigh, but you can't get much bullshit out of a bruise down at Le Pub - or wherever happens to be the 'in' place to hang out in Chamonix now that the Bar National has gone up-market and employed a garçon with slicked-back hair and a dickie bow - can you?

Within an hour I'd retrieved all the various piles of equipment and stood wheezing outside the Plan de l'Aiguille télépherique station.

You may think that my tribulations were now over. They were not. While resting from the exertions of hauling my rucksack up the concrete steps to the embarkation bay, I took the opportunity to glance through my recovered stock of French phrase books. It was then that I made an appalling discovery. That morning, in my articulatory enthusiasm, I'd inadvertently asked for a single ticket. A single ticket! The man behind the glass screen would demand an outrageous supplement for the return trip. What was to be done? I could hardly walk down to Chamonix with a plastic bucket jammed on each foot and the equivalent of a hundredweight sack of spuds strapped to my back, could I? There was no alternative: I would have to pay. I thumbed through my personal phrase book looking for the most apposite comment to make as I handed over the fifty-franc note. I found it on page forty-eight. "Has anyone ever told you," I mumbled throatily in perfect French, just so there would be no misunderstanding, "that your face looks like the maggot-ridden remains of a regurgitated par-boiled halibut head?"

He took my money with a smile. "Have a nice day," he said, in perfect English, exchanging the note for my down-ticket to Chamonix.

Within five minutes that tethered rocket of the cable car was transporting me back to earth; my adventure finished, my money and my enthusiasm spent. Back down to the miserable hovels of the valley. Back to the dust and to the grime. Back where I belong.

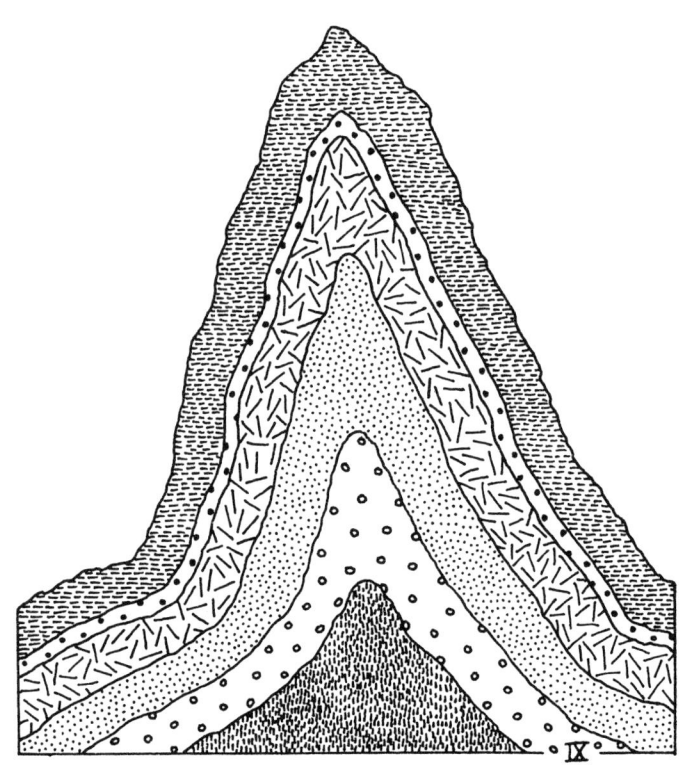

STANAGE, GOING SOUTH

by Libby Houston

One in green rich as holly on the watery white
and one whose harsh orange the mist has turned radiant,

friends that I follow, headed for the cloud on High Neb
at a pace harried by the wind as it bursts up the edge -

Off on the left a sheep bleats once or twice peevishly.
A grouse blows past, the trees are held down. Alone

I would still have had the blond grass glow, true, and the scud.
But the two I shadowed gave the landscape figures

and colour, colour the dark white intensified
and the figures scale, yes, as they would in a photo

or painting - those pointing groups on mountains; but now a
mirror too of the intricate steps quick judgments the delight

called up by fast going on uneven ground across wind
like this. Also I could know the cold I felt was shared.

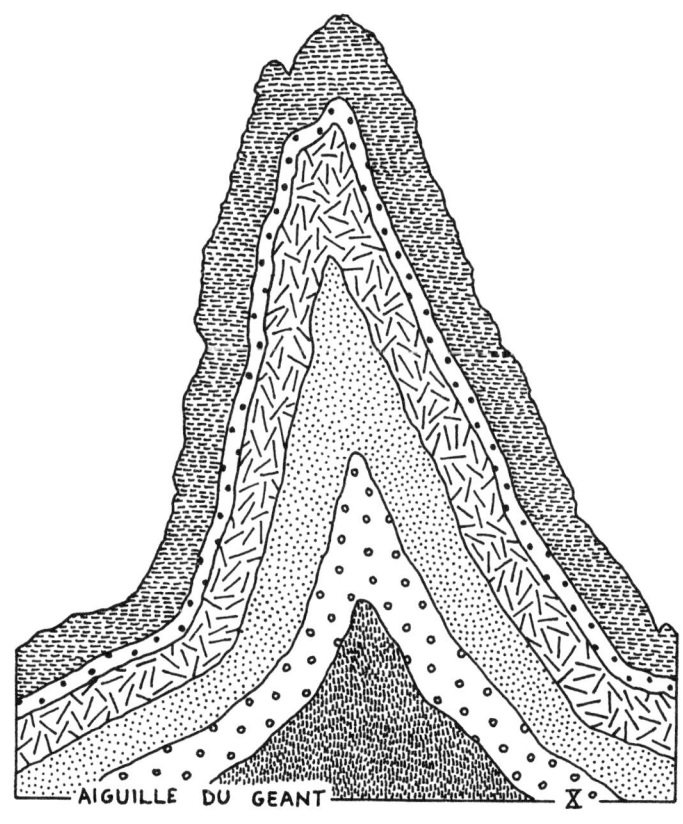

French Climbing Writing in French Mountaineering Culture

by Anne Sauvy

When I was asked to speak about "the features of *French Climbing Writing in French Mountaineering Culture"*, I was a bit nonplussed because I am unaware that there is any French Mountaineering culture.

So I could stop lecturing here, by simply saying - there is no French mountaineering culture. That would be very nice for me, because I have never lectured in English before, and perhaps it would be nice for you, too, because you would not have to put up with my accent too long... and my English!

But I think Terry Gifford would not be pleased with me if I did that. And so I shall try to talk about French literature on mountains. Already it is a large topic - and I shall confine myself to the *French* literature. So I shall not speak of Saussure, Topffer, Ramuz, Charles Gos and others. Swiss alpine literature is really another subject.

On the other hand, I shall include in my survey both fiction *and* works by travellers or climbers who have written from personal experience.

Some months ago, I thought I knew French alpine literature quite well. I have been collecting books about mountains since I was a teenager, and I have read a lot of them. But, in working for preparing this lecture, I was surprised, really surprised, because being obliged to organise, to classify, to look for the ins and outs, I discovered facts I had never thought about.

There is no book on the subject. Or, more exactly, there are a few books but each of them is confined to bits of the subject. No synthesis. So, what I am going to do now is to attempt a general survey - and try to give you, in thirty minutes, an idea of what has been our alpine literature.

It appears to me that there are three streams, three lines, corresponding to three periods. They might be entitled:

- The time of the travellers.
- The time of the writers.
- The time of the climbers.

The time of the travellers begins, for us, at the end of the eighteenth century, when, after Windham and Pococke, and particularly after Saussure, people went to the high valleys of the Alps to see peaks, glaciers and summer snow. It quickly became a fashion.

Everybody who was in a position to travel *had* to see Chamonix, or Switzerland, or both. And sometimes it produced books, or at least a few pages.

This period came to an end in the middle of the nineteenth century.

Strangely enough, in France, it is two women who begin and, in my eyes, end this period of travellers. I am not especially a feminist, but I think these two women are - with just one exception - the most interesting of the lot.

The first one is Manon Roland. With her husband, she travelled in Switzerland in 1787. She went to Grindelwald, was strongly attracted by the high mountains and tried to climb on moraines and glaciers.

She wrote:

A woman who can ride, walk for four or five hours, who is not afraid to have her complexion burnt by the sun, or to get soaked by the rain, can hope to travel in inner Switzerland if she has in her soul that kind of energy which thrives on difficulties...

Any person capable of undertaking this journey but who is held back by fear of fatigue and danger is a poor specimen whose habit of comfort condemns him never to know the greatest pleasures of all.

Madame Roland could have been the first woman to be a climber. She had the guts for it. But our French Revolution took place two years after her journey. She became active in

Revolutionary politics and paid for it by being beheaded in 1793. Now, she is only known through the Revolution, but I think it is a pity because, instead of being a rather rough and excitable Revolutionary as she was, she could have been a very good alpinist.

Then, by the beginning of the nineteenth century, all our famous writers and poets passed through Chamonix - as also did Byron and Shelley. Each of them felt obliged to record his travel by an account, or in verses. I shall just refer to four of them: Chateaubriand, Victor Hugo, George Sand and Alexandre Dumas.

The first one, Chateaubriand, is a very good writer and has the advantage of sincerity. Coming in 1805, he plainly *disliked* the mountains, and said so. True, he was travelling with his wife and that never put him in a good mood. But the fact remains he really disliked the wilderness of what he saw.

He missed air and space. He thought mountains were good as a distant skyline but "hideous when seen from too close". He said that all the traveller to Chamonix sees is "as though through a funnel, a little patch of hard blue sky... Depressing stay in which the sun could just be seen at midday, peeping over an icy barrier."

No romanticism for him. Even the country life, chalets, farmers and shepherds made a bad impression - he was principally struck by the piles of manure, the stench of cheese and fermented milk...

In short, his visit was not a success.

Victor Hugo travelled in 1825 with another writer, Charles Nodier, their wives, one child, a maid and a sketcher. They had succeeded in realising an author's dream: to have a wonderful trip paid (for all of them) by a publisher. On their return, they were expected to write a book. But, when they came back, the publisher had gone broke - and they did not have to write it...

Only some fragments, which were already completed, were published later. From these, the most interesting feature to emerge is that Victor Hugo, who was then only 23, nearly fell in a deep crevasse on the Mer de Glace: had he done so, the history of French Literature and even French politics would have been changed quite a lot...

As for George Sand - a woman with a male pseudonym - she travelled in 1836 in a party which included Liszt, the famous musician. They had great fun but were not really interested in the mountains.

Alexandre Dumas, the author of the *Three Musketeers* is the best of all. It can't be said he had a particular fancy for mountains but, in 1832, he travelled in Switzerland and the Savoy Alps (Chamonix was not French at this time) and wrote five excellent volumes about it, full of humour. There are great pages where he tells how he ate, in Martigny, a steak from a bear which - he learned at the last mouthful - had eaten the hunter, or when he describes a pillow-fight, in the dark, with other travellers.

He was a great walker and instead of staying down in the valley and doing just the Montenvers excursion, like the others, he used the few days he was in Chamonix in doing big tours. What is more, he was interested in everything about climbing. He saw Marie Paradis, the first woman to climb Mont Blanc and he saw Jacques Balmat, who made the first ascent more than 40 years before. He made real journalistic interviews with them and popularised their exploits all over France, purveying Jacques Balmat's account which took all the credit for himself!

Alexandre Dumas's contribution to alpine literature is a very good one.

Then came the second woman I mentioned, Henriette d'Angeville, who also travelled in Chamonix (in 1838), made long walks without getting tired, and started wanting to climb Mont Blanc.

Mont Blanc had already been climbed by Marie Paradis, but this first female ascent was almost a forced one. She had been persuaded to try it by guides, in the hope of making her a local celebrity and selling drinks to visitors. It was a horrible experience for her. Time and again she demanded, "Chuck me into a crevasse... Better die here than up there..." She was pushed, pulled and carried, and her only remembrance of the summit was that it was "white around and black elsewhere."

With Henriette d'Angeville, the approach was quite different. She was already 44 but she *wanted* to succeed and was as determined as the most sportive climbers of today. She recorded her ascent and all the events around it. It was *not* published *then* but, fortunately, her note-book was kept by her nephews and nieces, and then by their descendants, and was published four years ago: 150 years after it was written! It is a superb account, sometimes very humorous, describing the ascent almost hour by hour and it makes a full-length book.

Henriette d'Angeville explains her motives and how everybody tried to stop her from undertaking the ascent, saying that she would die, that she would lose her sight, that she would have her feet frozen, that she would burst a blood vessel... and so on.

"Even if the worst happens," replied Henriette, who was a very determined woman, "an icy tomb does not fill my imagination with terror... Once decided, one must only see the positive side and pursue it without paying attention to the criticism or plaudits of others. If not, life would pass in indecisiveness and uncertainty."

She had found six guides and six porters but the other guides of Chamonix were making bets on her failure. We know everything about the clothes and even the underclothes she wore for the expedition. And everything about the food taken: 2 saddles of lamb, 24 roast chickens, 18 bottles of St. Jean wine, 1 small barrel of ordinary wine, etc., etc. We know all the details of the ascent, its mishaps, its laughs, the songs sung by the guides at the first bivvy - where Henriette d'Angeville had asked for an "Evening Hymn", and it was rather drinking-songs that her guides knew - and of course all the details about mountaineering.

Having climbed without too many difficulties till the final section, Henriette was overtaken by drowsiness and felt very weak. But she wanted so much to succeed that she asked her guides:

"If I die before reaching the summit, promise me to carry my body to it, and leave it there."

But she recovered enough strength for finishing the ascent, and experienced the joys of the success. The guides decided she should go higher than everybody else, and lifted her the highest they could, on their alpenstocks. The return to the valley was quite a triumph but Henriette was realist enough to know that the same people who were congratulating her, would have said, if she had had an accident: "That silly woman paid dearly for getting talked about!"

The whole of Henriette d'Angeville's book is a much more living document about an ascent than most books - or films - which have been made since about mountains. It really is a small *chef d'oeuvre*.

But the period of the voyagers came to an end in the middle of the nineteenth century, when railways made access so easy to the Alps, that it was no more a topic to write an account. By that time, however, ideas about mountains and even mountaineering were becoming sufficiently widespread that it became possible to write fiction about it.

Some very good writers did so. As far back as 1860 there is a very amusing play by Ernest Labiche: *Le Voyage de Monsieur Perrichon* (Mr. Perrichon's Journey). It is a comedy about the visit to Chamonix of a tradesman, very full of himself, accompanied by his wife, his daughter and two young men competing for the girl's hand. It contains a well-known episode on the Mer de Glace, and it is a good play, still performed.

There is also, from Alphonse Daudet, in 1885, a famous

novel *Tartarin sur les Alpes*. Tartarin is an amusing type of boaster, typical of the South of France (for people who are, as I am more or less, from the North of France, all the people of the South of France are boasters). The plot is situated in Switzerland and is a hilarious mixture of climbing and Russian nihilists. The story ends on Mont Blanc, where Tartarin and a friend fall off on either side of a ridge - and each of them cuts the rope to save his own life. But of course, both of them are finally safe.

Alphonse Daudet knew Chamonix well. He asked a lot of questions about mountaineering to Chamonix guides. So, if the book is good for the story and style, the details about mountaineering are also very accurate.

Then, in 1887, in the book *Le Horla* by Maupassant, a short story *L'Auberge* (The Inn) was published that English readers may know because it has been recently translated in *One Step in the Clouds*, under the title of *Ulrich the Guide*.

As all the stories Maupassant wrote, it is brilliant and the atmosphere is beautifully set - but I am a little unconvinced by the circumstances of the plot.

Through these three works, mountains took their place in French literature - and then came the time of novelists - of second rate - who were mostly fascinated by accidents.

First and foremost, in 1886 is Paul Hervieu's *L'Alpe Homicide* (The Killer Alp), a title which became a cliché in the public mind of mountains not being a passive background but actively murderous.

The short story which gave its title to the volume ends with such lines, supposedly written by a man dying in the mountains:

I am finished... Already my feet are frosted... I shall die trusting in God... My frozen fingers can no more grip my pen... No longer can I keep my eyes from closing... Farewell, my beloved, until we meet again in eternity... My last breath shall be for thee.

And the other stories in the book are also a mixture of

accidents, crimes and love.

It was a time, in France, and probably also in Great Britain, where there was a fascination for the melodramatic. I have also brought a picture from a newspaper of this period showing an accident. Alpine literature had a similar tendency.

Others followed Paul Hervieu, with titles like *Le Vertige des Cimes* (The Giddy Heights); *Une ascension dramatique au Mont Blanc* (A Dramatic Ascent on Mont Blanc); *La Neige sur les pas* (Snow on the Footsteps); *Du sang sur la neige* (Blood on the Snow); *Les Jeux Dangereux* (Dangerous Games), and so on.

The most dramatic of these writers is Georges Casella. At the beginning of *Blood on the Snow*, he puts this quotation:

Dark blood makes such a beautiful effect on the sparkling snow...

In this book there is a dramatic mix-up of bodies, and also a debate around the theme "Is it justified to cut the rope?" In *The Giddy Heights*, the introduction says:

Mountains are suggestive of death..... The delirium for the peaks is a dangerous love which kills. The mountains take corpses unto themselves..... Every year they devour new heroes.

And so on... A very morbid outlook on climbing.

The other novelist of the first half of the twentieth century is Henry Bordeaux, a bit less tragic because he does not introduce murders in his novels, but who, nevertheless, uses the full literary devices of accidents and love.

And, during all this period, which covers nearly eighty years - from 1860 to 1940 - where there have been perhaps 80 novels using mountains, there were *very, very few* works written by real climbers.

Of course, the Club Alpin Français produced, from 1874, the *Annuaire du Club Alpin Français*, a kind of *Alpine Journal*, each volume being a book of 600, 700 pages. But it is surprising to see that climbing had relatively little importance in it. Most of the papers are geographical ones, or scientific ones or about low-level walking in the Alps, Pyrenees, Auvergne or Morocco..... About caves, geology, meteorology, hut building or in military topography... Very, very few about mountaineering. With *one* notable exception: the first ascent of la Meije by Gaspard and Boileau de Castelnau - yet it only occasioned a paper of *twelve* pages.

When the *Annuaire* gave place in 1906 to *La Montagne*, which was then a monthly magazine, there was no significant change in the nature of the contributions until at least 1920.

You can see the difference between French and English mountain literature. At this date, around 1920, we had no Ruskin, no Leslie Stephen, no Whymper, no Tyndall, no Mummery, no Coolidge, no Geoffrey Winthrop Young... Nobody! No real climber, at least who wrote about it.....Why? Are the reasons political? (Frenchmen were certainly longing to recover Alsace and Lorraine between 1871 and 1914, and political fights were also very sharp in the country itself.) Are they economic reasons? (Britain was much more industrialised and its towns had grown more quickly than in France.) Or are they reasons to be found in the differing mental structures and feeling of nature between the two countries? All these are possible, but I am unable to understand really where this difference comes from. It is sufficient here just to point it out.

It is only after the First World War that a little change began. French climbers became more interested in difficult ascents and in new first ascents, often without guides. But, during twenty more years, they did what I did myself later: they were more busy in climbing than in writing. Or they wrote some articles. Very few books.

Nevertheless, this period between the two World Wars presages change. There are still novels, but also books on the Alps, the first *guides Vallot* and some works about mountaineering history, like those of Claire-Eliane Engel.

The first real climbing book dates, I think, to 1929! *Sur les crêtes du Mont-Blanc* (On the Crests of Mont Blanc) by Jacques and Tom de Lépiney, two brothers who were very good climbers. And the introduction to the book summarises the situation. The first paragraph asks:

Why add another volume to the mountaineering bookshelves, already long enough?

But on the second page comes the answer:

French climbers have rarely recorded their story in any but specialised periodicals: nearly all the works which make up our libraries are by foreigners: Whymper, Mummery, Güssfeldt, Javelle, Guido Rey, Blodig, Finch, etc.

So, In France, it is the late twenties which saw the birth of personal writing about mountaineering (with the exception of Henriette d'Angeville and very few others).

The new tendency became more pronounced in the thirties, with some books about Karakoram expeditions, and a few books of essays or memoirs. But at this date, it still did not amount to much.

Then, in 1940, begins the third period: the time of the climbers. Fixing the date is easy, because the two books which probably remain the two major books of the whole French alpine literature were respectively published in 1940 and 1941: *L'Amateur d'abîmes* (The Void Lover) by Samivel (whose real name is Paul Gayet-Tancrède) and *Premier de Cordée* (First on the Rope) by Roger Frison-Roche. The two of them were great best-sellers and, 50 years after, they are still on sale.

Premier de Cordée is a novel, whose plot is set among the Chamonix guides. The author was himself a climber and a guide. He knew what he was speaking about. His plot is remarkably built and his characters are, more or less, inspired by *real* people. The book, on the other hand, tended to create, in France, a mythical image of the guides.

L'Amateur d'abîmes could have been called *Three Men in the Mountains* on the model of Jerome K. Jerome's *Three Men in a Boat*. It relates the summer season, in Chamonix, of three young climbers without guides, their routes, the atmosphere in the huts, the problems about the rope, and so on. The book is sometimes very funny, sometimes poetic, with beautiful descriptions.

For Frison-Roche and Samivel it was the beginning of a long literary career. By Frison-Roche there are at least three mountain novels: *La Grande Crevasse* (The Great Crevasse); *Retour à la montagne* (Back to the Mountains) and *Les Montagnards de la nuit* (Mountaineers of the Night). Samivel published two books of short stories: *Contes à pic* (Steep Stories) and *Contes des brillantes montagnes avant la nuit* (tales of the shining mountains before night/darkness). He also wrote a novel about environment, a very long one: *Le Fou d'Edenberg* (The Madman of Edenberg). And he is a painter and sketcher of mountains.

But there were not only these. After the appearance of their two first books, and following the end of World War Two, French alpine literature has been in a period of explosion. And the writers were all real and good climbers.

It is, of course, impossible to give a detailed account of what has been published since then. There are books of memoirs, books about expeditions, novels, short stories, mountaineering history..... A very large range. All I can do is mention those that are, for me, the most interesting and why.

Published in 1951, *Annapurna Premier 8000*, by Maurice Herzog (Annapurna First 8000) has been a great best-seller. Hundreds of thousands of copies. The book is said to have been mostly written by Gérard Herzog, the brother of Maurice Herzog, but that does not really matter because it relates a very exciting story and it gave the taste of mountaineering books to many readers.

I shall also mention, in 1955, *Victoire sur l'Aconcagua* by René Ferlet (Victory on Aconcagua) about an expedition which was interesting in many ways, even if the book had not the same success.

As for the personal memoirs of alpinists, there are a lot of them. Too many. Lachenal, Desmaison, Mazeaud, Yannick Seigneur, etc., etc. The problem is that a good climber is not necessarily a good writer. If he writes himself, it is often appalling. Or he uses a ghost, who works quickly and is sometimes very ignorant of mountaineering.

And many things may happen to the book...

I give you one example: it was Philippe Cornuau (who had made in 1955 the first ascent of the North Face of the Droites, with Davaille, and was a very scholarly young man) who was chosen by Lachenal for writing his memoirs. Lachenal intended to counter the account of Maurice Herzog in *Annapurna Premier 8000*. The work was nearly finished when Lachenal died in a crevasse of the Vallée Blanche, skiing. And the widow of Lachenal gave the manuscript notes to the Herzogs who, of course, suppressed what they did not like. So, it is not really *the* book of Lachenal.

A lot of things like that would have to be known about a book, when the 'author' has not written it himself, or has not seen it through publication. Even then, you don't know what the influence of the publishers may have been...

But we have in France, at least, three very good books of climbing autobiographies. In 1958, Georges Livanos' *Au-delà de la verticale* (Beyond the Vertical) - very humoristic accounts of rock ascents.

Then, in 1961, the book of Lionel Terray, *Les Conquérants de l'inutile*, which has been translated in English under the title *Conquistadors of the Useless*. Lionel Terray wrote his book himself. He was intelligent enough to succeed in this new adventure, and he did succeed. I was a student in literature when Lionel was writing and, when we met in the Club Alpin, I spent hours asking him about the way he worked and all the process of the making of a book by somebody who was not at all a professional writer. It was very enlightening.

Lionel said that when he thought about a route he had done, he had such a good memory that he could relive it, with all its details. And he worked a lot on his expression.

He said that very often he did the same passage ten times, or more, before succeeding in having one which satisfied him. So this book has been, for him, a lot of effort, but effort well spent because the book is excellent.

I must now mention another book, published in 1965 (the year Lionel died), but this book was written by a much older man, Robert Tézenas du Montcel, who was a climber of the twenties and thirties, but wrote his book much later. The title is *Ce Monde qui n'est pas le nôtre* (This World which is not Ours). If I had to take, on a desert island, only one book about mountains, I should take this one. The presentation was deliberately sober: no pictures, even on the cover. Only a very beautiful text. Unfortunately the book passed almost unnoticed. I love it so much that, one way and another, it happens that I have four copies of it: two well bound, two others to lend... It is a superb book.

Lionel Terray and Tézenas du Montcel were - it is interesting to mention it - not published by one of the French publishers of mountain books, but by Gallimard, the best publisher of literature in France.

I don't know really whether to mention Gaston Rébuffat. He began to write in 1954 with *Etoiles et Tempêtes* (Starlight and Storm), about six North faces he had climbed. Then came *Neige et roc* (On Snow and Rock) in 1959. He wrote about mountains all the rest of his life, and he began the "Hundred Best Routes" series. At the end of his life, a few years ago, he was even his own publisher.

Mountaineering fiction was also incredibly rich during this period, particularly between 1945 and 1970. Of course, Frison-Roche and Samivel were still writing and publishing a lot. But there are others like Saint-Loup, Georges Sonnier, Daumal, Henri Troyat, Max and André Chamson, etc. The case of Daumal is a strange one: he wrote one novel, *Le Mont Analogue*, which is unfinished because he died whilst he was writing it: it is a very literary text, and a symbolic one, considered as a mountain novel, but this unfinished story stops in the middle and so there is no passage really situated in the mountains.

But there is one particular author, almost forgotten now, who was probably the best of them all. His name was Etienne Bruhl. He had been, in the thirties, an excellent climber and a member of the G.H.M. He wrote two books. The first one, published in 1946, *Accident à la Meije* (Accident on the Meije), is a superb detective story, whose plot is brilliantly built on the topographical characteristics of the traverse of the Meije.

The second one, *Variantes* (Variants, 1951), includes seven excellent short stories, some of them dramatic, others humorous.

If I have written mountain short stories, it is in the steps of Etienne Bruhl. I have perhaps read each of his books ten times and I consider him as a really excellent writer.

While on the subject of detective stories, I should also mention one other, *Meurtre au sommet* (Murder on the Summit), published in 1964. The author, José Giovanni, mixed fictional characters and real climbers, like Desmaison.

Now, what can be told about the last twenty years and about the present?

It is the end of great figures. Gaston Rébuffat is dead. Samivel* and Frison-Roche are around 85 and may be considered as having stopped writing. In 1981, Frison-Roche published his memoirs under the title *Le Versant du soleil* (The Sunny Slope), which is not only about mountains but is also an entrancing book and, in effect, his swan song.

We also saw the publication, between 1977 and 1983, of a kind of irregular magazine, whose title was *Passages*: a very intellectual magazine, which ran for seven issues, written by very intellectual climbers who thought nothing had been written about mountains before them (and nothing except by them). I am perhaps a bit biased about *Passages*, but when I saw the title of the first paper of the first number (*Propositions pour une passion polyforme* (Propositions for a Polymorphic Passion)), and above all the subject of the fourth one (Alpinism and Politics) I decided not to buy *Passages*. For me, climbing was *not* a political act; for the writers of *Passages* it seemed to be extremely political to walk on a glacier, put on crampons, stick an ice-axe in a bergschrund or grip a block of stone. *Passages* looks to be a well-known magazine but I am afraid that the editors and writers have never gone beyond our 'revolution of May 1968'.

What else? We have had too many expedition books (I am speaking only of France!) and they have become so repetitive and boring that the genus is now dying out.

On the other hand - and it is by no means good for alpine literature in general - French publishers are often ready to publish very poor books by well-known climbers. It is a consequence of the fact that the best climbers, in France, always become professional. They are guides but they are also *stars*, looking for sponsors and publicity. That is not criticism of them as people. Lots of them are very nice. But they are in no way writers. Yet, they are almost obliged to publish books about themselves, which are sold a short period and are usually uninteresting. I shall not mention names, save to signal the exception of François Damilano, who is an excellent ice-climber but also a cultured young man.

We have had, in another way, a plethora of books of photographs, generally very beautiful but with rather poor texts.

So, in 1991, who are the mountain writers in France? They are two, or, if I dare count myself, we are three.

There is Bernard Amy, who is a computer engineer in Grenoble and also a climber. He has published a book about one expedition in Turkey (*La Montagne des autres* (The Others' Mountain), 1972) and, in 1985, a collection of stories called *Le Meilleur grimpeur du monde* (The Best Climber in the World). I think two stories in it have been translated into English. His stories are very well-written but perhaps, sometimes, they miss a real plot. He is excellent in descriptions of mountains and mountain atmosphere. I saw him last week and he is now planning a literary book about mountains for the publisher *Actes Sud*.

The second one is Yves Ballu. He is not really a climber

but he is a great collector of books and anything to do with mountains. He has written four or five books about the history of the Alps and climbing, the best-known being *Les Alpinistes* (1984). His approach looks more like a journalistic one than a real historian's. But he has a lively and efficient way of writing, a lot of documents and punch. He is planning a major history of climbing, with pictures, and a novel.

So, the third one is probably me and Ken Wilson has asked me to say something about myself. I wrote three books of short stories. It is not my main work, as I am a University lecturer in Paris. But I know well mountains for I did many routes in the Alps.

My first mountain book was *Les Flammes de Pierre*, including 14 stories, published in 1982. This book won the *Prix de l'Alpe* and was translated into German in 1983, where it won the prize of the German Alpine Club. It is the one which is now translated into English.

Then, in 1985, I published 16 other stories, under the title of *Le Jeu de la montagne et du hasard* (The Game of Mountain and Chance).

In 1989, I wrote the memoirs of an old guide I knew, Pierre Leroux, under the title *Guide*. And this year, in May 1991, was published my third book of short stories, *La Ténèbre et l'azur* (Darkness and azure) which won, last August, the *Grand Prix du Salon du livre de Montagne*.

So, I have now written 46 stories about mountains and mountaineering. I have lots of other ideas, for going on, but I think I shall do next something else. Probably a novel. Perhaps also an anthology of the most humorous texts about mountaineering, lots of them being, of course, translated from English.

A last point. Why choose fiction as a way of writing about the mountains? I think, personally, that it is a very good medium because experience shows that real adventures and souvenirs are often of limited interest. Sometimes, there is certainly a tremendous book, as was *Touching the Void*. But, in France, with a few exceptions, I can tell you what are our books. It is: "I put my left hand on the hold and so I could put up my right foot in the crack and the rope around the small block, for belaying. There, I could rest a bit. It was getting rather cold. I looked upwards and saw that the crack ended in a red wall which I thought I could reach..." And so on, and so on, for three hundred pages.

And, as I said, our expedition books were generally very boring also. The expedition itself was perhaps a big thrill, but not the book about it, in France at least. We have always: the approach march, the strike of the sherpas, the base camp, then camp 1, camp 2, camp 3, camp 4, cold, avalanches, problems, camp 5, bad weather, back to camp 1, again camp 2, camp 3, camp 4, snow tempest, one dead, back to base camp. And so on! And often a failure to reach the summit. Appalling books!

With fiction, you may choose what is essential, what is interesting, and recount it. Choose what is important, or funny, or dramatic - and highlight it, and organise everything in the story around it. Mountains are a good background for telling stories. Readers have a need of extreme examples, whence comes the success of detective stories and all the thrillers. In mountains, there is a place for efforts, fun, beauty but sometimes also for drama. Problems of life and death are much nearer, much stronger. It is a privileged background, out of any routine, which amplify, or magnify, the situations and the feelings. Good ones and evil ones. It communicates to every human event an intensity, a density.

And, if I choose to write fiction about mountaineering, it is also, of course, because I climbed a lot and know alpine circles well.

Why short stories? I think they are pleasant to read. If they are well done, well worked on, they are not boring. There is no need to spin them out, as there is with many novels. You may just say what is essential. Very often - and I learned this from my experience as a reader - I try to have a twist at the end - a new event, a sentence, a word which sometimes changes the whole story - or at least an interesting conclusion, so that the reader ends the story satisfied, and not waiting for something else, or being left floating in some woolliness.

I also often use the fantastic, or imaginary. Sometimes ghosts, or devils, or fairies, or statues brought alive, but mixed in a completely realistic background. Mountains lend themselves very well to fantastic stories. But some others I wrote are founded on pure facts, or on psychological situations.

Writing short stories, or any fiction, about mountains may also be, in a light manner, a way to speak about important matters, as for example the fight for the environment: all the problems about the development of buildings and new stations in the Alps. How promoters, real estate, cable-cars may endanger the mountains. I did it particularly in my last book. It may be short. But sometimes a good satire or epigram can be effective.

So, I think that the mountains are a good place for locating fiction stories. Ken Wilson asked me if, in France, other sports, sailing, or tennis, have inspired a similar literature as the one we have about mountains. I should answer - not really. The sea, of course, has inspired good writers, but, as far as I know, not recently. Sailing: some novels, I have been told, but I don't know them. Tennis, certainly not. I think that the main reason is that mountaineering is *not* a sport. It is partly a sport, of course, but also it is much more. And it is not the sport itself, nor the technical aspects, which inspire a literature. It is all that is around: what is in the landscapes, and in the atmosphere, and in the past *and* in the minds of men. I try to look for that, use that. And if I wish to interest climbers, I wish also to interest readers who are foreign to the mountaineering world. When I succeed in doing that, I feel it is a real achievement.

*Since this talk was given, Samivel has died.

Cuillin Bivvi

by *Kevin Borman*

Gas hisses towards a dusk coffee.
The squat turret of Mhic Choinnich
darkens just north of
our tightrope sleeping platform.
Alasdair and Thearlaich
are black pinnacles south.
We haven't said much all day,
mostly just selected individual lines,
soaked up views, negotiated rock.

We talk briefly and sip hot liquid
in a quiet euphoria at being here.
In the west improbable
horizontal fireworks on The Minch,
slowly evolve like a sixties lightshow.
East, cloud drapes itself over Marsco
in a wild white banner.
Our finger ends sing
from the abrasion of gabbro.
Guessing progress, we hope for a clear dawn,
knowing we'll wake almost before we've slept,
to reach the Inn Pinn at six
before the crowds arrive.

We udge around, working towards
a best fit for alien human shapes
on the few grass blades here.
One bivvy in this place
is a fair reward for the average life.

You are cocooned in down, asleep, quite still.
I lie awake, not cold, not troubled by midges,
mulling over all the nuances
of our mountain days, our urban nights,
seventeen years
of compromising, arguing, settling,
reflecting, learning, laughing.
Finally, turning again to fit the gabbro,
the last thing I am aware of is
two trajectories, drifting,
parabolas into the future,
a little unsure of their destinations.

Boardman Tasker Memorial Award for Mountain Literature Chairman of the Judges' Speech

by Livia Gollancz

Good afternoon. My fellow judges, Ronnie Wathen and Harold Drasdo, join me in welcoming you, and we have decided that you should be told something about each of this year's submissions.

In reaching our decision we faced two main problems. In the first place I, as an ex-publisher, have a rather different view of books to that of my two colleagues, who are writers. Secondly, there was an immense variation in the type of book that was on offer. Of course, differences in our personal tastes led to lively argument and stimulating ideas; and I think I reflect my colleagues' view that the exercise was extremely enjoyable and interesting. Our thanks to Dorothy and Chris and all concerned.

Now, let me reiterate our brief: the book has to be published in the current year, with its central theme the mountain environment, and above all it must display literary merit. But here we ran into the problem of diversity. Most literary prizes are for books of a similar nature: we were confronted with six or seven different types of book - and I should say, right away, that we did not feel that any one of them was a flawless masterpiece. However, looking back at previous winners, few (if any) come into this category, and we thought that a number of this year's titles compared quite favourably with several of these previous winners.

As you know, we eventually decided on a shortlist of four books: those by (alphabetically) Brown & Mitchell, Curran, Diemberger and Fell.

Now I propose first to discuss those we did *not* put on the shortlist. Three of these books were very largely photographic; two of them, *The Secret Life of Snowdonia* by Michael Leach and *Eyes to the Hills* by Gordon Stainforth had texts that could not really be called 'full length', so we did not feel they should be seriously considered for a *literary* prize. I may say, though, that in all three the standard of photography is very high and Stainforth's is exceptionally so. Leach, in his book on Snowdonia, has contributed an excellent introduction to the ecology of one of our most important mountain regions. The third photographic book, *Wainwright's Favourite Lakeland Mountains* benefits from magnificent pictures taken by Derry Brabbs, but the text is personal and somewhat limited in scope, though it will give much pleasure to those many who have read Wainwright's other books or followed in his footsteps on the hills.

Another type of book we felt could be justly dismissed was Sonia Melchett's *Passionate Quests* - an account of five women's present-day adventurous lives, but only one of her subjects actually travelled in the mountains.

There were five autobiographical books, two of which are short-listed. Of the other three, all have points of great interest, but are uneven in their appeal. Reinhold Messner has written a great deal, and his *Free Spirit* does not add very much to he previous output except at the beginning when he is telling of his childhood and the early climbs he did with family and school friends. John Hawkridge's *Uphill all the Way* shows astonishing determination and an amazingly courageous tenacity of spirit in his conquest of physical disability, but only part of the book is relevant to the hills and to mountains as such. Andy Fanshawe's *Coming Through* deals largely with his Himalayan expeditions and will give much enjoyment to devotees of this genre, but the writing is uneven. However, the book is particularly notable in showing the development of a rather happy-go-lucky youthful climber into someone with a fully adult and responsible outlook and approach to mountains. Jim Perrin's essays *Yes, to Dance* represent yet another type of publication. From the literary point of view this is probably the most polished offering, and we had a good deal of discussion as to whether or not the rules of the Award would allow us to short-list it. But we decided that, as most of these pieces had already appeared in print in journals, it could not be said to be entirely published in the current year. But it is an important book, full of information, and ramming home its points, particularly in the section on conservation; it undoubtedly contains some of the best writing on offer this year.

And so to our shortlist. And here we have two extremely interesting and unusual autobiographical accounts, and two books unlike any others. To take them in alphabetical order, *A View from the Ridge* by Brown and Mitchell is a delightfully written series of anecdotes, somewhat nostalgic, of early working-class climbing in Scotland. It goes on to show Scottish climbers, later in life, sampling travels further afield but always returning to home ground. It is a beautiful celebration of Scottish hills told largely in witty dialogue, sometimes with a regional accent, and a completely natural gift for humour and poetry. Many of its protagonists must by now be very old, and the authors have done a grand job in capturing their memories for posterity.

Jim Curran's *Suspended Sentences*, comprising some remarkable pen portraits, is most amusing and entertaining, and is told in an engaging, self-deprecatory style. It outlines the author's life as a mountain and expedition photographer. It is a celebration both of his own experiences and of the personalities of his friends. I particularly liked the way he led up to the 1986 K2 tragedy and then charmingly excused himself, having, of course, already published a book-length account of it.

Kurt Diemberger's *The Endless Knot* is on an altogether more serious and memorable plane. He draws together two threads - that of his own attraction to K2, from his first viewing of the mountain when he was on Broad Peak as a young man, and that of his friendship and collaboration with Julie Tullis. He outlines their film-making expeditions over the years, and gives the reader a deep insight into Julie's personality that, under the circumstances, is most moving. He himself comes through as a simple, straightforward mountain man, and his account of the K2 affair will, I hope, lay this devastating tragedy finally to rest. The book is written with real craftsmanship, is well translated and is one that many people have been waiting for. They won't be disappointed.

Alison Fell's *Mer de Glace* is probably the first novel about climbers that sets out to be overtly post-modern. The plotting is somewhat obscure, the writing was described by one judge as beautifully poetic and by another as overly purple but it shows a romantic triangle situation that will strike to the hearts of many climbers. It is interesting in its observation of the climbing world from the outside, and, while some may complain that the book depends more on the delineation of an ageing relationship than on its mountain background, the story displays a basic truth that has a wide appeal.

Now, over the years, the popular view of a mountain book has become synonymous with the expedition book - or, at least, the mountain biography or autobiography. Of all the winners of the Boardman Tasker prize most have fallen into this category. This year we have sensed a change towards a broader type of mountain book - no poetry, but a great variety of literary styles and types of writing. Your judges applaud such a trend and wish to encourage it. We have therefore decided not to award the prize to one of the more traditional accounts - even though there is one of these that incorporates an emotional and exceptionally brave voice. We have therefore decided to divide the prize between *A View from the Ridge* and *Mer de Glace*. *A View from the Ridge* because it captures a slice of British climbing history just in time, before it might have been lost for ever; it is delightfully written and great fun to read and it is in the true tradition of good story-telling.

Quite different, but equally unusual, is *Mer de Glace*. Here is an author who puts a certain responsibility on the reader to decide on the exact details of her story, a novel within a novel, the blurred outlines of which seem to be deliberately vague; and yet it displays powerful images and a truth of feeling towards the mountains that will not fail to strike a chord. At times it may appear undisciplined, and at times its digressions may seem irrelevant, but it attempts to take mountain writing into a new form and could lead to some interesting and exciting developments in the future.

In only now remains for me again to thank Dorothy Boardman and the Committee for having invited me and my colleagues to take part in this fascinating exercise and to wish our winners all success in their future writing careers.

Kaçkar Mountains

by Ronnie Wathen

I'm humouring my new leather boots
Hammering hell out of the heavy brutes
I take them for a walk up the routes

Into the mountain towers and steeples
To break them in and to make them supple.
My boots are pleased with the boots of the couple

Danièle, Jean Michel with whom I'm trekking
Their boots ask do my boots leak
My boots ask do their boots squeak

When first made to kick rocks
By feet in thick smelly sox?
"And how do you feel about Nikwax

Smeared into your pores and airways?"
We love it they squeal but we blister the toes
Or the heels of feet according to sizes:

Undersizes we make 'em look really silly
Hobbling downhill in hilly
Country with their toes like jelly,

Oversizes we rub at the heel
Till the whole skin begins to peel
The torture they tell us is hell.

Twisting ankles because laces are loose
And kicking up dust are our other vices.
All six boots then started a race

Danièle's pair up front by a furlong
Mine in the middle stumbling along
Jean Michel's in the rear not feeling strong.

So we turned back within sight of the peaks
Towards which we'd travelled for weeks and weeks
In a boot that blisters and a boot that leaks.

Climbers, their Writing and History

by Paul Nunn

There are two stereotypical roles to be avoided in performing in this slot, if at all possible.

The first is what I might call the Jonathan Ross know-all role, typified in the shallows of Thatcherite culture by institutions like the Late Show, or for younger ravers by artier pop programmes from Manchester, reifying the Hacienda night club five years after it was interesting (Maria Coffey had left).

In this fast-moving and disintegrated post-modern existence, life passes so fast that a young, fast-talking and preferably fast-moving Michael Ignatieff or Sarah Dunant are needed to guide bemused consumers through the bewildering display of art, artefacts, mere products or toys that the popular media industry honks up for their gratification. In typical British deferential way a mentor of taste, ironical, even banally sarcastic, informed but bloated to excess by the variety, deigns to hint at the satisfactions to be obtained from the variety of climbing-related merchandise, whilst avoiding the slightest personal dishevelment. The presenter is the only REAL object of attention, a power and sex symbol projected by undemonstrated assumed knowledge onto the bemused and supposedly uninformed AUDIENCE. For audience most of us are, condescended to by these ruthless commodifiers. The commentator stands or falls by only one capacity in reality. Obliged to ease the pain of time passing by making us laugh, like the chapatti sellers on Indian stations who dispel the fatigue and heat of endless plains by regular refuelling for a rupee or two, so they manipulate our laughter as we swarm towards the grave. The sphinx-like solemnity of their powdered faces gives the lie to their clowning.

Climbing writing and history has its equivalent of this disintegrative process. Not least of the causes is the quantity of material produced, serving an enormous range of tastes and interests, among climbers and the broader public. At almost any time in the last thirty years it was possible to read material on climbing which made wildly differing demands of the reader. The range has always spanned from the intellectual posh to the utilitarian, as in simple guide-books.

The first collection of books on climbing I met belonged to an uncle. Stricken with polio in his youth he spent his later life as a member of the BBC Northern Light Orchestra in Manchester. As so often with disabled people, he thought nothing of a daily three-stage twenty-mile commute to work, in both directions. A shelf in his front room contained accounts of the early Everest attempts and the recent 1953 success jostled with Scott and Shackleton. From there I graduated to Macclesfield Public Library, the blue guide-book to Kinder and the Roaches and, almost at a stroke at fifteen, Herman Buhl. It seemed beyond practicality that I would ever see Nanga Parbat, but it was from Buhl that I first heard the lines from Hans Hartmann, who had died in the 1930s on that mountain:

Though the frost be fierce and the pain be dire,
My oath shall be my burning fire.

The English edition of Buhl's book *Nanga Parbat Pilgrimage*, translated by Hugh Merrick, was probably the strongest single influence on an adolescent consciousness, and I think not mine alone. Published in 1956 it circulated before Buhl's ascent of Broad Peak with Kurt Diemburger, and death in the same year on Chogolisa. Indications of its influence include the frequency of British visits to the Kaisergebirge, Wetterstein, Karwendel, Berchtesgardener Alps, Dolomites and Bregaglia in the early to mid-1960s, and the death of a sixth former and his girlfriend in the Karwendel from my Manchester school while I was in the fourth form. Buhl's book, and our experience, was to make some of us adherents of *Alpinismus* in the early 1960s, while the ethos of the SUMC or Alpha Club was probably nearer München than London.

One shock of disillusion in early adolescent climbing at the Roaches was the realisation that Sir Philip Brocklehurst, who had paid Shackleton £1000 to join the Nimrod, was the landowner who had the place keepered. It did not seem to help him understand our desire to scramble on his magical red rocks. There was even the blasphemy of a new ugly Texas barbed wire fence for a time.

A literature ought to function. In the rich diet of the late 1950s, Noyce's writing was peculiarly important to many. *Snowdon Biography* bridged from the world of Brown and Whillans to crinkly but articulate Oxbridge. As a book, it is demanding upon youthful patience, but for me it summed up the divided pre-1959 North Welsh World.

Of course that division was an artefact, based upon class lines that were in part already a comforting fiction. Joe Brown had stood with George Band atop Kangchenjunga in 1955, and was undisputed Grand Master of the climbing world.

There was an element of anglo-centricity in this view, but few disputed it in the English-speaking firmament.

For climbing writing there were some important implications of artisanal mastery. Scribes or photographers were secondary to action, throughout the 1960s. Climbing culture was extroverted but primarily oral. Though Pete Crew ghosted Joe Brown's autobiography, he had to do it quietly on Sunday evenings.

The early BBC Outside Broadcasts, Llithrig on Cloggy in the rain with Robert Paragot, and at Anglesey, projected action and monosyllabic dialogue to a fascinated yet uncomprehending public. MacNaught Davis and Chris Brasher's voices relaunched the "uman fly' in accents which the BBC could understand, and the telephenomenon persisted until our times, including 'Old Man of Hoy 1 & 2' in 1967 and 1984. The first, following upon the Eiger direct in 1966, projected a particular view of climbing on the public, and helped launch Chris Bonington into the big time, as well as airing that magnificent wit and climber Tom Patey to a wider audience. The second was really a reiteration of Brown's longevity as the symbolic baron of British climbers, the happy rubber-legged hero still swarming over overhangs and now accompanied by Zoe, an equally lively and idiosyncratic daughter.

In that era, books about climbing were fewer. John Hunt's *Ascent of Everest*; Wilfrid Noyce's *South Col*; Houston and Bates' *K2 The Savage Mountain*, were probably among the most popular. Expeditioning appealed in a world of decolonization where a passage to India still involved ships..

An important addition was Ralph Barker's *The Last Blue Mountain* in 1959. Its account of death and disaster on Haramosh worked against Noyce's romanticism. The latter mentality rubbed off more readily with the general public than with the climbers.. It was at the same time deeply chilling, a sort of black shiver, for those enraptured by big mountains. Barker brought home to enthusiasts like me the likely consequences of our fixation.

Many times during the past few weeks each member of the party had asked himself whether the expedition had been worthwhile. Now they had their answer. It was worth coming all this way and enduring all the discomforts and privations for this view alone. And there were many, many other compensations. They sat there chewing chocolate, relaxed and happy, all their difficulties forgotten, laughing at former strains, a team as never before. For some weeks now, these men had been shedding something of their individualism, pooling their resources, drawing strength from each other, becoming a team...

Throughout August they had each kept a personal diary. But in the first few days of September, one by one they had stopped writing, all within two or three days of each other. It was as though they could no longer keep secrets, no longer express themselves except together.

Emery roped up with Jillott, and the two men prepared to move off. It was in keeping with their mood of elation that they should want to reach just one more dominant point before going down...

Emery was taking a particularly firm belay with the cornice in mind, and Jillott had covered the last few yards to the pinnacle and had almost reached the point at which he was going to stop, when there was a muffled explosion which seemed to come from under their feet, followed by a crunching tearing sound, and almost simultaneously the snow on which Jillott and Emery were standing began to move.

For a fraction of a second it seemed to Streather and Culbert that the two climbers were simply playing about; their first reaction was to laugh at the comical way in which they were throwing their arms and legs about, jerkily, like puppets, their weight not properly planted on the ground. But in the same instant they understood the awful significance of the muffled explosion, the tearing sound and the tell-tale crack in the snow a few feet above Jillott. They stood like statues, dumbfounded, fearful to move lest the avalanche spread, horrified by the ghastly sight of their two comrades being swept helplessly past them with sudden and terrifying acceleration, down the convex slope and away out of sight.

Eventually Streather moved across to the point of the avalanche... From here he was able to look down the slope into the snow basin below. .. [Flurries of powder snow were still settling, but as he looked he thought he detected...] *movement. Then to his astonishment and joy, he saw a figure moving about in the snow...*

He watched incredulously, as Jillott seemed to bend over and dig his hands in the snow; soon like a chicken hatching from an egg, another figure broke out of the snow... By some miracle both climbers had survived the fall.

This miraculous escape paved the way for the worse fate that was later to afflict the party. The Last Blue Mountain was tragedy in the true sense, raising the reader's emotion and hope then dashing them in pathos. Is this merely another adventure story? I think not, for it seems to me to meet literary criteria of competence and to far transcend mere entertainment. Would that the same could be said of all that has followed. Not that all since is dross, but it, and a few others of its ilk, were a hard act to follow.

In truth few tried to do so, for a long time.

In the 1960s the honest John wrote guide-books to crags as an adjunct to climbing. Even this had to be undertaken with modesty and decorum, and subjected to the debates of various collectives in the Peak and elsewhere. Crew and Collomb did their own thing in Wales, and John Wilkinson ably remodelled the Lakes guides with a very talented bunch of writers. In Scotland nothing much happened for a long time. Robin Smith's promise was cut off, in the Pamirs with Wilfrid Noyce, two great literary talents in one fall.

Photographers were mercenaries and not to be trusted in the 1960s. They tried to immortalise honest climbers with broken backs, selling their snaps to the Daily Express. Newspapermen too were abhorred as vermin. They seemed only to pry into sensational horrors like the multiple deaths on Mont Blanc in 1966. Only a few penurious climbers, like Chris Bonington or Don Whillans, seriously considered exploiting the media rather than being their victim. Rockclimbing and mountaineering offered a continuum of danger prior to the improvements of protection - deaths on crags were not numerous, but were probably disproportionate to the small number of climbers active. There was an introversion about this social world which sought to avoid exhibitionism for public titillation except on our own terms. Somewhere beneath the surface there lurked fear of divine retribution upon those who flaunted themselves. By self-definition they became inauthentic. The only people who seemed to revel in publicity were the increasingly specialised and often bumbling 'boy scouts' of the rescue.

There were notable exceptions to the refusenik view. John Cleare's *Rock Climbers in Action in Snowdonia* was widely acclaimed as combining innovatory pictures and a thoughtful text. It became a model which most imitators have miserably failed to emulate. Some did the photographic spade work, like Bob Keates in the Peak, but moved on before the work could be finalised. Ken Wilson's monumental *Hard Rock* (1975) and its later brethren, *Classic Rock, Cold Climbs* and *Extreme Rock*, occupied the photographic Chronicle of climbing in Britain with an unsurpassed authority for more than a decade, an extension of the sheer power of *Mountain* magazine 1969 - 1979. This hegemony conditioned the thinking of a generation, adopting a sharply moralist tone in evaluating world climbing development and squeezing out from below it more or less radical small magazines of which *Rocksport, Crags* and *On the Edge* are the best examples in Britain. These have tended to be the vehicle for a pursuit of supposed modernity in each generation of climbers which has been blithely unaware of the post-modern condition and thus occasionally looked like re-inventing the wheel. Similar innocence has been characteristic of much of the recent bolt debate...

Mountain retains the role, more difficult amidst post-modern fragmentation and cynicism, of the magazine of record, alongside the major annual journals, amidst a pretty froth of British and external ephemera.

Since the 1960s there has been a huge outpouring of books, articles and films about climbing. They range from the honest blow-by-blow chronicles, like *Sacred Summits* by Pete Boardman or *Savage Arena* by Joe Tasker, rich in insights yet essentially expedition accounts, via standard expedition books like Chris Bonington's *Everest South-West Face*, which are essential to the economics of expeditions (every Barclays Bank Person had to have one, and their mothers, fathers, uncles, aunts etc.) to the experiments and poetry of Ed Drummond, David Craig and their ilk.

In reality all these works perhaps ought to find their level amidst literature in general, rather than remaining in the swaddling clothes of a particular sub-culture. Joe Simpson's *Touching the Void* did that, but it remains a rare occurrence.

Yet this is one of the criteria inescapable for climbing writing like all other.

Such niceties are lost at times amidst the avalanche of 1980s publishing in Britain. Here I am at risk of falling into the alternative stereotype, to that which I sought to evade at the beginning. This is the equally obnoxious role of the great panjandrum, the eminent Victorian so pilloried by Lytton Strachey and ubiquitous personality and bore. Climbing writing has always had some of these, from Virginia Wolff's father Leslie Stephen, whose Playground of Europe was bible to many early twentieth-century alpinists, via Winthrop Young, to Bonington himself.

Nevertheless it is necessary after twenty-odd years of writing and reviewing to reveal an opinion or two. In my view recent times have seen a sad failure of many publishers to maintain their own critical standards or even, some might say, their sanity, resulting in an outpouring of poor counterfeits of books, unthought, unwritten and unedited. These should be well on the way to the dustbin of history already, and others of their ilk, and sadly even some better, will follow in the present slump. That is no bad thing, as there were signs of 'bad money' driving out 'good'.

This suggests to me that future books will need to be prepared to higher standards by authors and produced more carefully by editors and their employers. This is a tall order, when costs remain high and expectations of the reading public likewise. No amount of word processing or speed of production will compensate for quality of thought and adequacy of language in this process.

There are some stirrings of imaginative writing of both fiction and memoirs, no matter how disguised, with A View from the Ridge, a good example of thoughtful use of the latter, and Dermot Somers' work of the former. More thought about what a good adventure book might contain is also needed, to ensure that the formula including photo copy of Everest South-West Face gear list does not bore us all to death. There seems little reason to assume that good writing about large scale ambitious mountaineering will not remain at the centre of the stage. The extreme effort and concentration involved in success or involvement at this level is likely to produce the commitment to write well too, among at least some of its activists. Everything in the innovative tradition of British climbing and its writing supports this view, from Leslie Stephen to Stephen Venables.

Meanwhile, at the poetry and experiment level, there is little to fear, for there it seems to me there is confidence, experiment and involvement greater than in the recent past, though there is too much inhibition about pushing it into the daylight. Only a 'Little Englander' lack of confidence has induced the occasional exaggeration of the value of this cultural form to the exclusion of others. Such volkischness should not be allowed to detract in judging the undoubted interest and quality of much of this, from Menlove Edwards to aspects of Ed Drummond and his successors in poetic vein, or Tom Patey and others in prose. Done well these transcend the restrictive confines of any pretended English canon, and of stifling 'Englishness' in itself.

A Hymn to Harnesses

by Dennis Gray

Last night I got to thinking seriously about harnesses,
something I had never really dared to do previously.
I wondered why are they now so colourful and erotic,
who develops them and how are they named and
tested?
Presumably Mr Pat Littlejohn fell an awful long way,
and Don Whillans suffered gelding to test their
designs?
But how did those responsible produce The Black
Master,
by belay bondage using whips, steel chains and
leather?
I suppose the Alpinist was developed out in the Alps,
and the Competition in some UIAA organised
contests?
Is the Technician the brainchild of an outstanding
jammer,
or the Freestyle by some climber who fell off all alone?
The longer I sat and looked at my equipment
catalogues,
the more I began to wonder and worry about these
matters.
Who named The Bod, and why is the 'X' such a dark
mystery,
is it for illiterate beginners or star-struck lovers?
The Venus I read is only meant to be used by ladies,
presumably because it holds things up instead of

down?
The Canyon is intended solely for the caving fraternity,
for which I feel a more appropriate name could be a Trog?
But what are we intended to make of the Salto, Vario and Koala?
The latter I know to be a furry tailless arboreal marsupial.
We used to say in the days when you tied on the rope direct,
"You can always tell a good climber by the state of his hands!"
But in my bed last night unable to sleep thinking harnesses,
I suddenly realised these might be the new badges of merit?
An old and revered climber will now equip himself with a Guru,
a sprog buy a Cadet, and an overactive activist obtain a Dynamo.
But who is supposed to wear a harness with a name like Aero,
or even more of a puzzle are the Vario, Oxygen and Super Belt?
Presumably out on the outcrops and crags of Great Britain,
are a whole host of climbers wearing their models with pride?
However I will definitely avoid those sporting The Gunfighter,
but snigger at anyone I see encased in an Air Time Hangdog!
I will doff my cap if I should meet a jock in a Hone

Master,
or a lady wearing a Sky Pilot or the fantastic, futuristic
9a.
Oh God it is all just too much and I cannot take any
more,
perhaps tonight I'll go home and look at my
catalogues again?
And come to think of it rock boots might now be just
as erotic,
for are not the feet where the libido is most easily
located?
A whole new problem awaits attention in the form of
stickies,
for is there a secret link between the harness and rock
shoes?
Is there a correlation between the type used and their
owners,
can an Eagle happily wear a pair of Megas, Run Outs
or Aces?
I do not know yet whether such liberties of style are
possible,
and to come up with an answer will mean doing more
research.
I shall have to send away for yet more colourful
catalogues,
and suffer further sleepless nights before I can be
certain.

Avoiding the Touch

by Moira Viggers

He didn't have to cut me off like that... I'd never have hurt him. I loved him. I still do.

You know what it's like when you're young - all the dreams and plans you have for the future. I always knew I'd be with a climber, but I saw myself on sun-soaked rock with some muscular lad, flashing E7s; or possibly someone older, a father figure, not so hard, but with a wealth of experience of rock. An adventurer? An Alpinist perhaps? I didn't want to grow old, left on the shelf - I wanted to stretch myself - to live life to the full.

There I was, hanging out in Joe Brown's shop the way I usually did when he walked in. I think it was love at first sight. He wasn't a hard man, or a respected figure, but he was tall and blonde, and I'm sure he felt the same way about me as I did about him, because after he'd picked me up we went straight down to Pete's Eats. I think he wanted to show me off to his friends - well, though I say it myself, I was pretty good-looking in those days. Of course, I was younger then - bright and wilful, but I guess he found me easy enough to handle.

We went climbing that first day together, and when he fell, and I held him, I knew that I'd discovered what I was made for. We were blessed with sun in the Pass, but even had it rained I know it would have been the same. And after we had finished climbing, the way he touched and caressed me... I knew this was a partnership that would last a lifetime.

Of course, it wasn't all sweetness and light. I wasn't the only one in his life. I can't pretend I wasn't jealous when he went out without me, or that he was overly tolerant of my tangled lifestyle, but as the months went by we became closer. I knew he felt safe with me, and I felt tied to him, safe, secure.

I can remember when the idea of the trip to the Andes was first mooted. We'd lived together from the start, and his friend was visiting for the weekend. It was the first time I'd met him, and the three of us went out to Stanage and climbed together. They started talking about a lightweight trip and what an adventure it would be. One thing led to another and it was practically decided then and there that we would all go to the Andes. We got together many times over the next few months and spent long hours sitting by the fire, talking and planning. One night his friend told us of an epic he'd had in the Alps when his bivouac ledge collapsed, leaving him hanging in space, convinced he was going to die. I shuddered when I heard this, and prayed nothing like that would happen to us in the Andes.

I'd been to the Alps with him before, but this was a different ball-game. However, I'd have followed him to the ends of the earth if he'd asked, and I knew the two of them would look after me, and that I could play a part in the expedition. The only thing that rankled a bit was that I never had a chance to be involved in the decision-making, that somehow I was being used. But just to be there with him was enough, and I soon got used to my supporting role.

Siula Grande was indescribably beautiful, and when we established Base Camp the enormity of it all finally sank in. I'd never been to such a big mountain. I was knotted with fear, and yet I couldn't wait to get started. I was so proud to be part of their team - I guess I could have stayed at Base Camp with their trekking friend, but I knew they both wanted me along, and trusted my abilities.

I expect you may know what happened on the mountain. We made it to the summit, but the snow was soft and climbing was a nightmare. Just as we started down, part of a cornice collapsed, taking us by surprise. It happened in an instant, but his friend was quick enough to hold the two of us. This shocked me to the core - one slack moment and I'd nearly lost him.

My relief was short-lived - worse was to follow. His friend was climbing down an ice cliff when his axes lost their grip, and he fell, landing heavily on a ramp below, breaking his leg. It was me that held him, you know; it was me that saved him. With hindsight, I wonder if I'd have been better to let him go, but at the time it never even crossed my mind - I'm just not made like that.

What can I tell you about the descent? We've all had our epics, but this was the most serious situation I'd ever been in. His friend was in agony as we lowered him, pitch by pitch, down the face. A storm had set in by now, and I was stiff with cold, but I was still functioning, still remembering that they trusted me to keep them safe. Ironically, it was now that I realised, in a blinding flash of jealousy, that whatever he felt for me, the bond he had with his friend was infinitely stronger.

We'd been doing so well, and then he lowered us over a deep crevasse. There was no way back. His friend was hanging free, half unconscious with cold and pain. I knew the weight would be pulling at the belay, that he would be wrenched from his seat, into oblivion. I felt pulled between the two of them - I didn't want to hurt either of them, but I knew where my loyalty lay. I'd just about decided that I'd let his friend drop, when he got out the knife. I couldn't believe he'd cut me off like that... I'd never have hurt him. I loved him.

That night in the crevasse his friend cried. I wished I could have wept too. We coiled around each other, for warmth, for comfort, but my tears would not come. There was only one thing left to do. I had to help his friend back to the world, back to him. Perhaps then he would at least remember me with affection.

I know his friend was abseiling to die as we went down into the crevasse, but once he hit the snow platform I held him as he crawled up to a slot in the crevasse. I don't think there was much I could have done to save him, but psychologically I was important. And then he was out, and I was alone.

His friend wrote a book you know. A best-seller I'm told. Me? I'm still in the Andes. I came out of the bottom of the crevasse, and an old man took me in. I help him now with the loads on his llama, but sometimes I look back at the mountains, into the past, and recoil from his rough, thoughtless hands, avoiding the touch...

He didn't have to cut me off like that... that's no way to treat a good rope.

Borrowdale Evolution

by Terry Gifford

And when they turned at last
In the Jaws of Borrowdale and cried
"After the whale, Save the Saxifrage!"
The fenced paths were white stairways
Onto purple fells fertilised for perfection,
Climbing crags were chalk polished
And made safe with BMC bolts,

Fields farmed rare species
Of nearly lost sheep behind
Electric fences sheathed
In Leisure Park green.

And in the Leisure Park office
After many meetings,
Consternations of conferences,
The committee came up with
The Borrowdale Crag Plan:

Upper Falcon Crag to the ornithological interest,
Beth's Buttress to the botanist, refurbishing the ferns,
Castle Crag to the photographer - National View 5003,
Nitting Haws to the scrambler whose guidebook made history,
Shepherd's Crag to the climber who has coughed up the fee.

Now the climber with her National Certificate
Never envies the ornithologist his Borrowdale permit,

And the windsurfer displaying her Derwentwater Disc
Never speaks to the botanist with his SSSIC.
But sometimes a walker with Self-leadership Grade 3
Applies for a day on the Ecological Trail
In triplicate, for next year, if the geiger count is clear.

Hanging by a Thread

by David Craig

Briefly a spotlight shines on Gimmer, making
The wall below the overlap on Springbank
Warm almost hospitably. It moves on, glows
On the salad-green of hayfields newly tedded
Down-dale from Stool End - climbs the skirt of Crinkle,
Making the scree speckle like Donegal tweed.
Shorn Herdwick ewes have moved up here already
With their black lambs - agile as goats they browse
From one precarious blaeberry ledge to another,
Cleansed of their lowland panic, ignoring us.

Our goal is the North Buttress of Bow Fell.
Terra incognita. That must be Flat Crag,
Striped like great bolts of corduroy turned to stone.
There is *the* Buttress, its laid-back prow
Dwarfing the gaggle of climbers at its toe.
There's nothing else but a scrappy, flaked-out cliff,
Darkling as mussels in a tidal pool.
We climb a little further, a little further -
It gets to its feet, an ogre standing up -
Its trunk is armed - its forehead rears to a notch
Sharp as the Needle above the Shelter Stone.

It wasn't so daft to find the crag elusive.
Only raven and peregrine knew its crannies
Until one day in the early 1950s,
When they were climbing The Plaque Route on the
Buttress,
Don Hopkin remarked to Peter Greenwood,

"That crag over the way - there must be something
Goes up there," a d Dolphin came to help them,
Half a century after Craig and Shaw
Had played their tune all up and down the Buttress
And thousands followed. Now it's Craig and Crawshaw
Eyeing the height where Damocles hung his sword.

Greenish chunks and blades as rough as pumice,
Padded with blaeberry and dewy grasses,
Defend the base of the scarp. Pad up those valleys
Blank-jointed like the armour of Lochnagar,
Sink fingers in roots, pull onto an alp
Whose headwall is a twenty-foot curved rim -
Grasp that, set edge to tiny ledge, trust forearms
To the black mouth above, it's cold and smooth
As a crawl in the gut of Gaping Ghyll - reverse
And jump back down - ram in a hulking Hex,
Haul up and monkey, grow suckers on your feet,
Stride way-way rightward to a scoured green gutter -
Too far, too far - what now? - sink head and shoulder
Like a badger bolting into its sett,
Palm yourself upward, making it be a mantel,
It is, lunge over gasping like a fish
Onto the ladder of scree behind a pinnacle,
Plant feet in the mass of gungy tussocks stranded
By floods from the upper reaches. Bring Rob up.

He checks nuts, borrows quick-draws, rises neatly
On little steps, wires a crack on the left,
Turns his left leg into a telescope
And does the splits in mid-air, planting wires
Like a prodigal matador, arrives
At the 'semi-hand-traverse' (so what *do* you use,
Hands, knees, boomps-a-daisy?), spans the space
Tense as a flying buttress, swings through air
(Gripping on what?), and homes on a little eyrie.

I reach the semi-Thing, I pull up hard,
Nothing above for godsake, sink back down,
Fit extra joints to the leg, stretch out, it barely
Touches the opposite wal¹ - "Little hold *there*,"
Commandment from on high, I am clay, I obey,
This jug is heavensent, it's sharp, I rise
Onto a slope of stone bleached white by downpours -
Which the tip of the Sword must nearly have touched
Until in the Eighties, on a winter day,
The battered Buttress wearied, weakened its grip,
And the blade of its weapon crunched down into the
scrapyard.

Everything narrows here. Your toes have pointed
To a kind of claw. Your eyes are focused slits
For estimating distance. Words are sharp
And imperative, your mind a skeleton key
For easing into the wards of the vertical.

Fit feet into crevices next to blades
(Miniatures of the Sword), pinch edges, balance up
To where the hilt stemmed from the mother-rock,
Finger the rim of a shield and scrabble into
The whitish-greenish scabbard - there must be
Some crack - it's closed as the joints in an Inca wall -
Brace yourself in a bridge and think *think* THINK,
Key fingers into the neuk above the shield,
Mould thigh and buttock to the scabbard, udge
With the last gasp of faith-and-friction, rise
(Waiting for toes to skid) and cling those flakes -
Horrors, no points - reach-up-and-fall/*don't*-reach-
Stay-here-forever - make yourself six feet tall,
Expand those rubber tendons, the rock is budging
Slowly-slowly downward past your eyeballs,
The Crawshaw feet are jutting over the eave
Like beaks of fledglings peering out of a nest

Of ropes and trousers - no room to perch or swap,
Go with the flow, make for the guillotine-blade
On the wall of the channel where a jammed old Friend
Signals a possibility, grip its edge,
It's fine as ice, clip Friend, curl fingers round the -
Round nowt, the crack has closed, now I am done for,
Can't downclimb this, elasticate that arm
Three - six - nine inches, ahhh, the beloved crack
Is opening, it's staying open, it's magnetising
Hands to rock firm as a magnet's keeper.
"Jugs!" I yell and Rob hears only the cry,
None of its meaning, braces himself for a plummet -
All's upward now, fine edges carve the air
Sheer as the arrowing wings of a peregrine.
Yank an original Moac into a crack
(Last rite to placate the falling of the Sword),
Lay-away in a levitation so turned-on,
So happy that there's time to cruise, to want
All this to happen in slow-motion, in minutes
Not flashing seconds, even to go back down
And do it all (blade, scabbard, and hilt) again.

Answers to 'A Quotes Quiz'

A   Herman Buhl (*Nanga Parbat Pilgrimage*, 1956)
B   R.L.G. Irving (*The Romance of Mountaineering*, 1935)
C   Lindley Henshaw (writing about the first ascent of Pigott's Climb in the *Rucksack Club Journal*) c. 1928.
D   J. Menlove Edwards (Lliwedd, 1946)
E   Graham West (*Rock Climbs on the Mountain Limestone of Derbyshire* 1961)
F   Maurice Herzog (*Annapurna*, 1951)
G   Peter Boardman (*Sacred Summits*, 1982)
H   Jim Perrin (*Climbers' Club Journal*, 1976)
I   Edward Whymper (*Scrambles Amongst the Alps*, various editions)

Letter to *Crags*   Gary Gibson, *Crags* No. 20, Aug/Sep.1979

BIBLIOGRAPHY

Where we have been able to trace them, first publication dates are given.

Accident à la Meije by Etienne Bruhl. France 1946. Susse (Paris)

Aconcagua: South Face (see **Victoire sur l'Aconcagua**)

Adventure of the Misplaced Eyeglasses, The by Robin Campbell. UK 1979. *Scottish Mountaineering Club Journal*

Against Looting by David Craig. UK 1987. Littlewood Arc (Todmorden, Lancashire)

Alpe, L' Homicide by Paul Hervieu. France 1903. Lemerre (Paris)

Alpine Byways; or Light Leaves gathered in 1859 and 1860 by A Lady (Mrs. H. Freshfield). UK 1861 (London)

Alpinistes, Les by Yves Ballu. France 1984. Arthaud (Paris)

Amateur d'abîmes, L' by Samivel (Paul Gayet-Tancrède). France 1940. Stock (Paris)

Angels of Light by Jeff Long. US 1987. Beech Tree Books/William Morrow (New York)

Annapurna, a Woman's Place by Arlene Blum. US 1980. Sierra Club (San Franacisco). UK 1981. Granada (London) - softback edition

Annapurna: Conquest of the first 8000-metre peak by Maurice Herzog see **Annapurna Premier 8000**

Annapurna Premier 8000 by Maurice Herzog. France 1951. Arthaud (Paris). UK 1952 as *Annapurna: Conquest of the first 8000-metre peak*. Translated from the French by Nea Morin and Janet Adam Smith. Cape (London). US 1953. Dutton (New York)

Ascent edited by Allen Steck and Steve Roper. US/UK 1989. Sierra Club Books (San Francisco)/Diadem (London)

Ascent of Everest, The by John Hunt. UK 1953. Hodder (London). US 1954 as *Conquest of Everest*. Dutton (New York)

At the Rising of the Moon by Dermot Somers. UK 1994. Baton Wicks (London)

Au-delà de la verticale by Georges Livanos. France 1958. Arthaud (Grenoble)

Auberge, L' short story by Guy de Maupassant. France 1887 collected in *Le Horla*. UK 1896. *The Strand Magazine Vol. XI* and collected as *The Inn* in *The Mountain Inn and Other Stories* and in *A Treasury of Mountaineering Stories*, and as *Ulrich the Guide* in *One Step in the Clouds*

Backing Off by Dave Roberts. US 1976. *Climbing* Jan/Feb

Best New SF2 edited by Gardner Dozois. UK 1988. Robinson Publishing (London)

Beyond the Mountain by Elizabeth Arthur. US 1983. Harper Row (New York)

Borders of the Impossible: from the Alps to Annapurna by Lionel Terray see **Les Conquérants de l'inutile**

Bronx Plumber, The by Guy Waterman. US 1976. *Off Belay* October and collected in *One Step in the Clouds*

Camp Six by Frank Sydney Smythe. UK 1937. Hodder (London)

Case of the Great Grey Man, The by Robin Campbell. UK 1986. *Scottish Mountaineering Club Journal* and collected in *One Step in the Clouds*

Ce Monde qui n'est pas le nôtre by Robert Tézenas du Montcel. France 1965. Gallimard (Paris)

Chaos. Making a New Science by James Gleick. UK 1988. Heinemann (London)

Classic Rock by Ken Wilson. UK 1978. Granada (London)

Climber's Fireside Book, The compiled by Cuthbert Wilfrid Frank Noyce. UK 1964. Heinemann (London)

Climbers by M. John Harrison. UK 1989. Gollancz (London)

Cold Climbs by Ken Wilson et al. UK 1983. Diadem (London)

Collector, The by Anne Sauvy. France 1982. Editions Montalba (Paris). Collected as *Le Collectionneur* in *Les Flammes de Pierre* and *Le Jeu de la montagne et du hasard*. US/UK 1989. *Ascent*. Translated from the French by Franco Gaudiano.

Conquérants de l'inutile, Les by Lionel Terray. France 1961. Gallimard (Paris). UK 1963 as *Conquistadors of the Useless* (translated from the French by Geoffrey Sutton). Gollancz (London). US 1964 as *Borders of the Impossible: from the Alps to Annapurna*. Doubleday (New York)

Conquistadors of the Useless see Conquérants de l'inutile, Les

Contes à pic by Samivel (Paul Gayet-Tancrède). France 1951. Arthaud (Grenoble)

Contes des brillantes montagnes avant la nuit by Samivel (Paul Gayet-Tancrède). France 1980. Arthaud (Paris)

Déva by Michael Tobias. US 1982. Avant Books (San Diego)

Don Quixote by Miguel Cervantes see *Ingenioso Hidalgo Don Quixote de la Mancha, El*

Doubt by Les Ellison. US 1983. *Climbing 79*

Dream of White Horses, A by Ed Drummond. UK 1987. Diadem Books (London)

Du sang sur la neige by Georges Casella. Switzerland 1918. Payot (Lausanne)

E5 6b First performed in 1989 by the Cragrats at the Gracemount Leisure Centre, nr Edinburgh

E5 6c Performed in part at the International Festival of Mountaineering Literature 1990 and in part also at the British Mountaineering Council Buxton Conference 1991

Egyptian Book of the Dead translated from the Egyptian by Thomas George Allen and prepared for publication by Elizabeth Blaisdell Hauser. US/UK 1974. University of Chicago Press (Chicago: London)

Elusive Summits. Four Expeditions in the Karakoram by Victor Saunders. UK 1990. Hodder & Stoughton (London)

Endless Knot, The: K2, Mountain of Dreams and Destiny by Kurt Diemberger. UK 1991. Grafton (London)

Etoiles et Tempêtes by Gaston Rébuffat. France 1954. Arthaud (Paris)

Everest - Kangshung Face by Stephen Venables. UK 1989. Hodder & Stoughton (London)

Everest South-West Face by Christian John Storey Bonington. UK 1973. Hodder (London). US 1973 as *The Ultimate Challenge*. Stein & Day (New York)

Everest the Hard Way by Christian John Storey Bonington. UK 1976. Hodder (London). US 1976. Random House (New York)

Expeditions and Explorations by Nigel Gifford. UK 1983. Macmillan (London)

Extreme Rock compiled by Ken Wilson and Bernard Newman. UK 1987. Diadem (London)

Eyes to the Hills by Gordon Stainforth. UK 1991. Constable & Co. (London)

Face, The by Al Churcher UK 1987 in *Mountain* 117 (Sept/Oct issue)

Fall, The by Albert Camus France 1956 (published as *La Chute*). UK 1957. Hamish

Hamilton Ltd. (London) and collected in *The Collected Fiction of Albert Camus,* Hamish Hamilton (London) 1960

Falling by Colin Thubron. UK 1989. Heinemann (London)

Faustus, Dr. see **Tragicall History of the horrible life and death of Doctor Faustus, The**

First on the Rope by Roger Frison-Roche see **Premier de Cordée**

Flammes de Pierre, Les by Anne Sauvy. France 1982. Editions Montalba (Paris). UK 1991. Diadem Books (London)

For Everything Its Season by John Long. US 1989. *Rock and Ice* 31 and collected in *One Step in the Clouds*

Fou d'Edenberg, Le by Samivel (Paul Gayet-Tancrède). France 1967. Albin Michel (Paris)

Fourche, La by Anne Sauvy. France 1982. Collected in *Les Flammes de Pierre.* UK 1985 in *The Alpine Journal* and collected in *One Step in the Clouds.* Translated from the French by Jane Taylor.

Free Fall by William Golding. UK 1959. Faber & Faber (London)

Free Spirit - A Climber's Life by Reinhold Messner. UK 1991. Hodder & Stoughton (London). Translated from the German by Jill Neate

Games Climbers Play, The edited by Ken Wilson. UK/US 1978. Diadem (London)/Sierra Club Books (San Francisco)

Gearfreak Caper, The by Guy Waterman. US 1976 (by Rex Slim) from *Off Belay* and collected in *This Climbing Game*

Give me the Hills by Miriam Underhill. UK 1956. Methuen (London). US 1971. Chatham Press in association with Appalachian Mountain Club (Riverside, Colorado) - enlarged edition, adding a final chapter and many more illustrations

Grand Crevasse see **Grand Crevasse, La**

Grande Crevasse, La by Roger Frison-Roche. France 1948. Editions Arthaud (Grenoble and Paris). US 1951 as *Grand Crevasse.* UK 1952 as *Last Crevasse* translated from the French by Janet Adam Smith and Nea Morin. Methuen (London)

Great VS Climbs of the Lake District by Tim Noble. UK 1989. David & Charles (Newton Abbot)

Greatest Climber in the World, The by Bernard Amy. UK 1978. *Mountain* 24 and collected in *The Games Climbers Play.* Translated from the French by Beverley Davitt

Green Mars by Kim Stanley Robinson. US 1988. Tor Books (New York) in *Tor Double* paired with Arthur C. Clarke's *A Meeting with Medusa*

Guide (book about Pierre Leroux) by Anne Sauvy. France 1989. Arthaud (Paris)

Guys and Dolls (short stories) by Damon Runyon. UK 1932. Jarrolds (London)

Hard Option by Gwen Moffat. UK 1975. Gollancz (London)

Hard Rock by Ken Wilson with ed. assistance from Mike and Lucy Pearson. UK 1974. Hart-Davis, MacGibbon (London)

Headwall by Tim Ahern. US 1989 in *Ascent.* Sierra Club Books (San Francisco)

Her Two Doors Up by Dave Gregory. Hitherto unpublished

Here and There Among the Alps by Hon. Frederica Louisa Edith Plunket. UK 1875. (London)

High Alps in the Winter, The by Mrs. Fred (Elizabeth Alice Frances) Burnaby. UK 1883. Sampson Low & Co. (London)

Hollow Men, The by Thomas Stearns Eliot. US 1925. Can be found in *T.S. Eliot - Selected Poems.* UK 1954. Faber and Faber (London)

Horla, Le by Guy de Maupassant. France 1887.
Ice Chimney, The by Barry Collins. UK 1990 collected in *One Step in the Clouds*. Diadem (London). First presented by The Lyric Studio Theatre at the Traverse Theatre Club, Edinburgh on 19 August 1980. First broadcast on BBC Radio 3 in 1982.
Impressions de voyage en Suisse by Alexandre Dumas. France 1837 (1st edition). 2nd edition 1838 Dumont (Paris)
In Another Tongue by Greg Child. US 1988. *Climbing* 110 and collected in *One Step in the Clouds*
Indian Alps and How we Crossed them, The, being a narrative of two years' residence in the Eastern Himalaya and two months' tour into the interior by A Lady Pioneer. UK 1876. (London)
Ingenioso Hidalgo Don Quixote de la Mancha, El by Miguel Cervantes. Spain 1605. I. de la Cuesta, vendese en casa de F. de Robles (Madrid). UK 1612 as *The History of the Valorous and Wittie Knight-Errant, Don-Quixote of the Mancha*. Translated out of the Spanish by Thomas Shelton. William Stansby for Ed. Blount and W. Barret (London)
In Gentle Combat with the Cold Wind by Jeff Long. UK 1977. *Mountain* 56 and collected in *One Step in the Clouds*
Inn, The by Guy de Maupassant see **Auberge, L'**
Jackson's Way see **The Jackson Route**
Jackson Route, The by Gerard Herzog. France 1976. as **La Voie Jackson**. UK 1978. Translated from the French *La Voie Jackson* by Hilary Davis. Collins (London). US 1978. as *Jackson's Way* Farrar Strauss and Giroiux (New York)
Jane Eyre. An Autobiography edited [or rather, written] by Currer Bell [pseudonym for Charlotte Brontë]. 3 Vol. 8°. UK 1847. Smith, Elder & Co. (London)
Jeu de la montagne et du hasard, Le by Anne Sauvy. France 1985. Editions Montalba (Paris)
Jeux Dangereux, Les by Henry Bordeaux. France 1926. Plon (Paris)
K2, Triumph and Tragedy by Jim Curran. UK 1987. Hodder and Stoughton (London)
K2: the Savage Mountain by Charles S. Houston and Robert Bates. US 1954. McGraw-Hill (New York). UK 1955. Collins (London). UK/US 1979. Softback edition with additional material and more illustrations. Diadem (London). Mountaineers (Seattle)
Komin Pokutników by Jan Dlugosz. Poland 1964. Iskry (Warsaw)
Lady's Tour round Monte Rosa, A by Mrs. Henry Warwick Cole. UK 1859. (London)
Land of the Snow Lion. An adventure in Tibet by Elaine Brook. UK 1987. Jonathan Cape (London)
Last Blue Mountain, The by Ralph Barker. UK 1959. Chatto & Windus (London). US 1960. Doubleday (New York).
Last Climb by Martin Berry. UK 1964 collected in *The Climber's Fireside Book*
Last Crevasse by Roger Frison-Roche see **Grande Crevasse, La**
Legends of the Fall by Jim Harrison. UK 1980. Collins (London)
Llithrig, Cloggy outside broadcast by BBC Television. 1963.
Llanberis by Paul Williams. UK 1987. Climbers' Club
Lliwedd by J. Menlove Edwards. UK 1946. Climbers' Club
Meilleur grimpeur du monde, Le by Bernard Amy. France 1985. Glinat

(Grenoble)
Menlove by Jim Perrin. UK 1985. Gollancz (London)
Mer de Glace by Alison Fell. UK 1991. Methuen (London)
Meurtre au sommet by José Giovanni. France 1964. Gallimard (Série noire)(Paris)
Moby Dick by Herman Melville. US 1851. UK 185 as *The Whale* (London). First
    included in Everyman's Library, UK in 1907
Moments of Personal Peril by Pat Ament. US 1986. *Rock and Ice* 15
Mont Analogue, Le by René Daumal. France 1952. Librarie Gallimard (Paris). UK
    1959 as *Mount Analogue*. Translated from the French by Roger Shattuck. Vincent
    Stuart (London)
Montagnards de la nuit, Les by Roger Frison-Roche. France 1968. Arthaud (Paris)
Montagne des autres, La by Bernard Amy. France 1972. Arthaud (Paris)
Mother Goddess of the World by Kim Stanley Robinson. UK 1988. Robinson
    Publishing (London) in *Best New SF2* and collected in *One Step in the Clouds*
Mount Analogue by René Daumal see **Mont Analogue, Le**
Mountain Craft edited by G.W. Young. UK/US 1920. Methuen (London)/
    Scribner's (New York)
Mountain Inn and Other Stories, The by Guy de Maupassant, translated by H.N.P.
    Slowman. UK 1955. Penguin (Harmondsworth)
Mountaineering Literature by Jill Neate. (First published as **Mountaineering and
    its Literature** by W.R. Neate UK 1978.) UK 1986. Cicerone Press (Milnthorpe,
    Cumbria). US Mountainbooks (Seattle)
Mountains and Other Ghosts by Dermot Somers. UK 1990. Diadem (London)
My Home in the Alps by Mrs. (Elizabeth Alice Frances) Main. UK 1892. Sampson
    Low & Co. (London)
Nanga Parbat Pilgrimage by Herman Buhl. UK 1956. Hodder (London) translated
    from the German by Hugh Merrick. US 1956 as *Lonely Challenge*. Dutton (New
    York)
Native Stones - A Book About Climbing by David Craig. UK 1987. Secker &
    Warburg (London)
Neige et roc by Gaston Rébuffat. France 1959. Hachette (Paris)
Neige sur les pas, La by Henry Bordeaux. France 1912. Plon (Paris)
Night Out by Al Alvarez. US 1971. *New Yorker* (New York). UK 1985 in *High* 27
    and collected in *One Step in the Clouds*
Nightfall by Dermot Somers. Eire 1983. *The Irish Climber* (Dublin). UK 1990
    collected in *Mountains and Other Ghosts*
No Gentlemen in the Himalaya by Greg Child. US 1985. *Climbing* 89 and
    collected in *One Step in the Clouds*
Nothing So Simple as Climbing by G.J.F. Dutton. UK 1993. Diadem (London)
Obsesja by Michal Jagiello. Poland 1978. Wydawnictwo Literackle (Krakow)
Obsession see **Obsesja**
Old Man of Hoy outside broadcasts by BBC Television. 1967 and 1984.
On Snow and Rock by Gaston Rébuffat. Translated from the French by Eleanor
    Brockett with technical assistance from J.E.B. Wright. UK 1963. Nicholas Kaye
    (London)
One Green Bottle by Elizabeth Coxhead. UK/US 1951. Faber (London)/
    Lippincott (Philadelphia), and collected in *One Step in the Clouds*
One Step in the Clouds edited by Audrey Salkeld and Rosie Smith. UK/US 1990.
    Diadem Books (London)/Sierra Club Books (San Francisco)
Outcrops by Terry Gifford. UK 1991. Littlewood Arc (Todmorden, Lancashire)

Passionate Quests: Five Modern Women Tranvellers by Sonia Melchett. UK 1991. William Heinemann (London)

Playground of Europe, The by Sir Leslie Stephen. UK 1871. Longmans (London). US 1909. Putnam (New York)

Premier de Cordée by Roger Frison-Roche. France 1941. Arthaud (Grenoble and Paris). UK 1949 as *First on the Rope* translated from the French by Janet Adam Smith. Methuen (London). US 1950. Prentice-Hall (New York)

Red Peak by C.G. Malcolm Slesser. UK 1962. Hodder (London). US 1964. Coward-McCann (New York)

Red Wall, Anglesey outside broadcast by BBC Television. Easter 1966.

Rescue at Stoney by Nick Barrett. UK 1983. *Oxford University M.C. Journal*

Retour à la montagne by Roger Frison-Roche. France 1957. Arthaud (Paris). UK 1961 as *Return to the Mountains* translated from the French by Hugo Charteris

Return to the Mountains by Roger Frison-Roche see **Retour à la montagne**

Ridiculous Mountains, The by Geoff Dutton. UK 1984. Diadem (London)

Rock Climbers in Action in Snowdonia by Anthony G. Smythe and John Cleare with Robin G. Collomb. UK 1966. Secker & Warburg (London)

Rock Climbs on the Mountain Limestone of Derbyshire by Graham Thomas Wilfred West. UK 1962. published by Cade for Manchester Gritstone Climbing Club

Romance of Mountaineering, The by Robert Lock Graham Irving. US/UK 1935. Dent (London)/Dutton (New York)

Sacred Summits by Peter Boardman. UK/US 1982. Hodder (London)/ Mountaineers (Seattle)

Satanic Verses, The by Salman Rushdie. UK 1988. Viking/Penguin (London); Viking/Penguin Inc. (New York)

Savage Arena by Joe Tasker. UK/US 1982. Methuen (London)/St. Martin's (New York)

Scrambles Amongst the Alps in the years 1860 - 1869 by Edward Whymper. UK 1871. Murray (London). US 1872. Burrows (Cleveland)

Secret Life of Snowdonia, The by Michael Leach. UK 1991. Chatto & Windus (London)

Seven Pillars of Wisdom, The by T.E. Lawrence. UK 1922. (Oxford). UK 1935. Jonathan Cape (London)

Sky Burial by Graham Mort. UK 1989. Dangeroo Press

Snowdon Biography by G.W. Young, Geoffrey Sutton and Wilfrid Noyce. UK 1957. Dent (London)

Soldiers and Sherpas by Brummie Stokes. UK 1988. Michael Joseph (London)

Solo Faces by James Salter. US 1979. Little Brown (Boston), Collins (London) and collected in *One Step in the Clouds*

South Col by Cuthbert Wilfrid Frank Noyce. UK 1953. Heinemann (London). US 1954. Sloane (New York)

Speak to the Hills ed by Hamish Brown and Martyn Berry, with introduction by Norman Nicholson. UK 1985. Aberdeen University Press

Starlight and Storm. UK 1956. Dent (London) translated from French by Wilfrid Noyce and Sir John Hunt. US 1957. Dutton (New York)

Stefano, przyjdziemy jutro by Adam Skoczylas. Poland 1958 in *Burza nad Alpemi*, an anthology edited by Jozef Nyka. Poland 1958. Iskry (Warsaw). UK 1962 as *Stefano We Shall Come Tomorrow*. Poets' and Painters' Press (London)

Stefano We Shall Come Tomorrow by Adam Skoczylas see **Stefano, przyjdziemy**

Jutro

Stone Spiral, The by Terry Gifford. UK 1987. Giant Steps (Clapham, N. Yorks)

Sur les crêtes du Mont-Blanc by Jacques and Tom Lépiney. France 1929. Dardel (Chambéry)

Suspended Sentences by Jim Curran. UK 1991. Hodder & Stoughton (London)

Take It to the Limit by Lucy Rees and Al Harris. UK 1981. Diadem (London)

Tartarin sur les Alpes by Alphonse Daudet. France 1885. Calmann-Levy (Paris). France 1887. Editions du Figaro (Paris). UK/US 1887 as *Tartarin on the Alps*. Routledge(London/New York)

Ténèbre et l'azur, La by Anne Sauvy. France 1991. Les Editions Arthaud (Grenoble and Paris)

The Sea, The Sea by Iris Murdoch. UK 1978. Chatto & Windus (London)

This Climbing Game edited by Walt Unsworth/illustrated by Ivan Cumberpatch. UK 1984. Viking (London). Penguin paperback 1985

Three Men in a Boat by Jerome K. Jerome. UK 1889. UK 1957 published by Penguin (Harmondsworth)

Three Musketeers, The by Alexandre Dumas. France, date unknown, published as *Les Trois Mousqetaires*. UK/US 1893-97. J.M. Dent & Co. (London)/Little, Brown & Co. (Boston, Mass.)

Total Control video by High Film Productions made by Alun Hughes. UK 1986 or 1987.

Touching the Void by Joe Simpson. UK 1988 Jonathan Cape (London) and in numerous editions worldwide.

Tragicall History of the horrible life and death of Doctor Faustus by Christopher Marlowe. UK 1609. imprinted by G.E. [George Eld] for Iohn Wright (London)

Treasury of Mountaineering Stories, A ed. by Daniel Talbot. US 1954. Putnam (New York). UK 1955. Davies (London)

Tremadog and the Moelwyns by Mike Mortimer. UK 1978. Climbers' Club

True Tales of Mountain Adventure for non-climbers and old by Mrs. Aubrey (Elizabeth Alice Frances) le Blond. UK 1903. T. Fisher Unwin (London)

Ulrich the Guide by Guy de Maupassant see **Auberge, L'**

Under Ararat by Ronnie Wathen. Mallorca 1988. Es Clot Press (Deià)

Une ascension dramatique au Mont Blanc (unable to obtain details)

Uphill All the Way by John Hawkridge. UK 1991. Michael Joseph (London)

Variantes by Etienne Bruhl. France 1951. Arthaud (Grenoble)

Versant du soleil, Le by Roger Frison-Roche. France 1981. Flammarion (Paris)

Vertige des Cimes, Le by Georges Casella . Ollendorff (Paris). Date unknown.

Victoire sur l'Aconcagua by René Ferlet and Guy Poulet. France 1955. Flammarion (Paris). UK 1956 as *Aconcagua: South Face*. Constable (London)

View from the Ridge, A by Davie Brown and Ian Mitchell. UK 1991. The Ernest Press (Glasgow)

Voie Jackson, La see **The Jackson Route**

Vortex by David Harris. UK 1990. Diadem (London) as part of *One Step in the Clouds*. UK 1991 Diadem (London) as hardback

Voyage de Monsieur Perrichon, Le; play by Ernest Labiche. France 1860.

Voyage en Suisse by Manon Roland. France 1800 in *Oeuvre Vol. III*. Bridault (Paris)

Wainwright's Favourite Lakeland Mountains by A.W. Wainwright with Derry Brabbs. UK 1991. Michael Joseph (London)

White Eagle, The by Stanislaw Piasecki see **W potrzasku, Powiesc**

White Graph, The by Dermot Somers. UK 1990. collected in *Mountains and Other Ghosts*, Diadem (London) and collected in *One Step in the Clouds*
White Spider, The by Heinrich Harrer. UK 1959. Hart-Davis (London). US 1960. Dutton (New York)
Woman's Reach, A by Nea Morin. UK 1968. Eyre and Spottiswoode (London)
W potrzasku, Powiesc (The White Eagle) by Stanislaw Piasecki. Poland 1929. Wydawnicktwo Polskie (Poznan)

INDEX

Θ Denotes article/poem published
in this book

Copyright acknowledgements, first publication dates and references
for articles and poems appearing in *Orogenic Zones*

Listed in order of their appearance in this book:
(where specific titles are referred to in articles, please see entry in bibliography)

Running on Empty by Dave Cook. UK 1988. *Climber and Hillwalker* January issue

A Quotes Quiz by Mike and Marjorie Mortimer: please see answers to quiz on page 246.

Report of the First Festival of Mountaineering Literature by Terry Gifford. UK 1988. *Mountain* 120. March/April issue

Report of the Second Festival of Mountaineering Literature by Tim Noble. UK 1989. *High* 74 January issue

Women and Climbing Writing by Jill Lawrence.
The following references are made:

p31	Quote by Jim Masters. Unable to trace.
p32	A Couple of Climbs with Coco by John Barry. UK 1987. *Climber*, March issue
p32	Bill Birkett's interview of Alison Hargreaves. UK 1984. *Climber and Rambler*, April issue
p40	No Spare Rib by Rosie Andrews. UK 1984. *Mountain* 97. May/June issue
p41	**A Peculiar Eclipsing: Women's Exclusion from Man's Culture by Dorothy E. Smith.** 1978. Unable to trace exact source
p42-43	Stella Adams' review of the Women's Issue of *Climbing* appeared in High 62, 1988, January issue

Ladies' Mountaineering Books is from *Books in my Life (the Collection of Janet Adam Smith and Michael Roberts* - Contemporary Collectors XXI) *The Book Collector* Vol. 37. no. 4, Winter 1988. Janet's talk was based around this piece, and included also readings from various books.

Report of the Third Festival of Mountaineering Literature by Roy Bennet. Previously unpublished

Climbing Fiction - The State of the Art by Audrey Salkeld and Rosie Smith
The following are referred to in this piece:

p55	Quote from Climber and Hillwalker, 1989 November issue

p58 On the Rock with Cathy Powell by Jim Perrin. UK 1988.
Climber and Hillwalker. December issue
p59 Alpine Journal, Vol. 87. No. 331 (1982)
p64/65 Her Two Doors Up by Dave Gregory. Hitherto
unpublished and used with his kind permission.
Midges by Geoff Dutton. UK 1990 collected in *One Step in the Clouds.*
Originally read at the Third Festival of Mountaineering Literature,
Bretton Hall, 1989. UK 1993 collected in *Nothing So Simple as
Climbing.* Diadem (London)
**Boardman Tasker Memorial Award for Mountain Literature
Chairman of the Judges' Speech** by Geoff Dutton. UK 1989. *Mountain*
130. November/December issue
Sean's Story by Terry Storry. UK 1990. High 87. February issue.
Mind Games by Ian Vickers. UK 1990. High 87. February issue
Climbing at Heptonstall Quarry by Graham Mort appeared in his 1989
Dangeroo Press collection *Sky Burial* and is reproduced here with their
kind permission
**Report of the Fourth International Festival of Mountaineering
Literature by** Kevin Borman. UK 1991. *High* 98 January issue
A Tale of Spendthrift Innocence by Dermot Somers. Originally read at
the Fourth International Festival of Mountaineering Literature, Bretton
Hall, 1990. UK 1994 collected in *At the Rising of the Moon.* Bâton
Wicks (London)
Climbing Language by Tony Lopez. UK 1994 in *Stress Management*
Boldface
Diff in the Afternoon by Andy Anderson. U.K. 1991. *High* January
issue, No. 98.
All for Love by Martin Owen. U.K. 1991. *High* 98. January issue
The Case of the Vanishing Hangers by Dave Gregory. U.K. 1991. *High*
98 January issue
**Report of the Fifth International Festival of Mountaineering
Literature by** Andy Popp. UK 1992 *On The Edge* 28. February issue
On Falling Off by Harold Drasdo is a reading from a work in progress
provisionally titled "The Ordinary Route".
Scafell Pike by Chris Whitby won second prize in a poetry competition
run by the Kaleidoscope programme on Radio 4 in 1991 (theme:
Arrival and Departure)
Back Where I Belong by Steve Ashton originally read at the Fifth
International Festival of Mountaineering Literature, Bretton Hall, 1991
and was published in *High* 110, 1992. January issue.
Stanage, Going South by Libby Houston first published in *High on the
Walls* (Bloodaxe, 1990)
French Climbing Writing in French Mountaineering Culture by Anne
Sauvy
The following reference is made:

p198-199 Manon Roland *Voyage en Suisse* in **Oeuvre** Vol. III, Paris,
Bridault, 1800.

Kaçkar Mountain by Ronnie Wathen. Mallorca 1988. collected in
Under Ararat. Es Clot Press (Deià)

Climbers, Their Writing and History by Paul Nunn
The following reference is made:
p226   The reference to the 'Nimrod' is to the Nimrod Antarctic
Expedition, 1908

Avoiding the Touch by Moira Viggers. UK 1992. *High* 111. February
issue

Borrowdale Evolution by Terry Gifford. UK 1991 in *Outcrops.*
Littlewood Arc (Todmorden, Lancashire)